African Feminist Hermeneutics

An Evangelical Reflection

Copyright 2016 Rachel NyaGondwe Fiedler

All rights reserved. No part of this publication may be reproduced, stored in a retrieval system, or transmitted in any form or by any means, electronic, mechanical, photocopying, recording or otherwise, without prior permission from the publishers.

Published by

Mzuni Press
P/Bag 201
Luwinga, Mzuzu 2
Malawi

ISBN 978-99960-45-20-2

Mzuni Press is represented outside Malawi by:
African Books Collective Oxford (also for e-books)
(orders@africanbookscollective.com)

www.africanbookscollective.com
www.mzunipress.blogspot.com

In memory of Dorcas Olu Akintunde, Ibadan (1961 - 2011)

African Feminist Hermeneutics
An Evangelical Reflection

Rachel NyaGondwe Fiedler
Johannes W. Hofmeyr and Klaus Fiedler

MZUNI PRESS

Mzuni Books no. 18
2016

Contents

Introduction	7
Chapter 1: African Feminist Theologies as an 'Irruption within an Irruption'	10
Chapter 2: Introducing African Feminist Hermeneutics	27
Chapter 3: An Evangelical Feminist Biblical Hermeneutic of the Old Testament	61
Chapter 4: An Evangelical Feminist Biblical Hermeneutic of the New Testament	97
Chapter 5: Malawian Evangelical Feminist Hermeneutic	117
Chapter 6: Conclusion	152

Acknowledgements

Firstly, we would like to acknowledge the University of the Free State. This book is informed by a PhD thesis submitted by Rachel NyaGondwe Fiedler in 2010 at the University of the Free State under the supervision of Prof. J.W. Hofmeyr, professor extraordinary in the Department of Ecclesiology, University of the Free State. The title of the thesis was 'The Circle of Concerned African Women Theologians: History and Theology (1989-2007).'

Secondly, we acknowledge the Circle of African Feminist Theologians in Africa and the Diaspora. This book is about their academic reflections on African Feminist Hermeneutics.

Thirdly, we acknowledge fellow scholars and students in theology over the years. Their ideas have enriched this book.

Introduction

The discourse on African Feminist Hermeneutics is the brain child of the Circle of Concerned African[1] Women Theologians (Circle) that was officially launched in 1989, Accra, Ghana. Through the concerted academic efforts of these theologians, we can now celebrate what we call African Feminist Theologies. African Feminist Hermeneutics is one of the five courses in African Feminist Theology that is offered at Mzuzu University under the Department of Theology and Religious Studies. The other courses include: Religion and Feminist Theology, History of African Feminist Theology, African Feminist Theology and Human Rights and lastly African Feminist Theology and Development. These courses provide a platform for practical and academic reflection on women's empowerment and gender equality based on Circle writings in Africa and in the Diaspora.

This book has six chapters: The first Chapter deals with a brief history on the genesis of African Feminist theologies as an 'irruption within an irruption'[2] of Feminist theological movements in the world including a reflection on its relationship to the secular Feminist Movement, and to similar theologies such as Contextual Theology, Liberation Theology and the Holiness Feminist Movement. The second chapter deals with an introduction to African Feminist Hermeneutics. In this chapter, the three branches of African Feminist Hermeneutics, the general theories, principles and approaches to African Feminist Hermeneutics are highlighted. The third chapter deals with an Evangelical Feminist Biblical Hermeneutics of the Old Testament. The fourth chapter deals with an Evangelical Feminist Biblical Hermeneutics of the New Testament. The fifth is about how Malawian Christian women interpret culture, Bible and power relations to realize their own liberation and chapter 6 concludes the book.

Although there are several examples of how African Feminist Hermeneutics can be applied to the Bible, chapters three to five of the book provide only one example, an Evangelical African Feminist Hermeneutics approach to the Bible, culture and gender relations. Since the term "Evangelical" is some-

---

[1] The word African does not refer to black Africans only but to all women that are born and socialized into any African Culture. Therefore African women include women of colour, black women and white women.

[2] In current theology the coming of Third Word Theologies is considered an irruption from First World Theologies. Feminist Theologies are seen as an irruption within this irruption. Others refer to this as an 'eruption within an eruption.'

times misunderstood, this is our understanding of it. Evangelical is not defined by membership of a specific church, maybe with the word "Evangelical" in its name, but Evangelicals can be found in any Christian denomination. For us Evangelical theology is defined by five emphases: (1) The love of the Bible (and the habit to take it seriously), (2) Emphasis on the personal confession of faith (3) Emphasis on mission, (4) the "translation" of personal faith into action and (5) the fellowship of all who believe in Jesus Christ as their Saviour and Lord.[3] The views we present in this book as Evangelicals may not be shared by all who claim that name for themselves, but it is definitely *one* Evangelical approach.

From this Evangelical theological base, we have come to the following conclusions regarding African Feminist Hermeneutics:

(1) African Feminist Theologies to a certain extent are the grand children of the Holiness Movement and the Euro-centric Feminist Movement

(2) Women's liberation is not only about leadership (or maybe ordination) in the church, but to occupy any position they feel satisfied with. In the Bible there is a spectrum from women as leaders (like the prophets Deborah and Huldah or the church founder Lydia) to women majoring in hospitality like Dorcas. All such positions liberate if they satisfy the women who hold them. Women's oppression must therefore be defined as barring women from positions they want to occupy in church and society.

(3) Cultural hermeneutics as an exercise of continuities and discontinuities must also be applied to cultural elements that malign adherence to the Christian faith and promote holistic liberation to women.

(3) Feminist liberation offers only partial solutions to women's liberation and in some cases it is in conflict with central women's aspirations for a satisfying Christian life.[4]

(4) Liberation of women must not be to the detriment of the liberation of men, as both women and men are equally (and fully) created in God's image.

---

[3] Klaus Fiedler, *Missions as the Theology of the Church. An Argument from Malawi*, Mzuzu: Mzuni Press, 2015, p. 8.

[4] For example to keep a marriage (and the family and the children) may be more important than any liberation Feminist theories may advocate.

(5) African Feminist Theological Hermeneutics is not just a domain for women but equally so for men.

Currently African Feminist Hermeneutics created by the Circle have been echoed by many women and men, even outside the Circle, and we offer this book, authored by a member of the Circle and two non-members as a contribution to the discourse on Evangelical women's theologies in Africa.

Chapter 1: African Feminist Theologies as an 'Irruption within an Irruption'

African Feminist Theologies should be understood as a continuum of the Eurocentric Feminist Theologies that originated from the secular Feminist Movement as well as the Holiness Movement in the world. On the other hand, African Feminist Theologies have a distinct character of their own similar but also different from other Feminist movements. They are an African baby born in a Ecumenical surroundings.[5]

This chapter has the following components: The relationship of Feminist Theologies to the Secular Feminist Movement; The relationship of Feminist Theologies to Contextual Theologies; The relationship of Feminist Theologies to Liberation theologies; The relationship of African Feminist Theology to the Third World Feminist theological movements and the relationship of Feminist Theologies to the Holiness Feminist Movement.

Feminist Theology and Secular Feminist Movements

Feminist Theologies are a discourse that seeks women's liberation from a religious perspective. The early Feminist Theologies have their roots in the wider secular Feminist Movement. This wider secular Feminist Movement is popularly known as the Women's Liberation Movement that started in the 18th and 19th centuries in countries such as America[6], Canada,[7] England, France and Germany.

The beginnings of this movement were radical and some felt that as much as it dealt with patriarchy, its approach was bordering on the promotion of matriarchy.[8] The justifications for such assumptions were many. Firstly, the early movement was characterized by hate for men. The men were considered to be the cause of the injustices that women went through. The men were called upon to repent of injustices they perpetrated against women

---

[5] Rachel NyaGondwe Fiedler and J.W. Hofmeyr, "The Birth and Growth of the Circle of Concerned African Women Theologians in Malawi 1989-2011," *Studia Historiae Ecclesiasticae* XXXVII(2) – September 2011.

[6] The Declaration of Sentiments was published in 1848 in New York.

[7] Doris Anderson was already an editor of a women's magazine that promoted feminist ideologies in Canada in 1963.

[8] See Betty Steele, *The Feminist Take Over. Patriarchy to Matriarchy in Two Decades*, Richmond Hill: Tercet, p. 6.

including those by their fathers and grandfathers. The results of such tendencies were severe. Some argued for lesbianism. Women such as Simone de Beauvoir, argued that pregnancy was a female trap and that it was necessary to find ways to free women from such biological traps. There were many propositions made in this regard. Shullamith Firestone, for example, argued that childbearing could be done through technology.[9] The Women's Liberation Movement promoted the formation of Sisterhood movements at the exclusion of men as fora for women's liberation. This exclusion of men was the basis of why some men resented the Feminist agenda. Some men became misogynistic against those that promoted the Feminist agenda. Other men withdrew to themselves and passively watched what women did.

In the 19th century, there were attempts by the "women only" movement to begin to persuade men to join them in the fight against patriarchy.[10] Since this implied that women would be equal to men, the agenda received resistance by some Feminists. The argument was that they could not be equal to men who were evil.[11] Others became suspicious as to whether men would really press for liberation of women as such an exercise would rob them of opportunities filled by women.

Inasmuch as the movement promoted women's to access higher education and become leaders in the work place such as becoming lawyers, doctors and even presidents, it was later discovered that such women's progress was not without major sacrifices as men still clung to their patriarchal mindset. Men still considered women as the caretakers of the families and households. In this context women that occupied positions in the public spaces had to place less value on family and marriage roles. Women who enjoyed their traditional roles such as taking care of their homes and being mothers had to forgo or postpone such roles in the event that they wanted to occupy key positions in the public spaces. Thus women who occupied key positions in the public spaces often lost their marriages to divorce.[12] Some of the women did not even attempt marriage. The result was that there

---

[9] Ibid., p. 17
[10] Ibid.
[11] Ibid., p. 14-15.
[12] The 50% percent divorce rate in 20th Century America has been attributed to a world view where both partners are conditioned to absolute independence (Betty Steele, *The Feminist Take Over. Patriarchy to Matriarchy in Two Decades*, Richmond Hill: Tercet, p. 111).

was an increase in the prevalence of single women among them single mothers.

Single motherhood was complicated in situations where the mother had full time employment. In certain cases, children from such families suffered psychological problems and some became drug and alcohol addicts. Cases of teen age suicide also increased. Although such incidences were not restricted to children of single mothers, research in Canada confirmed that the highest number of victims were children of single mothers[13] and young adults that suffered divorce or separation.[14]

Even though the Feminist movement excluded men in the fight for women's liberation, it was not uncommon that some men got involved in pushing the agenda of women's liberation forward. In the Declaration of Sentiments for example, there were men such as Robert Smallbridge, who were among the many women that signed.[15] Some men were involved in pushing for legislation to protect women in the work place. One key legislation was about paid maternity leave and pension provision for women that worked part time because of caring for children.

African Feminist Theologies and Contextual Theology

In this section you will be introduced to the relationship of African Feminist Theology to similar movements such as Contextual Theology, Liberation Theology and the Holiness Feminist Movement.

Feminist Theologies are part and parcel of Contextual theologies. The context of Feminist Theology is women. There are several strands of Feminist Theology in the world, but each strand borrows a leaf from another. This is especially reflected in methodology and goals of all Feminist Theologies. Their main goal is to bring liberation to women so that they realize their God given potentials in their societies and religions. The earliest Feminist

---

[13] 33% of all the children that attempted suicide in Canada in the 20th century came from single parent families (Steele, p. 137).

[14] A Canadian 12 member task force found out in their research that young women and men who are divorced or separated are the high risk groups (Steele, p. 118).

[15] Declaration of Sentiments, Seneca Falls, New York, July 19-20, 1848.

Theologies are popularly called First World Feminist Theologies.[16] All other Feminist Theologies are later generation Feminist Theologies.

Feminist Theologies fall under the discourse on Contextualization Theology.[17] The word Contextualization is related to Inculturation and sometimes these words are used interchangeably although they do not mean exactly the same. Martin Ott reflects on the three sociological terminologies on which the meaning of Inculturation is based. These are Enculturation, referring to primary socialization an individual goes through; Acculturation referring to secondary socialization; and Transculturation that refers to the process of mutual transfer of culture when the gospel is preached to people.[18] When the early missionaries preached the gospel, there was a common assumption that there would be a one-way transfer of culture, that of the missionary and that of the gospel to the people receiving the gospel. The culture of the recipients was often considered demonic. This meant that the African culture was completely condemned with no possibility of it having an inspiration to the Christian message. By reinterpreting the Bible, culture and power balance, Feminist Theologians are questioning the way European Christian Thought Systems influenced the way African women learned the Christian message. This is what African Feminist Theologians are doing. They reflect and construct theology that is relevant to African women by critically analyzing these received theologies and making the Christian message more relevant to African women and their culture.

The processes of Inculturation and Contextualization in general started a long time ago. This process dates back to John Mbiti and Kwesi Dickson, who led a movement of African Theology in reaction to earlier theological works, which were Eurocentric. In fact for Kwesi Dickson the principal task in this process of Inculturation was to study the nature of the theological task that faced the African Church in its time.[19] In this, he critically looked at reinterpreting received theology in relation to the questions that Africans posed. These were questions relating to how Africans can make the church

---

[16] See Susan Frank Parsons (ed), *The Cambridge Companion to Feminist Theology*, Cambridge University Press, 2002, p. 24.

[17] For more details on contextualization, see Martin Ott, *African Theology in Images*, Blantyre: CLAIM-Kachere, 2000.

[18] See Martin Ott, *African Theology in Images*, Blantyre: CLAIM-Kachere, 2000, p. 25.

[19] See Kwesi A. Dickson, *Theology in Africa*, London: Darton, Longman and Todd; Maryknoll: Orbis, 1984, p. viii.

authentic in the African context.[20] While African Feminist Theology acknowledges these efforts of African men, the women are also searching for an African Feminist Theology that would be authentic to the African women in their context.[21] This same approach was characteristic in developing Feminist Theologies by women in other Third World Countries. Asian women and Latin American women did the same.

African Feminist Theology has two brands: Political Feminist Theology and Religio-Cultural Feminist Theology. Political Feminist Theology started within the context of Black Theology, a theology that takes the class and race of the Black people into consideration when constructing theology. This theology is within the context of the past history of apartheid. This is not a dominant African Feminist Theology. However, it is prominent in some South African women theologians. These women write from the perspective of how apartheid affected women in church and society. In this, white South African women are viewed from a privileged position compared to women of colour and black women. The white minority is seen as believing to have the right to dominate the other races who are a majority. This state has brought about the struggle of Blacks and women of colour for liberation from this oppression.[22] With many challenges women in politics face in the world, Political Feminist Theology is becoming more prominent in Africa and in the world at large. Political Theology is used to bring solutions of participation of women in politics.

African Religio-Cultural Feminist Theology has a different emphasis. "Its main concern is the relationship between different religions and African culture and women's liberation. This strand of Feminist Theology begins from the conviction that all cultures are God given, and are part of the natural revelation of God to mankind and that they are not meant to oppress women. African culture, far from being 'pagan' or satanic, therefore provides a genuine, if limited, knowledge of God and in this case is not to compromise the dignity of women. The fact that African cultures are regarded as being a preparation for this gospel,"[23] they must reflect the love of Christ

---

[20] Ibid., p. 2.

[21] Mercy was amidst various Feminist scholars when at Harvard. See Chapter on the Birth of the Circle.

[22] See Bonganjalo Goba, "Emerging Theological Perspectives in South Africa," in Virginia Fabella, M.M. and Sergio Torres, (eds), *Irruption of the Third World Challenge to Theology*, New York: Orbis Books 1983, p. 19.

[23] John Parrat (ed), *A Reader in Christian Theology*, London: SPCK, 1987, p. 7.

for women and men. Nevertheless, African Religio-Cultural Feminist Theology seeks to transform or eliminate African culture that oppresses women. Thus African Religio-Cultural Feminist Theology does not accept African culture as wholly divine; it takes a selective approach which calls for removing cultural elements that are oppressive to women and retaining those that are liberating. Even this selection of what is liberating and what is not lies in the hands of African women depending on the context they hail from as it is shown in this book.

A further contribution to African Theology is the exposure of how approaches and methodologies used in constructing African Theology differ or are similar to those that African women use in constructing African women's theology.

Feminist Theologies and Liberation Theology

Liberation Theologies are a group of Contextual Theologies that are related to Feminist Theology. The context of Liberation Theologies is the poor. In one way, women are also placed in the category of the poor because of their disadvantaged status. However, Feminist Theology is not a product of Third World Liberation movements that sought to fight against the socio political oppression of the Third World by the First World countries.[24] Feminist Theologies make a contribution to Liberation Theologies by highlighting methodologies, approaches, models, and case studies of liberation work among women. While some of the methodologies are similar to those used in Liberation Theology, the Feminist Theologians make a concrete application to women.[25] Liberation Theology for women must therefore highlight the importance of interpreting patriarchal theologies as promoting poverty in the world. Even though the Feminist Theologies provide methodologies, approaches and models from the women's perspective, such discussions also becomes a 'point of academic quest' on how they are relevant to men's

---

[24] French sociologists coined the term 'Third World' in the fifties. It refers to countries that are at the periphery of the world, where the rich Western countries are the First World and the Communist Bloc the second. See Leonardo Boff and Virgil Elizondo (eds), *Concilium. Theologies of the Third World. Convergences and Differences*, Edinburgh: Page Brothers, 1988, p. 3.

[25] An example is where African Liberation Theologies take the situation of the Africans as an important factor in creating African Theology. See Leonardo Boff and Virgil Elizondo (eds), *Concilium. Theologies of the Third World. Convergences and Differences,* Edinburgh: Page Brothers, 1988, p. 9. Circle theology also takes the situation of African women seriously in creating their theology.

liberation. In addition, Feminist Theology presents a theology of women's struggle against gender inequalities. In this theology, women are seen as victims of wrong interpretations of culture, the Bible and "power balance." As victims, they seek to oust such injustices, the very target of liberation theology.

Although the movement of Liberation was present as early as the 1950s, the work of Gustavo Gutierrez published in the 1970s sensitized the world to Liberation Theologies. The new movement coincided with similar movements in Africa and Asia. For Africans, their goal was to answer the question how the Christian faith could be better understood by Africans. They realized that their theologies ought to be different from (Euro-centric Feminist Theologies), those theologies constructed by their brothers and sisters in the First World. This is because of the realization that African contexts are different from those in Europe and North America.[26] Thus the African church had theological questions that could not be answered by traditional theologies from the First World. They felt it was time to develop their own theologies. According to Gustavo Gutierrez, "Liberation involves the total person and embraces three different interrelated levels of meaning."[27]

Gutierrez' concept of liberation involving the total person, has some similarity to feminist theologizing: These women argue, for example, that church teachings that promote women into leadership roles of the church but promote subordination of women in the home are not liberating to women. Philomena Njeri Mwaura, one of the key contributors to African Feminist Theology, is one of the women who clearly show this line of thinking. In the research she conducted in the Charismatic and Neo-Pentecostal churches in Kenya, she discovered that women in Charismatic churches enjoy leadership roles in church while they are taught to submit to their husbands in the home.[28] The meaning she provides for the experience of such women is that they are not liberated because their health is at stake especially if they are wives of abusive husbands.[29] This is because these women are not only spiritual beings but they are also physical, emotional, psychological beings. For these women to experience liberation, such liberation must involve the

---

[26] See Roberts J. Schreiter, *Constructing Local Theologies*, Suffolk: SCM Press, 1985, p. 2.

[27] Gustavo Gutierrez, "The Meaning of the Term *Liberation*" in Deane William Fern, *Third World Liberation Theologies. A Reader,* New York: Orbis Books, 1986.

[28] See Philomena Njeri Mwaura "Perceptions of Women's Health and Rights in Neo-Pentecostal and Charismatic Churches in Kenya," Malaka-le Theologies, 2005, p. 7

[29] The fuller account of this detail is in Chapter 7

total person (woman). Thus for such women to be liberated they must not only be liberated spiritually by being leaders in the church, but must also be liberated from psychological, physical and emotional trauma that they might face in their homes. However, liberation at the grassroots is also construed differently depending on the context of women.

The three levels of meaning of Liberation stated by Gustavo Gutierrez also relate to Feminist Theology. Gustavo Gutierrez argues "In the first place, liberation expresses the aspirations of the oppressed peoples and social classes, emphasizing the conflictual aspect of economic, social, and political process, which puts them at odds with wealthy nations and oppressive classes."[30] This thinking is not unequivocally related to all Feminist Theologies. African Feminist Theologians for example are not largely preoccupied with economic, social and political oppression by wealthy nations. There is a small contribution to fight class oppression in the Feminist theological writings of women of South Africa. However, even though such a contribution is small, it is clear that South African Feminist women take class oppression as an important issue in their writings. An example of such writers is Elna Mouton. She is a white South African who writes from the position of the oppressed by ideologies of the whites who were in a privileged position in the history of apartheid. Her contribution, which is also echoed by Madipoane Masenya, is that the way the Bible was used by those in privileged positions in South Africa was oppressive. She argues that it was even used to sustain oppression by those in control during apartheid. The Bible, then, was used as a "sword" as well as a "healing tool."[31]

In addition, Feminist Theology relates to this second level of meaning by Gustavo Gutierrez where he argues that "liberation expresses the aspirations of oppressed people."[32] All Feminist Theologies spring from the aspirations of women who are oppressed and emphasizes how women can rise above politics, religion and culture that puts them in subjection to men. In this women argue that politics, religion and culture largely put women at

---

[30] Gustavo Gutierrez, "The Meaning of the Term *Liberation*" in Deane William Fern, *Third World Liberation Theologies. A Reader,* New York: Orbis Books, 1986.

[31] Elna Mouton, "'From Woundedness towards Healing'. Rhetoric or Pastoral-Theological Vision?' 14th National Conference: Southern Africa Association for Pastoral Work, Cape Town, 12-14 May 2003. See also Madipoane Masenya, "The Bible as a 'Sword' and a 'Tool for Healing'," Malaka-le Theologies, 2005.

[32] Gustavo Gutierrez, "The Meaning of the Term *Liberation*" in Deane William Fern, *Third World Liberation Theologies. A Reader,* New York: Orbis Books, 1986, p. 16.

the bottom while men are usually at the apex of liberation. This is the whole essence of why Feminist women engage themselves in Liberation Theology.

Gustavo Gutierrez puts the second level of liberation in this way: "At a deeper level, liberation can be applied to an understanding of history. Humankind is seen as assuming conscious responsibility for its own destiny. This understanding provides a dynamic context and broadens the horizons of the desired social changes."[33] In this perspective, the unfolding of all the dimensions of the human person is demanded as the gradual conquest of true freedom leading to the creation of new women and men and a qualitatively different society. The vision provides, therefore, a better understanding of what in fact is at stake in our times.[34] This argument is also at the heart of Feminist Theologians. It is the spirit of these women that the transformation they seek today will contribute towards the creation of a new world for their daughters and sons in the coming generation. If they do not engage themselves in this transformation work, the destiny of their daughters and sons as equal human beings will be at stake.

Gustavo Gutierrez finally argues that the word 'liberation' allows for another approach leading to the biblical sources that inspire the presence and action of humankind in history. In the Bible, Christ is presented as one who brings liberation."[35] This relates to Christian Feminist Theology where the Bible is used as a source of inspiration to liberate both women and men in the world. It is in this vein that Luke 4:8[36] is often quoted by Feminist women as a basis for creating a particular paradigm of women's liberation. Thus the spirit of Feminist theologians to appeal to the Bible as a source for inspiration regarding liberation of women is a contribution to Liberation Theology. The women have also provided approaches and models in reading the Bible that are liberating to women.

Further, the women address the "masks" in the reading of the Bible that have prevented women from seeing a liberating 'word of God' for them. Some of them are: Failing to recognize women characters in the Bible, con-

---

[33] Ibid.
[34] Ibid.
[35] Ibid.
[36] "The Spirit of the Lord is on me, because he has anointed me to preach good news to the poor. He has sent me to proclaim freedom for the prisoners and recovery of sight for the blind, to release the oppressed, to proclaim the year of the Lord's favor" (NIV).

doning Bible culture that oppress women, an emphasis on inclusion of wrong models of women in theologizing, misinterpreting passages or words in the Bible to oppress women and so on. The women have also provided a way to interpret the Bible that is liberating to women, but also shapes a liberating destiny of their daughters and sons. These women suggest the following: To recover stories of women in power in the Bible, recover stories of men that affirm women's empowerment and so on. Even though feminist theology is providing approaches and models of liberation for women, they provide a point of discussion and example to the liberation of men as well.

Feminist Theology and Political Liberation Theologies

The question of political liberation has a long history. There have been works in the field of how the oppressed people groups can be included in the political consciousness of the nations. Here we have many examples ranging from the inclusion in American and South African politics to the inclusion of women in positions of decision making in politics. Feminist Hermeneutics is crucial in leveling the ground for promoting women's and men's equal partnership in politics in world. We need Feminist methodologies, approaches, and models to contribute to the liberation of women. Such a relationship is clear from the perspectives by Caroline Ramazanoglu. She looks at the relationship between Feminism and Political Liberation in this way. She argues that there is indeed a sisterhood between Political Liberation and Feminism but that there are also differences between those that are committed to Political Liberation in general and those that are Feminists. Further she adds that the goal of Feminism is Women's Liberation Movement [women's lib as commonly said in short among Feminist women] from oppression by men.[37] In this way we can argue that Feminism provides a partial social theory to liberation. This is because Feminist Theology only targets forms of oppression from patriarchy related to religion and culture. Thus Feminist theories cannot "explain the connections between different forms of oppression. But the problem remains that the oppression of women is complex and occurs in many ways, enmeshed in all

---

[37] Caroline Ramazanoglu, "Feminism and Liberation," in Linda McDowell and Rosemary Pringle, *Defining Women, Social Institutions and Gender Divisions* (eds), Cambridge: Blackwell, 1992, p. 176.

the other forms of oppression that people have created."[38] However, Feminist theory can also provide reasons for women's liberation from other forms of oppression such as political and social economic causes.

African Feminist Theology and Third World Feminist Theological Movements

Although all Feminist Theologies are related, they are also different from each other. Their similarity is that all Feminist Theologies are theologies about women and constructed to liberate women. However, there are two main braches of Feminist Theologies: First World Feminist Theologies and Third World Feminist Theologies. First World Feminist Theologies are also known as European Feminist Theologies, These are more linked to dealing with oppression related to Marxist capital/production ideas where women see themselves as being used to gain more capital. European Feminist women are also privileged in distribution of wealth and belong to colonial masters of Third World countries. On the other hand some Feminist theories developed by European Feminism are often used in an adapted form even by Third World Feminist scholars.

Third World Feminist Theologies are a later group of Feminist Theologies. They developed after the First World Feminist Theologies. This is because women from Third World Countries realized that although they shared the same passion of liberating women with First world women, they belonged to different contexts. This therefore required that they develop Feminist Theologies that are relevant to their different contexts. However, within Third World Feminist Theologies there are also different strands. This is because the context of Third World is also different. As such Third World Feminist Theologies have the following strands: Latin American women, Black American women, Asian women and African women. These groups of women have also named their Feminist Theologies differently. Latin American women have named their theologies as Mujerista Theology. The first organized meeting of Latin American women discussing Feminist Theology took place in 1979 in Mexico.[39] Mujerista Theology is about women crying

---

[38] See Caroline Ramazanoglu, "Feminism and Liberation," in Linda McDowell and Rosemary Pringle, *Defining Women. Social Institutions and Gender Relations,* Cambridge, 1992, p. 277.

[39] See Mary Judith Press, "Feminist Christians in Latin America" in *Voices from the Third World Women,* Colombo: EATWOT, vol. VIII, no. 3, p. 55.

for justice in a context where justice is denied to them.[40] Right at the beginning Latin American women identified church structures as reinforcing women's oppression through powerful patriarchal structures.[41] Latin American women at this time were concerned with the fact that men controlled decision-making processes including on what should be binding for faith, conscience and practice.[42] The women were committed to the redefinition of such patriarchal structures in order to create a model of the church that encourages participation of women and men. In this processes, patriarchal structures were relativized.[43] African women named their theologies as African Feminist theologies. Some call these "African Women's Theologies." These African Feminist Theologies have been developed by the Circle. These women are concerned about issues of women's oppression in Africa and they have developed theologies to liberate them in religion and society. These women are also concerned about issues of justice in decision-making in politics, religion and society. Further, African Feminist Theologies are different from Latin American Feminist Theologies because of their commitment to dealing with social justice as part of the struggle for women's liberation.[44] The other Third World Feminist Theology is that developed by women from the Black minority in North America.[45] This women's movement is based on the assumption that White women oppress Black women in America. Further, Black North American women accuse White women as posing themselves to be the norm of the women in America while perceiving Black women as second-class citizens. According to Ogbu U. Kalu, North American Black Women's Theologies are named Womanist Theologies because in the black culture to which these women belong "to say that a girl is acting womanish is to affirm that the person is beginning to exercise agency, act as grown up, and show a creative, adult sense of initiative."[46] This movement of Black women therefore develops this theology to liberate

---

[40] See Susan Frank Parsons (ed), *A Companion to Feminist Theology*, Cambridge University Press, 2002, p. 26.

[41] See Mary Judith Press, "Feminist Christians in Latin America," in *Voices from the Third World Women,* Colombo: EATWOT, vol. VIII, no. 3, p. 55.

[42] Ibid.

[43] Ibid., p. 56.

[44] Ibid., p. 59.

[45] See Alice Walker, *In Search of Our Mothers' Gardens*, New York: Harcourt, Brace, Jovanovich, 1983, pp. xi – xii.

[46] See Ogbu U. Kalu, "Daughters of Ethiopia Constructing a Feminist Discourse in Ebony Strokes," In Isabel Apawo Phiri and Sarojini Nadar (eds), *Women, Religion and Health, Essays in Honour of Mercy Amba Ewudziwa Oduyoye*, Pietermaritzburg: Cluster, 2006 p. 262.

themselves from their disadvantaged position. They also show the White North American women that they are grown up. These women's theologies are similar to those by Black women in South Africa where issues of race and class are still real due to the history of apartheid. However, they differ with Black women in South Africa because Black women in South Africa link their theologizing to religion and culture. This is different from Black Theology in America, where religion is not always part of their reflection.[47] The rise of different feminist theologies within different contexts demands different names.[48]

The origins of Third World Feminist Theologies are common. They trace their origins from Ecumenical Association of Third World Theologies (EATWOT).

The African Feminist Movement and the Holiness Movement

So far we have shown relationships to other current Feminist movements. These have fuelled the demand for female equality among Christian women in Africa. Important as these influences are, there is another line of influence, that of the Holiness Revival that originated in the 19th Century and which produced the Evangelical discoveries described below.

Evangelical Discoveries

These Evangelical discoveries, though Evangelicals were not the very first to do so (as the case of Chrysostomos shows), came way before the advent of the Women Liberation Movement, which increased women's visibility in the church. These discoveries were made in the context of evangelism, mission, and the quest for scriptural holiness. These were the main emphases of the great revival, which some call the "Second Evangelical Awakening" and which can also be called the "Holiness Revival." It started in America in 1858 and in Britain in 1859. As usual in revivals, the Holy Spirit blurred the distinctions between laity and clergy, between classes and races, and between male and female. So estate owners would pray together with their servants, black Americans would be accepted as missionaries, laymen would preach and lead, and women would take up positions of influence at home and (even more so) on the mission field.

---

[47] Ibid.

[48] See Isabel Apawo Phiri, "African Women's Theologies in the New Millennium," *Agenda* 61, 2004.

The "Holiness Revival" provided a fertile ground for new discoveries in ministry and biblical studies, since one of its major roots was in the Holiness Movement, which in turn had its roots in the Methodist Movement. The Holiness Movement's origin can be attributed to two sisters, Phoebe Palmer and Sarah Lankfort (1835), and ever since these original days, women played a major role in the Holiness Movement. But even John Wesley treated women very much differently from how he should have treated them being the Anglican clergyman that he was.[49]

The central concern of the Holiness Revival was conversion, and therefore evangelism (home) and missions (foreign) were of top importance. If salvation is needed by everyone, then missions become paramount, the faster the better, the more effective the more beautiful.

Revival usually enhances the role of women, and many felt the call to missionary work (at home and abroad), and many of the leading men were very happy to observe this development, and some published their thoughts and observations. Still, the first to publicly demand for women the right to preach, was a women (though she had no intention to preach herself): Catherine Booth. She wrote to defend Phoebe Palmer's activities in Britain. Among the men connected to the Faith Missions within the Holiness Revival it was perhaps the American Fredrik Franson (of Swedish origin who published in German) who was the most elaborate early male defender of women's rights to preach. And the first Free Methodist Bishop wrote the most far-reaching book, demanding that women even should be ordained.

The early Evangelical missiologists and expositors all used the historical approach to the biblical evidence. Though most of them were not Baptists nor of similar faith, all of them had a very close and direct relationship to the Bible, which allowed them, despite their official denominational allegiance, to ascribe to what they found in the New Testament a normative character, at least to the extent that all that was obviously practiced in the primitive church can not be forbidden to today's church.

This was summed up by Titus Roberts, the first Bishop of the Free Methodist Church:

---

[49] Paul Wesley Chilcote, "John Wesley and the Women Preachers of early Methodism" (PhD Duke University, 1984 (Ann Arbor: UMI). This dissertation deserves much more attention than it has received so far.

> Though Christianity has greatly ameliorated the condition of women, it has not secured for her, even in the most enlightened nations, that equality which the Gospel inculcates ... The dominion which God gave to man at the creation was a joint dominion. It was given to the woman equally as to the man. God created woman a female man— nothing more—nothing less. She had all the rights and prerogatives of the man ... In the New Testament church, woman, as well as man, fitted the office of Apostle, Prophet, Deacon or Preacher and Pastor. There is not the slightest evidence that the functions of any of these offices, when filled by a woman, were different from what they were when filled by a man.
>
> If woman, in using her voice, in praising God, or declaring His truth in our churches, is a transgressor, then silence her at whatever cost. If she is doing right, then remove all shackles and give her the liberty of the Gospel.
>
> All restrictions to positions in the church based on race have been abolished; it is time then that those based on sex were also abolished ... Men had better busy themselves in building up the temple of God, instead of employing their time in pushing from the scaffold their sisters, who are both able and willing to work with them side by side.[50]

Female Missionaries

When the modern Protestant missionary movement got underway in 1792 as a fruit of the Great Awakening, women were part of it, first of all as missionary wives, but increasingly also as single women.[51] Their Feminist concern was not fuelled by "liberal" political and social ideas, but by the deep desire to serve Christ and to make his name known all over the world, and in doing so they carved out the "*First Feminist Movement in North America*,"[52] well before the (secular) Women's Liberation Movement established itself there.

---

[50] Benjamin Titus Roberts, *Ordaining Women* (Earnest Christian Publication House, 1891, reprinted by Light and Life Press in 1992, second reprint by Light and Life Communications, Indianapolis, 1997), p. 10.

[51] For America described with deep insight by Dana Roberts, *American Women in Mission. A Social History of their Thought and Practice,* Macon: Mercer University Press, 1996.

[52] R. Pierce Beaver, *American Protestant Women in World Mission. A History of the First Feminist Movement in North America*, Grand Rapids 1980. The first edition of this book was published in 1968 under the title: *All Loves Excelling.*

The most famous of these independent minded single women missionaries of he 19th Century in Africa was probably Mary Slessor (1848-1915), called "the White Queen of Calabar", who specialized in rescuing twins whom the Efik would leave to die in the forest, in stopping local wars and promoting good laws in her country. She adopted a number of the children she rescued as her family,[53] and she never needed the help of a man in her pioneer missionary work.[54]

An even stronger "Feminist" influence came through some of the women missionaries of the Evangelical Awakening who were influenced by the Holiness Movement that had been started in 1835 by the sisters Sarah Lankford and Phoebe Palmer in Boston[55] and which became one of the defining forces in the Evangelical Revival (also Holiness Revival) which gave birth to the interdenominational Faith Missions.[56] One of the defining institutions in this movement was Mount Holyoke College, founded by Mary Lyon in 1797, which trained many women missionaries.[57]

The missionary impulse of the Holiness Movement liberated women. Malla Moe, a factory girl like Mary Slessor, evangelized Swaziland based on the her Gospel Wagon,[58] Catherine Booth (co-founder of the Salvation Army) evangelized the heathen of London's East End,[59] and when she was pregnant with her fourth child, she wrote a book demanding for women the

---

[53] For a picture of her and her children see Wikipedia "Mary Slessor."
[54] At one stage in her life she wanted to marry, but since the man was younger than her, the missionary society refused her wish. An easy to read biography is: Miller, Basil, *Mary Slessor. Heroine of Calabar*, Minneapolis: Bethany, 1974.
[55] Phoebe Palmer was a prominent evangelist in the Holiness Movement of the mid-19th century. She wrote the strongest early defence of women's right to preach the Gospel: "The Promise of the Father" (1859). For Phoebe Palmer's role in the early Holiness Movement see Klaus Fiedler, *The Story of Faith Missions*. Regnum/Lynx: Oxford, 1994, ^{2}1995. For her theology see: Phoebe Palmer, *The Way of Holiness*, Boston, ^{50}1867
[56] For ecclesiology and history see: Klaus Fiedler, *Ganz auf Vertrauen. Geschichte und Kirchenverständnis der Glaubensmissionen*. Gießen/Basel: Brunnen, 1992, 605 pp. Out of print, now available for free download through http://tinyurl.com/fiedler. The English version is: Klaus Fiedler, *The Story of Faith Missions*. Regnum/Lynx: Oxford, 1994, ^{2}1995.
[57] Malawi was influenced from Mt Holyoke mainly through its South African equivalent, in which most of the Nkhoma missionary women had been trained, both married and single. The most famous "female" mission station was Morgenster, 7 km from the ruins of Greater Zimbabwe. Googling "Morgenster Mission" yields informative results.
[58] Maria Nilson and Paul Sheetz, *Malla Moe*, Chicago ^{8}1980(1956).
[59] For the history of the Salvation Army in Malawi see: Godfrey Kamwendo, The Salvation Army in Malawi: Its Origins and Development, BA, University of Malawi, 2003.

right to preach the Gospel,[60] and Frederic Franson, the "World Evangelist" encouraged hundreds of women to become missionaries, many of them in the China Inland Mission, but equally so in Sweden and Germany as pioneer missionaries.

These Holiness missionaries would not have felt at home in the Women's Liberation Movement, but there are similarities, and through these women missionaries the Christian Church in Africa received much impetus for women's liberation.

---

[60] Catherine Booth, *Female Ministry; or, Woman's Right to Preach the Gospel*, London: 1859.

Chapter 2: Introducing African Feminist Hermeneutics

African Feminist Hermeneutics is not only about how women and men interpret the Bible to realize liberation of women. It is a diverse discourse that also deals with how African culture and power relations in the church and society are interpreted to realize liberation of women.

The diverse relationships of African Feminist Theologies to other Feminist theologies demand mixed African Feminist Hermeneutics. This chapter presents key aspects in interpreting the Bible (Biblical Hermeneutics), African culture (Cultural Hermeneutics) and power relations between men and women (Relational Hermeneutics) in church and society to realize liberation of women. These key aspects include: (1) General theories of Feminist Hermeneutics (2) General principles of Feminist Hermeneutics and an introduction to African Feminist Hermeneutics.

General Theories of Feminist Hermeneutics

Whether it is Biblical Hermeneutics, Cultural Hermeneutics or Relational Hermeneutics, the starting point is that women are not always liberated and that men, on the other hand, are mostly privileged over them in all sectors of society. In order to balance this inequality Feminist Theologians use various theories. Basing on the diverse relationships of Feminist Theologies to other Feminist Movements, this section has two theories from Feminist Theology and the third one from the secular Feminist Movement that is widely accepted and used within African Feminist theological reflection.

The first theory from Western Feminist Theology was developed by Rosemary Radford Ruether. It states that Feminism should promote the full 'humanity' of women and that this should not be achieved at the expense of the full humanity of men [children, the poor].[61] The underlining principle for this theory is that we are all created in the image of God, and equal in the 'fallen state,' all needing redemption.

The second theory is developed by Elisabeth Schüssler-Fiorenza. It states the importance of naming tangents of oppression such as androcentric Bible texts, patriarchy, kyriarchy, and androcentric scriptures in constructing

---

[61] See Rosemary Ruether, *Sexism and God-Talk; Towards a Feminist Theology*, Boston: Beacon Press, pp. 18-20

feminist theology.[62] These tangents describe some of women's oppression in the world.

The third theory is from the secular Feminist Movement by Rosa Salinas-Hultman. She states that Feminist theory must be critical and advocate for women's Liberation, seeking to produce a better world for women—and humankind.[63] The theory argues for advocating what can still be done to create a better world for women and men from women's perspectives. This concerns changing the conditions of women in society including within the different kinds of religions and cultures.

An example of this theory is the "Feminist theory" developed by Patricia Madoo Lengermann and Jill Niebrugge-Brantley.[64] It states that the major "object" for [feminist] investigation, and the starting point of all its investigation, is the situation (or the situations) and experiences of women in society. Secondly, it seeks to see the world from the distinctive vantage point (or vantage points) of women in the social world.

Evangelical Feminist Theology subjects the above theories to Bible concepts and to women's experiences from their mission history. Some of the Bible concepts that are often alluded to in their hermeneutics are: That both men and women are created in God's image and Paul's *Magna Charta* in Galatians 3:28.[65] Further, women often use the motif of Jesus' mission to the women in identifying paradigms to be emulated by church and society in the engagement of women. Some of the concepts from Mission history include reference to women leaders such as Mary Slessor and Malla Moe.[66]

General Principles of Feminist Hermeneutics

There are two major ways on how information for any theological research is done. These are primary and secondary sources. The first principle in

---

[62] See Elisabeth Schüssler Fiorenza, *A Feminist Theological Reconstruction of Christian Origins. In Memory of Her*, New York: Crossroads, 1999 (1983), p. xxviii.

[63] Ibid., p. 447. Also see paper by Rosa Salinas-Hultman, "Hispanics, Catholics and Women in the 'Americas.' Possibilities of the Hispanic American Women's Perspective." University of Linköping, p. 8.

[64] Patricia Madoo Lengermann and Jill Niebrugge-Brantley, *Contemporary Feminist Theory, Sociological Theory*, Singapore: McGraw Hill, 1992, pp. 447-496.

[65] "There is neither Jew nor Greek, slave nor free, male nor female, for your are all one in Christ Jesus" (NIV).

[66] For details on both see section 1.6.

Feminist research is that primary sources are largely based on the experiences of women. If it is a Feminist research in the area of Biblical Studies, women's experiences with the Bible text are viewed to be reservoirs for revelation from God. Unless women experience the Scriptures for themselves, there is no revelation from God for them. Thus a Feminist researcher collects and recollects women's experiences with the Bible text in constructing such theologies. If the researcher is researching in the area of Church History or Mission History, she gathers her information on biographical studies of women,[67] stories of women[68] and even poems about women. A key device used in collecting such women's stories is the personal interview that deliberately seeks to uncover stories, experiences, myths, poems and so on about women. Story telling has an advantage in shifting women's roles from being objects of history to being its subjects.[69] Some of the material, because of its sensitive nature, is collected or recollected mainly through participatory observation.

The second principle in Feminist research is that certain Feminist research can best be done by women. The assumption is that though men can also research on such subjects, they may not comprehensively understand biological experiences that are best captured by women and not by men. This is based on the assumption that a woman has a vantage point in entering into such issues. An example of this might be the collection of women's experiences of menstruation in a particular church. Although a man might be given the chance to collect such experiences, he may not as fully understand the intricacies of the subject as a woman would. A woman who has gone through the girls' initiation in Chewa society will have a better chance to collect experiences of women in relation to their initiation. The key to such an investigation is the secret codes a woman has learned as she un-

---

[67] Examples are: Annalet van Schalkwyk, "The Story of Anne Hope: A White Woman's Contribution towards South African Liberation," in Isabel Apawo Phiri, Devarakshanam Betty Govinden and Sarojini Nadar (eds), *Her-stories. Hidden Histories of Women of Faith in Africa*, Pietermaritzburg: Cluster, 2002, pp. 279-304; Devarakshanam Betty Govinden, "'The Mother of African Freedom' – The Contribution of Charlotte Maxeke to the Struggle for Freedom in South Africa," in Isabel Apawo Phiri, Devarakshanam Betty Govinden and Sarojini Nadar (eds), *Her-stories. Hidden Histories of Women of Faith in Africa*, Pietermaritzburg: Cluster, 2002, pp. 304-326.

[68] Use of narrative methodology has much prominence in Circle theology (H.M. van den Bosch, "African Theology: Is it Relevant for Global Christianity? *NGTT*, 2009, pp. 530-537 [537]).

[69] Ibid.

derwent the initiation. In cases where men engage in such research, the men usually use women as bridges to collect information. This principle is currently under challenge and it is now common that men are collecting information in subjects that earlier on were only regarded as women's subjects.

The third principle is that Feminist research requires that **experiences of women** are collected according to their cultural contexts. Even if a wider study of women is carried out, a deliberate reflection on experiences of women in accordance with their cultural heritage is encouraged. It is within this paradigm that comparisons and differentiations of women's experiences in a particular study are done. The underlying principle here is that different modes of socialization and culture have an influence on women's experiences. It is argued therefore that experiences of a particular cultural group of women do not necessarily reflect theologies of all African women. The theologies of women in the Baptist Convention in Southern Malawi may or may not be the same as those of Baptist Convention women in Central Malawi. Their theologies are influenced by their different cultures.

The fourth principle that is more applicable to African Feminist hermeneutics is that Feminist theological research must always be placed in the **realm of religion** and the **socio-political** and the **cultural context** of the people. Subjecting Feminist theological research to religion enables the researchers to differentiate their research from secular Feminist research. Religion is enfolded in data collection by restricting research to experiences of women of faith with their religion and their different books of revelation. The dominant groups of women in the world are Christians and Muslims. There are also a few religions such as Buddhism, Rastafarianism, African Traditionalist Religion and Jews. Feminist theological research is distinctly different from secular Feminist research in that faith is part and parcel of these women's theologizing. Among African Feminist researchers, for example, it is argued that there could be no theology for African women if it is not hinged in culture and religion. This is because the majority of African women are believers in God as revealed in their respective religious traditions: Islam, African Traditionalist, Christian, and Jewish among others. However, Feminist theological research and Secular Feminist research borrow from each other the core principles of doing research.

The role of faith as an ingredient in doing Feminist theological research has two dimensions. The first is that the targeted women under research are women that have a belief in God. It is this faith that illuminates their experiences in their different contexts. This means that if one is writing about women and leadership in a particular context, the writer must know that leadership of women is influenced by the faith of women.

The fifth principle is that a Feminist researcher must disclose his or her religion and her relationship to the particular aspect of research. It is therefore necessary that, as part of the research design, the researcher must include a paragraph on their particular background of faith. The assumption is that as one conducts research, she or he puts on the glasses of their faith and their particular position in that faith. The product of their theology is therefore subjectively illuminated by their faith and their position. This makes them insiders when they are conducting research relating to their faith, and outsiders when they are dealing with research of women in other faiths. Both perspectives (being outsider and insider) have advantages and disadvantages in doing research that readers must be aware of. As an insider one has the advantage that he or she has much knowledge about the experiences of these people and their faith. This on the other hand can be a disadvantage in that it may blind him or her from certain issues of concern within the faith community one is researching on. Being an outsider does not necessarily imply that one is conducting a particular research objectively. One's subjectivity may be influenced by judgmental attitudes, which often arise due to the fact that many people view their particular faiths as superior to others. One of the advantages though is that one may bring out issues that the people belonging to the particular faith are not conscious about.

African Feminist Hermeneutics

In all the three main branches of African Feminist Hermeneutics: Cultural Feminist Hermeneutics; Biblical Feminist Hermeneutics and Relational Feminist Hermeneutics, a Feminist epistemology based on Feminist theories is used in constructing knowledge from the collected information. Although Feminist Theologians use women's experiences in conducting research, they do not do that blindly. They use critical inquiry based of the Feminist theories highlighted above in constructing theology. The role of critical inquiry for Feminist theological research is imperative. As Feminist Theologians collect and recollect women's experiences, they must not be just chroniclers of women's experiences; rather they must task themselves with ordering these experiences in a logical and sensible way that brings out a theology about God and women. To achieve this, women's experiences are subjected to tools of analysis that require much reflection. The tools of analysis are dependent on the academic field under which such Feminist research is placed. However, regardless of the academic field, within which the research is placed, Feminist researchers based on the Feminist theories above use a "gendered analysis" from a woman's perspective. The theories, though not limited to those documented above, guide this Feminist analysis. In this respect of ordering of women's experiences in a particular context research must be designed in such a way that it assesses how particular experiences of women reflect the Feminist theories. Therefore, an engendered analysis must be guided by questions such as:

> (a) Are these women's experiences affirming God's oracle about women's equality with men?
>
> (b) If there are discrepancies, who are the perpetuators of such inequality? (In an engendered analysis, reasons are first and foremost related to issues of patriarchy.)
>
> (c) What are the areas where women are facing inequality? (These may be, for example, in the area of church leadership and sexuality, among others). Issues of whether women are ordained or not are gender issues if and where only men are ordained. Marriages such as a woman not being given the chance to choose a husband (forced marriages, arranged marriages) are also gender issues because they demonstrate that a man is more powerful than a woman. After areas where women are facing inequality are highlighted, women must ask:
>
> (d) What ways can transform such inequalities from a woman's perspective?

The goal of Feminist research is liberation of women and promotion of gender equality between men and women from a women's perspective and that's where such questions are important. Liberation, though aiming at women, must aim at dignity of both women and men. This is crucial where dignity and power balance can sometimes oppose each other. An example of this contradiction is in the event that men gain economic empowerment at the expense of women's health. This is not God's talk for women according to feminist theological research. God's talk for women is where God brings both equality and dignity to the women and men. A scientific inquiry in these women's experiences seeks to create a Feminist Theology that will bring balance of power between men and women in church and society without compromising women's dignity. Such a gendered analysis is applied to all branches of African Feminist Hermeneutics. This section deals with how Feminist theories and approaches illuminate the particular branch of African Feminist hermeneutics with examples.

African Feminist Relational Hermeneutics

At the heart of gender relations is the issue of who holds the power between men and women. A Relational Feminist Hermeneutic is intended at bringing equality between men and women in church and society. The crucial aspect of this approach is to have a critical analysis of who holds the powers, factors that promote such dominance (referred to by Elisabeth Schüssler as tangents of oppression) and what could be done to have equal power between men and women (this is what Radford Ruether would refer to as creating a better world for the future for both men and women). Significant contributions on gender relations in the church and society are by historical theologians in the Circle. Philomena Njeri Mwaura, Christina Landman,[70] Mary Getui[71] and Isabel Apawo Phiri are probably leaders in this field. These have based their writings on the experiences of men and women in either African Independent Churches or Traditional Religions[72] or Presbyterian churches, Charismatic as well as Pentecostal churches.[73] Some have written on more than one religious context as stated earlier.

In addition, the subject of gender relations has not been limited to historical theologians. It has also been promoted by the other African Feminist Hermeneutics: African Feminist Biblical Hermeneutics and African Feminist Cultural Hermeneutics. However, these two hermeneutics do not only deal with the issues of gender equality in leadership roles but also addresses issues of women's dignity in church and society. However, an application of these theoretical frameworks vary according to the context of those that engage in Relational Hermeneutics and those that consume the products of

---

[70] See for example: Christina Landman, "A Land Flowing with Milk and Honey", Musimbi Kanyoro and Nyambura Njoroge (eds), *Groaning in Faith: African Women in the Household of God*, Nairobi: Acton, 1996, pp. 99-111.

[71] See for example: Mary N. Getui, "Women's Priesthood in Relation to Nature", in Musimbi Kanyoro and Nyambura Njoroge (eds), *Groaning in Faith: African Women in the Household of God*, Nairobi: Acton, 1996, pp. 31-39.

[72] See for example: Philomena Njeri Mwaura, "The Anthropological Dimension of a Patient's Treatment: a Response to Prof. Bernard Ugeux", *International Review of Mission*, vol 95, pp. 136-142.

[73] See for example: Philomena Njeri Mwaura, "Nigerian Pentecostal Missionary Enterprise in Kenya", Ogbu Kalu, Chima Jacob Koriah, G. Ugo Nwokeji and Obiama Nnaemeta (eds), *Religion, History and Politics in Nigeria*, University Press of America, 2005.

a particular Relational Hermeneutic. An example of this is chapter 5 which shows how Evangelical women appropriate such hermeneutics of power relations between men and women among Baptist women and men of Southern Malawi.

African Feminist Cultural Hermeneutics

African Feminist Cultural Hermeneutics has been applied to many African cultural studies that relate to women's empowerment. Culture here is not only about the primitive African cultures of the past but the current cultures as well, taking into account the fluidity of culture and the particular identities of different African cultures these women are exposed to.[74] Here also Feminist theories are used to interpret culture so that women experience liberation. The tangents of oppression within the African culture are named but also solutions to such tangents of oppression are provided. There are two main positions on African culture.

The first one is that African culture is evil and must be destroyed in order to realize women's liberation. This position is illustrated by advocacy research documented in the later paragraphs that was done by Nyambura Njoroge among the Gikuyu women of Kenya, and Margaret Umeagudosu of Nigeria.

The second position is that African culture should be kept but must be rid of negative elements. The example of this position is Literary Feminist research that was done by Mercy Amba Oduyoye among the Akan women of Ghana that we detail in later paragraphs. Further, some African Feminist theologians argue that the goodness in African culture has been compromised by outside forces. Here we point out a few of them:

Firstly that women and men do not allow God to be born within their cultures in order to liberate women. The argument is that God relates with the real world of women (all forms of culture) and utters oracles for them in accordance with their social, economic, political and traditional culture. The key question is not who God is, but how God manifests Himself/Herself in their world of social, economic, political and cultural liberation of women and men, from all forms of oppression in their world. It is here that some African Feminist Theologians have proposed that women must allow God to be born and grow within their hearts to deal with the tangents of oppression between men and women in their African cultures. This simply means

---

[74] See Isabel Apawo Phiri, "African Women Theologies," *Agenda 61*, 2004, p. 16.

that they should be "mothers of God." In this expression, African Feminist researchers emphasize that in a world where there is economic, social, political, and cultural oppression, it is because God is not there, and once women are willing to let God be born through them within such a cultural contexts, compassion, justice, peace and all forms of liberation will flourish. Eliza Jane Getman is representative of this view and argues: "we must allow God to work and grow and be born over and over again in our lives."[75]

Secondly, other African Feminist researchers argue that colonization has tainted the African culture. Thus the tangents of oppression are due to the political, social and economic contexts women are exposed to. This is because African Feminist women have been influenced by different colonial powers, some of which were more oppressive than others. For instance, women from countries with prolonged periods of war will probably articulate theologies of women with an influence from such hostile environments. Countries that have experienced such prolonged periods of war and have such women theologies include: Angola, Congo, Rwanda, Burundi and Mozambique. It is not only the theologies that are tainted with such an environment but also the kind of women's issues Feminist women zoom in on. Progress in women's theological training, for example, is a more crucial issue in countries that experienced war than anywhere else.

Similarly, research conducted by South African Feminist women differs from that conducted by Kenyan Feminist women. For a South African Feminist woman, political, social and economic as well as religious oppression women went through in the apartheid era becomes central in conducting their research. Even within the same context of South Africa, a woman of Colour will probably conduct research differently from a White South African woman. In the same way, African Feminist women are suspicious of research conducted by African men because African women come from a different gender context from that of the African men. Thus research of Feminist female theologians differs from Feminist male theologians. Feminist theologies by women are from the perspective of the women's world context, different from that of their own brothers.

On the other hand, among African women, despite differences in contexts, there are marked similarities in their research because, although African contexts are different, in essence they all fall under two major cultural cat-

---

[75] See Eliza Jane Getman, "Giving Birth to God Our Mother: Nurturing a Theology of Birth as Creative Power," Malaka-le Theologies 2005.

egories: patrilineal and matrilineal. The beauty of this is that in many countries these two categories exist. Since African women share a similar culture, they have a legitimate claim to construct theologies that are indeed African (African women theologies) even though their similarities are coloured by differences in political and economic contexts.

Thirdly, some African Feminist Theologians argue that much of the oppressive elements women face are not due to outside forces but within the African Traditional Culture (ATR). Such theologians view ATR as imposing multiple patriarchal forces on the women, thus necessitating reinterpretation. Some of the patriarchal oppression in culture that women deal with is related to one's identity,[76] belonging, marriage stability and religious misconceptions about women. It requires multiple interpretative tools to unsettle these culture related patriarchal oppressions. As the women engage in this game of interpreting culture, they grapple with the old issues of continuity and discontinuity of cultural elements in the light of what is liberating and what is not. Daisy Mwachukwu, for example, argues that religious customs that reject the development of a whole person and impede progress should be discontinued.[77] African Feminist Cultural Hermeneutics to a certain extent demands that women pay a price in order for them to realize liberation. For others it is a nightmare goal to realize liberation because of conflictual realities in the life of African women which present a challenge in making choices on what is liberating and what is not. Some discontinuities might result in a woman being rejected by her kin. Further, women face the realities of "low risk cultural choices" and "high risk cultural choices."[78]

While low risk cultural choices refer to those that require less sacrifice by women, high risk cultural choices refers to choices that would result in a woman sacrificing her means of survival or security. This would include loosing one's marriage and kinship ties among others. While this is a reality for African women, this may not be a preoccupation for feminists in Europe

---

[76] The issue of identity also features prominently in the agenda of African Theology. See H.M. van den Bosch, "African Theology: Is it Relevant for Global Christianity? *NGTT*, 2009, pp. 529-537 [530].

[77] See Daisy Mwachukwu, "The Context of African Women's Life," in Mercy Amba Oduyoye and Musimbi Kanyoro (eds), *Proceedings of the Convocation of African Women Theologians 1989*, Accra-North: Sam-Woode, 2001, pp. 118-121, also quoted by Helen Adekunbi Labeodan, "Women Reproductive Health in Nigeria, A Theo-Philosophical Approach," Malaka-le Theologies 2005, p. 9.

[78] "Low risk cultural choices" and "high risk cultural choices" are my own neologisms.

or America. In the African context, women that would find it easy to make high risk choices are likely to be those that have other forms of security or survival to replace those that they have chosen against. Urban women, for example, may easily make such choices as opposed to rural women because (1) they are somewhat removed from the grip of kinship and family to such an extent that the cultural prescriptions of their clan may no longer be binding to them. (2) They are likely to have other forms of survival or securities other than those offered through marriage, kinship or family. Employment is an example of such securities. Regardless of the challenge regarding cultural interpretation the Circle is providing an important model in African cultural hermeneutics that critiques African culture without denigrating it.[79]

Examples of African Feminist Cultural Hermeneutics

In this section we provide examples of both advocacy Feminist cultural research and Feminist Literary Research. The example of Feminist Literary research was done by Mercy Amba Oduyoye. She reflects on the relationship between women's empowerment and African culture in the context of her first theological work on the experiences of Akan women in Ghana.[80] In this work she analyses these women's culture in relation to what in them is empowering and what is not. In "Daughters of Anowa," Mercy uses the word "empowering" when she argues that informal socialization practiced by the Akan women influences their empowerment.[81] In this, she problematizes the issue of informal socialization in relation to women's empowerment. This is also outlined by other African Feminist women, especially in their discussions on girls' initiation.[82] Mercy highlights the meaning of "empowerment" further, namely as "liberation." This is done in her theological

---

[79] See Tinyiko S. Maluleke, "Half a Century of African Christian Theologies: Elements of the Emerging Agenda for the Twenty-first Century", *Journal of Theology for Southern Africa*, 1997, 99, pp. 4-23.

[80] See Mercy Amba Oduyoye, *Daughters of Anowa: African Women and Patriarchy*, Maryknoll: Orbis, 1995, p. 227.

[81] Ibid.

[82] See Isabel Apawo Phiri, *Women, Presbyterianism and Patriarchy*, pp. 62-70. See Rachel NyaGondwe Banda [Fiedler], *Women of Bible and Culture: Baptist Convention Women in Southern Malawi*, Zomba: Kachere: 2005, pp. 121, 145, 183f; Rachel NyaGondwe Fiedler, *Coming of Age: A Christianized Initiation among Women in Southern Malawi*, Zomba: Kachere, 2005.

piece "Introducing African Women's Theology."[83] In this work, Mercy calls African Women Theologians to attention concerning "Life cycles of African women" as affecting women's lives. Mercy refers to the word liberation in the same way as empowerment when she argues that cultural aspects that are liberating to women must be enhanced and those that are not liberating to women must be nullified.[84] African Feminist women researchers have widely used this definition to analyze culture. Thus the process of continuities and discontinuities of cultural elements to affirm women's dignity is the hallmark of liberation in African Feminist Theology. This may be different from other Feminist researchers, where such liberation is targeted at the class struggles, for example.

The second example is the Feminist advocacy research carried out by Nyambura Njoroge on an ethical resistance staged by the Gikuyu women in the Women's Guild of the Presbyterian Church of East Africa (PCEA), established among the Gikuyu people in 1891.[85] In this church, women struggled with a hazardous cultural practice, the circumcision of girls (female genital mutilation). The practice is a health hazard because those that undergo this ritual face death, because of the brutality of the act of circumcision. They also face difficulty in delivery, or even death of their unborn child.[86] However, the cultural practice was sanctioned by patriarchy, as it served the interests of men. Thus the cultural element became an ethical issue, as there was a controversy as regards the essentiality of the rite. For some this cultural aspect was essential in nurturing and protecting the network of relationships in the Gikuyu community. This was important as well as a moral responsibility.[87] The centrality of the practice is also seen by how difficult it was to resist it.

Nyambura Njoroge researched on how the medical attempts in hospitals and schools did not manage to wipe away the practice. Thus, even though right from the beginning of mission medical work in the area, there was a systematic teaching about circumcision that was started in 1906 by Dr John Arthur of Thogolo Hospital, there was little change in this cultural aspect.

---

[83] See Mercy Amba Oduyoye, *Introducing African Women's Theology*, p. 30-31.
[84] Ibid., p. 30-31. The critical stages that are imbedded in women's life circles are birth, puberty, pregnancy, marriage, divorce, remarriage etc.
[85] Nyambura Njoroge, *Kiama kia Ngo: An African Christian Feminist Ethic of Resistance and Transformation*, Legon: Legon Theological Studies, 2000, p. 173.
[86] Ibid., p. 21.
[87] Ibid., p. 23.

This is because as a missionary and a European, it is likely that locals questioned as to why an outsider would try to solve problems that were outside his experience.[88] Circumcision was also included in the syllabus of the schools with the idea to oppose it. Minnie Watson did curriculum development on this particular cultural aspect. It had to take an active group resistance from women in the same culture (Gikuyu) that reinforced the transformation. Indeed the women staged a protest against the rite.[89]

From the experience of Gikuyu women, it is clear that in reinterpreting cultural issues that have an ethical significance, the urgency of the matter might require much more than dialogue. In this case, the women had to protest the cultural aspect by staging a group demonstration. This, however, is best done by those from within, in this case, the women of that particular culture that staged the resistance. Such a group in turn forms a source of survival. Secondly, change is effective if solidarity is reinforced (the women resisted this cultural aspect as a group, not as individuals). Such actions might also gradually change notions of what may be culturally binding to women's identity, belonging and family security in that particular culture. This might be a positive development for the liberation of daughters in the future generation. Since some of the cultural elements that oppress women are reinforced by the church, it is important that women participate in the decision-making forum of the church. (Gikuyu women had to approach the leaders of the church that they were rejecting this cultural element).

Another similar example is the work by Margaret A. Umeagudosu on the experience of women suffering from VVF (Vesico Vagina Fistula) in Nigeria. VVF is a hotbed for stigmatization and suffering for women, yet it can be prevented by an active demonstration against early marriages. Leakage of urine is experienced especially among women that have early pregnancies, since these woman's pelvic girdles are not sufficiently developed to allow the passage of the baby.[90] Therefore the baby ruptures some of the bladder tissue, causing the condition. Women in this condition are restricted to

---

[88] For a discussion of the then missionary context, see Klaus Fiedler, *The Story of Faith Missions. From Hudson Taylor to Present Day Africa*, Oxford et al: Regnum, 1994, pp. 252-256.

[89] Nyambura Njoroge, *Kiama kia Ngo: An African Christian Feminist Ethic of Resistance and Transformation*, Legon: Legon Theological Studies, 2000, p. 5.

[90] See Margaret A. Umeagudosu, "'Act of God?' The Experience of Women Living with Vesico Vagina Fistula (VVF) among Women in Northern Nigeria," Malaka-le Theologies 2005.

their private homes, are chased from families and have difficulty in accessing medical help. While Margaret Umeagudosu suggests that increasing access to medical facilities will help these women fight stigmatization, it is clear that this medical approach needs to be complemented with a demonstration against this practice. The traditional pattern of delivering babies outside hospitals (*kunya*) must also be demonstrated against.[91]

Feminist Biblical Hermeneutics

Feminist Biblical Hermeneutics are primarily based on Reader Response Criticism. This is often linked to liberal theologies, but it is also in tandem with Evangelical Theology that centres on the individual's experiences with God and His word. The many branches of Evangelical and Charismatic movements to a certain extend are based on the emphasis on personal experiences with the Bible.

However, in this book we present one specific Evangelical Feminist Hermeneutic that subjects Reader Response Criticism to: (1) Historical Approaches (Criticism) as shown in chapter 4, for example, when applying an Evangelical Biblical Hermeneutics to the New Testament; and (2) the Literary Approach which takes each literary genre seriously in itself. The interpretation is about situating the message for women's empowerment within the particular genre. This approach has been demonstrated in chapter 3 in the application of Evangelical Feminist Hermeneutics to the Old Testament.

Firstly, we describe some methods of collecting Biblical Feminist information:

Contextual Bible Studies:

The common approach to collecting feminist information from the Bible in Reader Response Criticism is to conduct contextual Bible studies with a group of women. The focus is to record how women experience a particular text and respond to it.

The other approach to collecting Feminist information from the Bible in a Reader Response is by studying sermons by women or men on women's issues. These sermons bring out women's and men's experiences with the bible on women's issues.

---

[91] Ibid.

In both sermons and contextual Bible studies, the researcher must record the experiences on women's issues as a participant. However, contextual Bible Study and Sermon Experiences can also be studied by a non participant.

Examples of how to conduct contextual Bible studies include: choosing a passage for reflection or a particular theme in the Bible and deliberating on it as it relates to women in a particular context. In this regard, a Bible Study guide basing on the objectives of the Feminist research must be used. An example of a topic that would be dealt with using Contextual Bible Studies would be: A study of 1 Corinthians 7:1-7 on liberation of Yao women in Mangochi; or A study of Leviticus 14 on participation of Calvary Family Church women in Holy Communion Services.

Such research topics will focus on a particular text and the lived experiences of such a text among women from a particular context. A research topic on a thematic Contextual Bible Study would be like these: The understanding of NT teaching on women leadership among Baptist Convention women of Northern Malawi; the relationship between the understanding of women as pastors in the Assemblies of God church in Lilongwe and in the Book of Acts.

In these Feminist Biblical Hermeneutics, Feminist researchers subject their different approaches to the Feminist theories as they deal with the Bible texts. This is not only characteristic of research in Christianity. Highlighting tangents of oppression within the Biblical text and solutions to such tangents is what Feminist research does. This is also done in other religions such as Islam and Judaism in their hermeneutics relating to the reveled texts within their religions. Why is the Bible central in African Feminist Hermeneutics?

For researchers in Christianity in Africa one must know that:

> The Bible is central in constructing African women theologies because Africans identify with much in the Bible. In fact much in the Bible remains in their memory and becomes the basis for their reflection about God in their everyday life. Whether one is in a village, or studying in a university, the Bible is accepted as the source for the articulation of the Christian faith.[92]

---

[92] Madipoane Masenya, "The Bible as a 'Sword' and a 'Tool for Healing'," Malaka-le Theologies, 2005.

In the Old Testament Feminist research is useful in dealing with issues that are problematic to women. Examples of this are passages on Levirate marriages, or polygamy, which African Feminist women find dehumanizing.[93] Such issues are dealt with within the discipline of Biblical and Cultural Hermeneutics.

Some of the tangents of oppression include oppressive interpretations to the Bible. For example, some Feminist theological researchers argue that over the years, the Bible has been used as a "sword" and at the same time as a "healing tool."[94] The Bible has been used to legitimize slave trade, for example, as well as apartheid, among other atrocities. In fact some have even become skeptic about the use of the Bible in constructing theologies because of its contradictory usage. These argue that the Bible cannot be trusted, as expressed by Elna Mouton in this quote:

> Through a lack of credibility on the side of preachers and theological institutions mainly because of repressive ways in which the Bible has been used in the past, many people seem to have lost their trust and confidence in the liberating power of God.[95]

To this, pitfall, Feminist researchers argue that one must use the Bible as a source if she is a biblical scholar and is researching on a specific issue in the Bible. The approach here would be how it is understood in the Bible and how it is understood and lived by a particular group of women. If one is not in the discipline of Biblical Studies but in other theological disciplines, then it is imperative that the Bible as a source must be used from the application perspective and never as an admonition or exhortation at the end of a theological piece.

---

[93] On these two issues (male) African Theology seems to be more willing to compromise with traditional culture. — For a study that tries to reassess the Christian attitude to polygamy with special concern for the victims (especially women and their children) see: Moses Mlenga, *Polygamy in Northern Malawi. A Christian Reassessment*, Mzuzu: Mzuni Press, 2016.

[94] Elna Mouton, "'From Woundedness Towards Healing'. Rhetoric or Pastoral-Theological Vision?" 14th National Conference: Southern African Association for Pastoral Work, Cape Town, 12-14 May 2003. See also Miranda N. Pillay, "Luke 7:36–50: See This Woman? Towards a Theology of Gender Equality in the Context of HIV/AIDS," Malaka-le Theologies, 2005, p. 4.

[95] See Mary Getui, "Masanta: Traditional Healer among Abagushii of Western Kenya," Malaka-le Theologies, 2005, p. 9.

In other disciplines of study, the Bible can be used as a tool of application. In the writing of the history of women in the Baptist Convention, Rachel NyaGondwe Fiedler uses the Bible to reflect on the experiences of women in her church. The question she is relating the Bible to is how these women's understanding of the Bible has shaped their history. Further, the analysis of these women's history is guided by categories of leadership among women in the New Testament.

The other tangent of oppression African Feminist Theologians highlight is that the Bible is patriarchal. For this reason African Feminist researchers are opposed to literal(istic) interpretations of the Bible. The androcentric nature of the Bible is attributed to the following:

Firstly they argue that the majority of Bible authors are male. In this they are in agreement with Elisabeth Schüssler Fiorenza. Thus the majority of the African feminist theologians do not subscribe to the position that the Bible is "thus says the Lord" all the time, but rather that women, in finding meaning for themselves from the Bible, should ask: "what does the Lord say in this Bible passage for women?"

Secondly they argue that most Bible interpretations are androcentric and this hides the Word of God for women in their different situations. The only way women can get meaning for themselves is to find ways of unsettling this androcentric nature of the Bible.

Within this dominant view of biblical interpretation is Evangelical interpretation that has become visible since the advent of Evangelical Feminist women in Africa.[96] Evangelical feminist women are of two variations. The first groups agues that the Bible's position that men should lead over women is ordained by God and must be followed. The second group argues that the Bible does not teach that men are above women and that those who claim that the Bible is andocentric read scriptures wrongly. These show their argument by unveiling women of power in the Bible.

Examples of African Feminist Biblical Hermeneutics

This section provides five approaches to interpreting the Bible. Some examples are by biblical scholars and one is an example of how non biblical scholars can apply the Bible to research on women.

---

[96] Dorcas Akintunde from Nigeria was one of the prominent women on the Evangelical side.

Cheryl Barbara Anderson[97]

Cheryl Barbara Anderson is a biblical scholar. She uses the following technique in reinterpreting scripture: Firstly, she outlines lessons or meanings in front of the text (within a given faith community). Secondly, she outlines lessons learned in the text; and thirdly, she discusses lessons learned behind the text.[98]

Meaning in Front of the Text

The beginning here for interpretation is the issue that one has chosen to research on. This might be 'the position of women in the church,' or 'faithfulness in marriage' and so on. After choosing this topic, one must decide on a Bible passage on which her study will be based. The next point is how a particular community is experiencing the problem in the area under study. Cheryl Barbara Anderson demonstrates this model in her study on the HIV/AIDS pandemic. She considers *meaning in front of the text* as how a particular faith community is experiencing the HIV/AIDS pandemic. This is achieved through telling the story in her own words basing on how HIV/AIDS is a reality in her community. This, according to Cheryl Barbara Anderson, is the flesh and blood.

Meaning in the Text (Literary Analysis)

After retelling the story, one needs to focus on a particular Bible passage related to the topic under research. One must reflect on this passage guided by issues or categories that are crucial in the experiences of HIV/AIDS in that particular believing community. For example one can choose the passage on Naaman. In this case the retelling of the story of Naaman should be under selective issues in the believing community such as those of age and gender, and then the story should be linked to how these issues play a positive or a negative role in the spread of HIV/AIDS.

Lessons behind the Text

After the exercise on meaning in front of the text, and meaning in the text, the next step is to read what other researchers have written on the same issue. This contextualizes the issue under research. Cheryl Barbara Ander-

---

[97] Cheryl Barbara Anderson, "Lessons on Healing from Naaman (2 Kings 5:1-27): An African American Perspective," in Isabel Apawo Phiri (ed), *African Women, HIV/AIDS, and Faith Communities,* Pietermaritzburg: Cluster 2003, pp. 23-24.

[98] Ibid., p. 23-37.

son contextualizes the passage in terms of what other scholars have said on the same issue. She outlines implications of various scholars to the spread of HIV/AIDS. Here redaction and transmission history are a particular interpretation key.

Cheryl Barbara Anderson's is that though biblical interpretation can be used in isolation, for a fuller meaning of the text, a multifaceted approach should be used. Although Cheryl Anderson is an African American theologian, the fact that her methodology is outlined in a Circle book means that it is accepted as a valid methodology to use in the Circle.[99]

Dorcas Olubanke Akintunde

Dorcas Olubanke Akintunde was a Nigerian New Testament scholar and member of the Circle. The methodology she uses in biblical interpretation has similar steps to those used by Cheryl Barbara Anderson. The difference is that she begins with the "meaning behind the text", where consulting of commentaries is done. This step is simply a "redaction history rereading of scripture."

Though both Cheryl Barbara Anderson and Dorcas Olubanke Akintunde utilize primary sources in trying to assess how a specific issue is experienced by a believing community, Cheryl Anderson utilizes stories while Dorcas Olubanke Akintunde uses interviews guided by a questionnaire. Dorcas Akintunde uses these oral interviews to determine experiences of women sex workers in a given community. Cheryl Barbara Anderson calls this procedure "meaning in front of the text." The last stage that Dorcas Olubanke Akintunde adds is that of *appropriation*. This is the application stage where she interconnects the experiences of women sex workers with the Bible text.[100] In this way, Dorcas Akintunde also supports a multifaceted approach to feminist rereading of scripture. Her methodology also utilizes experiences of women as an important aspect in feminist biblical scholarship.

---

[99] In fact, the preceding passage shows how much this methodology is already used by key biblical scholars in the Circle. The difference is more in a name and that some women may use all or just some stages of the methodology.

[100] Dorcas Olubanke Akintunde, "The Attitude: A Model for Contemporary Churches in the Face of HIV/AIDS in Africa," in Isabel Apawo Phiri, Beverly Haddad, Madipoane Masenya (ngw'ana Mphahlele), *African Women, HIV/AIDS and Faith Communities*, Pietermaritzburg: Cluster 2003, pp. 94-110.

Musa Dube

She is a New Testament scholar from Botswana who has written widely in Circle books and other publications. She uses the same methodology.[101] She begins with the same paradigm of "reading in front of the text", then moves on to describing how others have interpreted the text (redaction and transmission history). Cheryl Barbara Anderson calls this: "reading behind the text." The third step Musa Dube deploys is "appropriation" and she uses it in the same way as Dorcas Akintunde. It is the same step Cheryl Anderson calls "reading in front of the text." Here Musa Dube relates the biblical context with the context of the believing community.[102] She then uses an engendered analysis to analyze the results.[103]

Denise Ackermann

She is a systematic theologian from South Africa. She follows a similar methodology as a tool in reinterpreting scripture. In discussing the issue of Tamar's cry, she begins by setting the context (literary analysis) as well as retelling the biblical story in view of the realities of HIV/AIDS (reading in front of the text) in this believing community. After this stage, she moves on to the "appropriation" stage where the Bible text interacts with the context of the believing community.[104] Just as in the above methodologies, this stage is where a possible theology of transformation is shown. It is a stage where grassroots women can gain insights into how the Bible can be made relevant to their situation. This is how the women can actually have God's word for themselves.

Sarojini Nadar

Sarojini Nadar is a Biblical scholar. She brings a different perspective on the above approaches of biblical interpretation outlined by Cheryl Barbara An-

---

[101] Musa Dube, "Grant me Justice: Towards Gender Sensitive Multi-Sectoral HIV/AIDS Readings of the Bible." In Musa W. Dube and Musimbi Kanyoro (eds), *Grant me Justice. HIV/AIDS and Gender Readings of the Bible*, Pietermaritzburg: Cluster, 2004, pp. 16-21.

[102] Ibid., p. 16-21.

[103] A gendered approach is from the women's perspective as outlined in the theology chapter.

[104] Denise M Ackermann, "Tamar's Cry: Re-reading an Ancient Text in the Midst of HIV/AIDS Pandemic," in Musa W. Dube and Musimbi Kanyoro (eds), *Grant Me Justice, HIV/AIDS and Gender Readings of the Bible*, p. 27-34.

derson, Dorcas Olubanke Akintunde, Musa Dube and Denise Ackermann. She begins with the step that the majority would deal with last. This step is the "reading behind the text." Using the same redaction and transmission history, Sarojini Nadar surveys works done by others on the topic. This is then used to identify points of identification in reading the text as a woman.[105]

Sarojini Nadar calls this methodology the Tripolar Model. The methodology involves three stages: *conceptualization*, *distantiation* and *appropriation*. Conceptualization refers to extracting meaning in front of the text. Whereas the above Circle women limit this exercise to experiences of women in a believing community without referring to the Bible, Sarojini Nadar guides the telling of the experiences of women in a believing community with questions relating to a Bible passage. Here the reader subjects the Bible text to questions that relate to the experiences of women. Thus she analyses the context of the women.

The second stage she deploys is called *distantiation*. In this stage, her task is to extract meaning from the text to the intended readers. This exercise tries to bridge the gap in the *conceptualization* exegesis where questions asked determine answers given. In *conceptualization* exegesis one can easily miss out the whole message of the passage. *Distantiation* helps the reader to recover some continuity with tradition.[106] In feminist scholarship, this stage helps women to have a critical eye towards their received theologies. It is a step that affirms an important aspect in education that no reader is a tabula rasa. Since some of the things the women have learned have not brought liberation to them, it is an important stage where women can reconceptualize a theology of liberation.

The last stage is that of *appropriation*. Appropriation refers to the meaning we get as our context dialogues with the text. This meaning is also influenced by the context of the reader/researcher. For example Patricia Frances Bruce in her article, "The Mother's Cow" interprets a text from the

---

[105] Sarojini Nadar, "Barak God: Women, HIV/AIDS and a Theology of Suffering" in Musa W. Dube and Musimbi Kanyoro (eds), *Grant Me Justice. HIV/AIDS and Gender Readings of the Bible*, Pietermaritzburg: Cluster, 2004.

[106] Patricia Frances Bruce, "The Mother's Cow: a Study of Old Testament References to Virginity in the Context of HIV/AIDS in South Africa" in Isabel Apawo Phiri et al, *African Women, HIV/AIDS and Faith Communities*, Pietermaritzburg: Cluster, 2003.

feminist perspective and uses stories of women as means for biblical theologizing.[107]

Evidence Women Give for the Androcentric Nature of the Bible and its Interpreters

Women in the Circle explain the androcentric nature of the Bible in many ways. The first argument is that the Bible is androcentric because women are not recognized in the Bible. In the words of Mercy Amba Oduyoye, the world of the first century in which the church was born was a "predominantly hierarchical-patriarchal world."[108] This influenced the production of an androcentric Bible text. This view is also shared by other African Feminist writers. Basing her exposition on Mt 8:14-17, Peggy Mulambya Kabonde shows that the wife of Peter and his mother in-law are neither named nor considered for their part in the ministry. The two women are also not named in Mark and Luke. The argument, which Peggy Mulambya Kabonde puts forward, is therefore that the Bible follows an androcentric pattern.[109] As such it does not always address correctly the issues of women today unless reinterpreted. In relation to service, Peggy Mulambya Kabonde argues that it is not liberating to see the woman (Peter's mother in-law) caring for people soon after being healed. She argues that the state of her health should have been recognized and maybe the very men the mother in-law was providing service to should have been the ones doing the caring ministry.[110]

Secondly, African Feminist women argue that the androcentric nature of the Bible is responsible for the inclusion of wrong models of women in the Bible. In addition to this, the early Bible interpreters who were mainly men constructed theologies basing on such wrong models of women. A common example is how the story of Eve is presented against woman's empowerment. The story is used by such early androcentric biblical interpreters to argue that because Eve is the one who gave the forbidden fruit to Adam she made Adam sin. This biblical reflection is taken as a reason why in some

---

[107] Ibid.

[108] See Mercy Amba Oduyoye, "Women Theologians and the Early Church. An Examination of Historiography," in *Voices from the Third World Women*, Colombo: EATWOT, vol. viii, no. 3, p. 70.

[109] See Rev Peggy Mulambya Kabonde, "Women and Health in Africa in the Face of HIV/AIDS Based on Mt 8:14-17, Malaka-le Theologies 2005.

[110] Ibid. p. 4.

churches women cannot be ordained as pastors. The other story is that of a woman caught in adultery and where Jesus asks those around to throw a stone at her if they did not sin. Here the biblical writer exposes the sin of the woman and hides that of the man that is later exposed by Jesus. The other argument is that there is failure to absorb women's wisdom from wrong models of women to promote the dignity of a woman. For example why not reflect on why this woman committed adultery? Was it due to lack of economic empowerment? The sin of this woman might point to deeper patriarchal forces that rob some women of the right to decent economic activities.

Thirdly, misinterpreting passages or words in the Bible to oppress women is another landmark for the androcentric nature of the Bible as well as that of early male interpreters of the Bible. These African Feminist women argue that certain male Bible interpreters have interpreted words or phrases in the Bible to undermine women. Beatrice Okeyere-Manu presents an example of this model. She argues that the words "woman as helper" to the husband have been used wrongly to imply woman's subordination to men.[111] The other examples are how verses or words such as these undermine women: Ephesians 5 about women submitting to their husbands; Man as head of woman; Woman as created from man's rib; God creating man first before woman and Paul's teaching on head covering. Such phrases and concepts have been used to promote patriarchal leadership in church and society. This point is also supported by non African Feminist Theologians. Phyllis Trible, for example, shows how the passage on how woman was created after man is wrongly used to construct a theology that women are inferior to men.[112]

Fourthly, African Feminist women argue that the practice of ignoring women that played an important role in the Bible is another product of the androcentric nature of the Bible as well as that of the biblical interpreters. An

---

[111] See Beatrice Okeyere-Manu, "Sacrificing Health for Well Being: Sex Work as a Livelihood Option for the Poor Women in Pietermaritzburg," Malaka-le Theologies 2005, p. 4. – This goes along with the original Hebrew, which reads literally: "a help into his eyes," or a help equal to him.

[112] See Phyllis Trible, "Depatriarchalizing in Biblical Interpretation," *JAAR* 41(1973), pp. 36 - 37, cf J. Muilenburg, "Form Criticism and Beyond; *FBL* 88 (1969), p. 9f. For a contrary interpretation of Gen 2 as emphasizing gender equality see: Janet Kholowa and Klaus Fiedler, *Pa Chiyambi Anawalenga Chimodzimodzi*, Blantyre: CLAIM-Kachere, 1999, pp. 22-25, translated as: *In the Beginning God Created them Equal*, Blantyre: CLAIM-Kachere, 2000, pp. 22-25.

example is the undue emphasis on male models of leadership in the church. An example is that Jesus chose 12 male disciples. Such androcentric texts have also influenced androcentric interpretations of the Bible.[113] From the passage of Jesus choosing only male disciples for example, some theologians conclude that women cannot be leaders of the church or be ordained, because they were not among the Twelve.

Evangelical Feminist Hermeneutics

Evangelical Feminist Interpretation is indeed a force to reckon with in Feminist writings. Othniel Mintang Yila in his category of the four waves of Feminism in the African Feminist Movement includes Evangelical feminism. Other categories are: Rejectionist Feminism,[114] Liberal Feminism and Hierarchical Feminism.[115] Evangelical Feminism relies on historical and literal (not literalistic) interpretation of the Bible text. It accepts that the Bible is valid and is the standard of faith. Those subscribing to this view argue that the Bible is not androcentric, but that the traditional interpreters of the Bible constructed theologies that oppressed women. Further Evangelical feminists argue that passages that portray women as inferior were historically conditioned and are not universally applicable to the Christian faith of today.

Within the arena of Evangelical interpretation lies also what Ogbu O. Kalu calls Hierarchical Feminism. He argues that this is part and parcel of African Feminist writings. It is based on the interpretation that scripture teaches hierarchy in the Christian home and in the Christian church. This hierarchy, however, does not imply that there is an ontological difference between women and men. Both sexes are equal in the eyes of God while maintaining different roles in a functional hierarchy.[116]

---

[113] See Mercy Amba Oduyoye, "Women Theologians and the Early Church. An Examination of Historiography," in *Voices from the Third World Women,* Colombo: EATWOT, vol. VIII, no. 3, pp. 71-72.

[114] These Feminists argue that both the Bible and the Christian tradition must be rejected. They seek answers for women's liberation through other means not based on the Bible. Some of such solutions include: Seeking structural change in society; viewing history as a massive plot against women; advocating an inclusive language, legalizing abortion among others; the entire Judeo-Christian tradition is sinful and unredeemable etc.

[115] Othniel Mintag Yila, "The Place of Women in the Church Ministry as Shown in 1 Timothy 2:9-15," MA, Nairobi International School of Theology, 1998.

[116] Ibid., p. 4.

Patriarchal Relationships not God's Design

One wing of Evangelical interpretation in the African Feminist Theology disagrees with the view that the Bible is patriarchal and androcentric. These try to recover stories of women of power in the Bible. An example of African feminist women who does this is Rhodah Ada James. In contradiction to the lack of representation of women leaders in top church structures, she argues that the Old Testament and the New Testament argue for women's leadership.[117]

Beginning with the Old Testament, she outlines the following examples of women who played an important role in the Bible: Miriam was a sister to Moses and Aaron (Micah 6:4, Hebrews 5:4); Deborah was judge and prophet (Judges 4 and 5:4); Esther was the wife of a king and a Jewish girl (Esther);[118] Hannah was a godly mother (1 Samuel 1:28; 2:19); Ruth became an ancestor of Jesus Christ (Ruth 4 and Mt 1:2-6); Rahab, Rebecca and Sarah and many others were women of importance in the Old Testament.[119]

Rhodah Ada James also refers to women who occupied important positions in the New Testament. In the Gospels, for example, she outlines Mary the mother of Jesus (Luke 1:26-55); Luke 2:34-35; 41-52; John 2:3-5; 19:25); Mary sister of Martha and Lazarus (Luke 10:38-42; John 11:17-44; John 12:1-3); Mary Magdalene, a friend of Jesus (Mark 15:40-44; Mark 16:1-8; Luke 8:2, John 19:25; John 20:11-18).[120]

Rhodah Ada James does not only see examples of such powerful women in the gospels, but also in the life of the early church. Phoebe (Rom 16:1-2) is one of them. She also argues that it is not true that Paul promoted the subjection of women. This is seen in his attitude towards women reflected in his ministry, as he often cooperated with women.[121] Rhodah Ada James argues that 1 Cor 14:34-35, which talks of Paul barring women from speaking in church, was culturally conditioned. She argues that Paul was offering ap-

---

[117] Rhodah Ada James: "The Scope of Women's Positions in the Church," in Mercy Amba Oduyoye and Musimbi Kanyoro (eds), *Talitha Qumi. Proceedings of the Convocation of African Women Theologians 1989*, Accra-North: Sam-Woode, 2001, pp. 192-200 [193].

[118] Ibid.

[119] Ibid., p. 194.

[120] Ibid., p. 194-196.

[121] A similar position is taken here in Malawi in: Janet Kholowa and Klaus Fiedler, *Mtumwi Paulo ndi Udindo wa Amayi Mumpingo* [The Apostle Paul and the Authority of Women in the Church], Blantyre: CLAIM-Kachere, 2001, pp. 7-14.

propriate solutions to the problems he was facing at that time. This teaching should not be applied to women in church today.[122] By highlighting women leaders in the construction of Bible theology these Circle women are trying to correct views regarding the androcentric nature of the Bible.

Secondly, such African Feminist women highlight the role of men in uplifting positions of women in church and society. Mercy Amba Oduyoye for example argues that certain men's behaviour in the Bible affirms women. If men could emulate these men today, women would be empowered. Some of the examples she gives are: Abraham, Joseph and Jairus. Abraham was criticized by fellow men when he lied that Sara was his sister. If men condemn fellow men, for example, those involved in activities that demean women, women would experience liberation. An example would be men condemning men who rape girl children and women.[123]

In the case of Joseph, the husband of Mary who became the mother of Jesus, Mercy Amba Oduyoye argues that Joseph chose to defend women's dignity even when it meant him going against culture. He demonstrated this when he found out that Mary was pregnant with Jesus even before he married her. He chose not to dump Mary as Jewish custom allowed, but went ahead and married her. If men were willing to go against culture for the sake of protecting women, women would be empowered. Jairus is an example of a man who takes care of his children. This wisdom could transform men who leave to women the responsibility of caring for children. Paul worked with women on equal level. His list of greetings in Romans 16 shows clear evidence of this.

Thirdly, African Feminist theologians argue that where teaching in the Bible does not affirm women's leadership, a search must be made whether such rules were followed or not. In the case of Jesus choosing the 12 disciples, for example, who were all men, one may get the message that He was against women's leadership in church. However, if this is checked by His

---

[122] Rhodah Ada James: "The Scope of Women's Positions in the Church," in Mercy Amba Oduyoye and Musimbi Kanyoro (eds), *Talitha Qumi. Proceedings of the Convocation of African Women Theologians 1989*, Accra-North: Sam-Woode, 2001, pp. 197-198.

[123] This resonates with the Men for Women campaign launched by the President of Malawi in 2015.

lived experience, it is clear that Jesus was not anti-women. In fact he taught positively concerning women's issues. So he was a Feminist.[124]

Fourthly, African Feminist women construct theologies of women by contextualizing texts that exclude women in the church tradition. Mercy Amba Oduyoye argues that in the Methodist Church of Ghana, at Easter, the pronouncement made in the church is: 'Jesus is risen, is risen indeed: He showed Himself to Peter'. But the pronouncement should read: 'He showed Himself to Mary and Peter'. This acknowledges the reality that some Bible accounts present the narrative in which Mary was the first person who saw Jesus after the resurrection. She is the one who transmitted the message to Peter and his fellow disciples who were in hiding.[125] Women are also reconsidering the formula in the sacrament of marriage that says: "until death do us part." African Feminist women argue that if a woman finds herself in an abusive marriage, she must not be forced to stay in such a marriage.

Fifthly, African Feminist women appeal to Jesus' message in reconstructing theologies that undermine women. In this they argue for inconsistency between Bible passages that oppress women and Christ's message. An example of this model is where the Leviticus passages that stipulate laws of uncleanliness are compared to the message of Christ that calls for new life. Helen Labedeodan Adekunbi deployed such a model. In this, she argues that the message of Christ decides what women should follow; and if there is a passage that opposes the message of Christ, then the teaching in that passage must be ignored. The laws of uncleanliness in Leviticus must be censored by Christ's teaching that the old has gone and the new has come. Laws of uncleanliness belong to the old and need not be followed. The other Bible passage that is used in opposing passages that oppress women in the church is Luke 4:8, which says: "the spirit of the Lord is upon me to preach good news and set the captives free." Isabel Phiri uses this motif in justifying why missionaries of Nkhoma Synod were wrong in denying women church leadership positions.

---

[124] The same argument is used in cultural reinterpretation. Paul taught about "head covering," but commended women in ministry such as Phoebe.

[125] Helen Adekunbi Labeodan, "Women Reproductive Health in Nigeria, A Theo-Philosophical Approach," Malaka-le Theologies, 2005.

Patriarchal Relationships as God's Design

For some Evangelical Feminist women, equality between men and women is only in being created in God's image and not in sharing leadership roles. These argue that patriarchal relationships are designed by God. However, this assertion is highly contested by the majority of African Feminist women. Their protest is eschatological. They argue that God's vision of the Church is that the Church is the image of the Kingdom of God, as it is illustrated in passages such as Mt 22:30.[126] For this reason, the church must get rid of distinctions between man and woman that do not reflect His Kingdom. The other verse that forms the Magna Charta of such an inclusive theology is Galatians 3:28.[127]

> There is neither Jew nor Greek, slave nor free, male nor female, for you are all one in Christ Jesus.

In the Kingdom of God both men and women are created in His/Her image and there is no distinction between men and women apart from biological distinctions. Even in God's eschatological dream, at the resurrection, there is neither husband nor wife. Thus there ought to be no distinction between man and woman now. It is for this reason that God uses people (men and women) as He/She likes according to the spiritual gifts showered upon them all. In this showering of gifts, God does not make distinction as regards which roles women should play and which roles men should play. Thus both men and women can be pastors, teachers, healers, prophets and so on, as God gives them grace.

On the other hand, African Feminist Theologians have seen that this image of God for the church is far from being realized in today's believing communities. There is often lack of inclusiveness of women, especially in areas related to Church participation. Men have often monopolized power in Church and society. These African Feminist women highlight the following ways in which patriarchy is expressed in the Christian church.

Firstly, hierarchical structures are viewed as patriarchal and negative to women's leadership in church. Hierarchical structures are the means by which the Church has systematically concentrated its power at the centre, whereby the majority become followers. In such a model, decision-making

---

[126] "At the resurrection people will neither marry nor be given in marriage."

[127] Othniel Mintang Yila, "The Place of Women in the Church Ministry as Shown in 1 Timothy 2:9-15," June 1998, MA Thesis, Nairobi International School of Theology.

is often top to bottom and for one to influence decisions of the church, it is easier to be at the centre. Unfortunately those on the top of the hierarchy are usually men, the clergy who are ordained. This therefore becomes a challenge to women, as those ordained are mainly men. It follows also that in many churches more men than women access theological training because it is often a prerequisite to ordained ministry. After the clergy there is the laity and this is the group that forms the majority. Almost everywhere in Africa more women than men are lay members of the congregations. Since hierarchal structures are often patriarchal, and depend on ordination, they are less empowering to women who are denied opportunities to ordination and church leadership. According to Teresa Hinga, such hierarchical structures have a tendency to practice absolutization of power and to centralize decision-making.[128] This implies that women become recipients of decisions, even those affecting them. Some African Feminist women see these patriarchal hierarchical structures as not empowering to women and also foreign to some African cultures. In such cultures it is viewed by some African Feminist women that patriarchal leadership has been inherited from the west via missionary Christianity.[129]

Secondly, the majority of African Feminist women see some church teachings as patriarchal. An example is in the area of marriage teaching that promote women to be inferior to men. These African Feminist women see that certain teachings on Christian marriage disregard God's vision of women as equal partners with men. This is visible, for example, in the fact that certain teachings encourage married women to be silent in the church as well as to submit at home to their husbands. In Charismatic ecclesiology, for example, Matthew Ojo, a leading analyst and scholar of Charismatic Christianity in Africa, observes that some of these churches prescribe silence of women literally in their practices. An example is that although a charismatic family may believe that a couple should have a joint account—which they call the common purse—to which all incomes go and from which all expenses are deducted, the financial responsibilities of the home are left to the husband, and the wife is expected to obey and submit completely to him. In fact this is a sure and unmistakable mark of a woman's spirituality. The other teaching on marriage that African Feminist women see as sabotaging equality of women is the insistence on the indissolubility of marriage even in the case of dangerous marriage relationships. This is expressed at

---

[128] Oral presentation, Addis Ababa, 4-9.8.2002.
[129] Isabel Apawo Phiri, *Women, Presbyterianism and Patriarchy*, p. 49ff.

the time when a couple ties the knot at a wedding ceremony; saying: "until death do us part," and in the time of HIV/AIDS this may well mean that the husband may bring HIV and death into the marriage and the wife has to submit.

Isabel Apawo Phiri outlines another evil that goes with this silencing of women in such churches using the case of CCAP Nkhoma Synod. Although this practice is dying away, it was common in the past that at their church women group meetings they had a man as a CID. These men were elected by the church to oversee the activities of the women. In this church, where Isabel Apawo Phiri conducted her research, the CID was called *mkhalapakati* (the one sitting in the midst).[130] This was usually a church elder.[131]

Further, in this model of women being subservient to men, some women are more involved in the practical work of the church. Women play the deaconate role of visiting the sick, comforting them and those bereaved. Some women engage themselves in projects aimed at intervening in social problems of the society such as hunger and orphans. However, women who are involved in such roles are often not economically recognized by the church. The majority is not paid for their work.

The other dimension that reduces women to subordinate positions is the common understanding that women lead women only. This problem has a long history. In the 1st to 6th century African church, the Catechetical School of Origen, for example, produced women such as Potamiaena who taught women only.[132] This trend continues even in sections of the modern missionary movement.

Suggested Reasons for Men's Leadership over Women

Apart from other reasons stated above, some African Feminist women see that women's confinement to minor roles in the church is a result of the internalization process women have gone through in their respective ecclesiologies. Churches, which have a history of women playing subservient roles, have impacted women negatively to such an extent that some of them have started believing that women ought not to be leaders. This state

---

[130] See Isabel Apawo Phiri, *Women, Presbyterianism and Patriarchy*, p. 97.
[131] Ibid.
[132] Though she taught only women during her lifetime, she appeared to a number of men after her martyrdom encouraging them to convert to faith in Christ, which they did.

has been realized through internalization of wrong interpretations of scripture and of cultural and social beliefs that reduce women to second class citizens in church and society. The side effect is that such women become a barrier to the liberation of fellow women who desire to come out of such situations. Such women disapprove fellow women to be leaders. This position is in contrast to the Evangelical position shown in the earlier paragraphs.

A delayed start in theological training for women has immobilized them from aspiring to church leadership at higher levels of the church government. Some women who have some kind of leadership in church only have "pastors' wives' training. Unfortunately, this is only accessible to those who are wives of the "to be" pastors of their different congregations. Some received training in Church related Theological Colleges or Bible Schools. Such training was often linked to promoting women to serving positions. The only other possibilities for theological training for laywomen often was the secular university. This, however, is now changing.[133]

Seeking an Alternative Theology to Promote Equal Leadership of Women and Men

Firstly, some African Feminist women argue that an approach where the church moves from centred hierarchy to people centeredness will enhance women's equality with men in participation in church and society. This will unsettle the reality of the majority of the women being at the fringe of the church. In Catholic theology, it would require the church to move in the direction of Vatican II that encourages participatory and authentic Christian communities. In this paradigm men and women have the privilege of participating in decision-making.[134] In this model women are seeking an ecclesiology that must allow both men and women to be actively and strategically consulted, involved and listened to as moral agents capable of critical engagement with church and society. Denise Ackermann, who champions this model, however cautions that she fears that if women are at the centre, they will behave in the same way as men and oppress others.[135]

---

[133] For a recent discussion see: Rachel NyaGondwe Fiedler, "Theological Education for Women in Malawi", *Studia Historiae Ecclesiasticae*, vol. 35, 2009, Supplement, pp. 119-134.
[134] Elisabeth Schüssler Fiorenza, *The Power of Naming. A Concilium Reader in Feminist Liberation Theology*, Maryknoll: Orbis, 1996, p. 213.
[135] Interview Denise M. Ackermann, Cape Town, May 2002.

Secondly, African Feminist women argue that the church should revisit the role women play in the church through a fresh interpretation of the same verses that are used to relegate women to support roles. The proponent of this model is Prof Elna Mouton.[136] In this argument, she refers to Genesis 3:20. "Adam named his wife Eve, because she would become the mother of all the living." Based on this Elna Mouton argues that Adam is given enormous responsibility to name Eve as mother of all human beings. By this Adam gave Eve space to become a significant and honourable figure in history. She further argues that this verse can be interpreted in both a historical and a metaphorical way. In a metaphorical way, what Adam did in naming Eve, was to ascribe to her the role of mother of all. Historically however, Eve has been ascribed female roles as opposed to something more in accordance to the gift God accorded her. Elna Mouton regrets that this verse is among those verses used to promote low positions of women in church and society; yet it has a liberating voice for women.

Elna Mouton argues that women must take the initiative to challenge men to give back to women full motherly roles both in the literal sense and in the metaphorical sense. In the metaphorical sense, it is not only the woman who is to be a mother, but also the whole church as a parent. She desires therefore that the church should build up an inclusive team of both men and women in the church. This can be achieved by bringing female experiences into the mainstream of the church through liturgy. These experiences should aim at converting men and bringing them aboard to explain their own experiences. Such an exercise would encourage healing and bridging the gap between men and women. This liturgy can include prayers to facilitate healing.

Concerning reasons why men do not participate freely in such an exercise of sharing experiences, Elna Mouton uses the analogy that distinguishes men from women, as regards freedom to share experiences. She argues that women are perceived to be "private." They focus on the body and are emotional. Men are perceived to be "public", with reason, and therefore their focus is on the mind. They enjoy being in authority. This distinction has led to an inferiority complex in women and a superiority complex in men. A mutual sharing of experiences by both men and women can bridge

---

[136] Prof Elna Mouton was lecturer at Stellenbosch University when I interviewed her in May 2002.

this chasm and bring healing for both sexes. Men will learn to share power with women and enhance each other's potential.[137]

Thirdly, African Feminist women present stories of women who have become leaders in their different churches to inspire other women that struggle to be leaders at higher levels of their church. Central items in these stories are the struggles that women go through; the perceptions from both men and women concerning their struggle, and the means of transforming such structures. Classic examples of women in leadership are those in the area of ordained ministry. African Feminist women also write concerning women leaders in politics. Their goal is to override the notion that women cannot be leaders.

Fourthly, women show how church women groups can bring transformation to such structures. The leader here is Beverly Haddad, who did extensive work on Mothers' Union in South Africa.[138] Several African Feminist scholars have shown how women's groups play a significant role in church. Many other African Feminist women have used this paradigm in Feminist theological writings, like Isabel Apawo Phiri, Esther Mambo from Kenya and Dorcas Akintunde from Nigeria. Some of their work is reflected in this book.

Fifthly, apart from writing stories of women in the ordained ministry, women have sometimes used action to realize ordination. The march in the Presbyterian Church of Malawi (CCAP Blantyre Synod) is one of them.[139] In lobbying for the ordination of women, issues of equal treatment between men and women are also discussed. Those elements that discourage ordi-

---

[137] When I visited Cape Town in 2002, it was an exciting time to meet Prof Elna Mouton in her splendid office at Stellenbosch University. She was most delighted to have me talk to her as one of the African Women Theologians. She was grateful that, even though she is a White South African, I had singled her out as an African Women Theologian. African Women Theologians of white descent have sometimes felt alienated by women of colour at times. A similar reaction was evident when I visited Denise Ackermann, a retired Professor at the University of Western Cape. Denise Ackermann showed concern over the fact that she is not informed about some of the regional Circle meetings in South Africa despite the fact that she has been involved in the Circle for a long time.

[138] See Beverly Gail Haddad, "The Mothers' Union in South Africa. Untold Stories of Faith Survival and Resistance," PhD, University of KwaZulu Natal, 2000.

[139] For a personal appraisal see: Isabel Apawo Phiri, "Marching, Suspended and Stoned: Christian Women in Malawi 1995," in Kenneth R. Ross (ed), *God, People and Power in Malawi. Democratization in Theological Perspective*, Blantyre: CLAIM-Kachere, 1996, pp. 63-105.

nation for women are challenged. Mary Getui, a Kenyan, gives the example of a church that at ordination commissions the women with such question as: "will you take care of the young girls?" while men are commissioned "to take care of the church."[140] The attempt of churches to ordain women to lesser positions in the church is written against by African Feminist women.[141]

Lastly, African Feminist Women promote women's exposure to the winds of liberation as one way of unsettling patriarchal hierarchy. Such promotion is done by encouraging women to study at secular Universities abroad and locally; or to participate at interdenominational meetings such as PACWA. Such an exposure provides an environment of learning from others that triggers liberation among women in contexts where women are subordinate to men.

Conclusion

African Feminist Hermeneutics is broad. The Evangelical Feminist Hermeneutics are part of this. There is need to provide a comprehensive reflection on all kinds of African Feminist Hermeneutics. In the later chapters of the book, we only provide a comprehensive reflection on *one* Feminist Biblical Hermeneutic, an Evangelical Feminist Biblical Hermeneutic.

While chapters 1 and 2 were an introduction to African Feminist Hermeneutics, chapters 3 and 4 apply principles of Evangelical Feminist Interpretation firstly to the Old Testament and then to the New Testament. Chapters 5 and 6 will be a contribution to the discussion on how elitist Feminist interpretations relate to grassroots interpretation, showing a relationship between Evangelical Feminist Interpretation and an interpretation by grassroots from an Evangelical context.

---

[140] Interview Mary Getui, The Institute of Religion and Culture, Ghana, 2005.

[141] Such lesser (non-) ordinations took place in Malawi in the Zambezi Evangelical Church to placate the women who were denied full ordination (Anthony Nkhoma, *Women in Search of Identity: the Case of Women's Ordination in Zambezi Evangelical Church,* Zomba: Kachere, 2005).

Chapter 3: An Evangelical Feminist Biblical Hermeneutic of the Old Testament

One of the marvels of the Bible is that so many different people at different times in history have called this book their own, in spite of so many different cultures, life styles and political systems. The process of translation has been part of Christian expansion and survival over the centuries. In this global process, everywhere lurks the danger of a cultural reading of the Bible, but the Bible has proved, in the long run, that it is able to put up quite some resistance to such cultural reading and has often hit back after periods of cultural suppression of part of its message to challenge what seemed to be the consensus of the custodians of its message.

The understanding of the "biblical role of women" is such a topic which seemed to be so clear and to be settled once and for all, to be either accepted (by the conservatives) or opposed (by the liberals or the feminists), or to be wriggled around by those who want to be in neither of the two camps. But all these approaches have in common that the biblical evidence is assessed on the background of the readers' concept of patriarchal European culture. Most older expositors would not be very conscious of their patriarchal bias, and some of the more "progressive" expositors after them would "unquestioningly" claim that the New Testament "unquestioningly" assumes a patriarchal culture.

The fact that patriarchal culture has been questioned and challenged so severely in many parts of the world in this century affords Bible expositors with a good opportunity to look anew at the biblical evidence, this time with more awareness of the possibility of cultural bias in exegesis (both ways: against our predecessors and against ourselves). In this chapter we explain how an Evangelical Feminist hermeneutic can be applied to the Bible. The reflection begins with an introduction to the claims on how the passages of scriptures are used to support women's oppression and then ends with an Evangelical Feminist explanation on such claims.

An Evangelical Position on the Old Testament as a Patriarchal Book

Earlier chapters have shown that there are many Feminist interpretations of the Old Testament (and even of the whole Bible). While in some Eurocentric Feminist scholarship extreme positions (including rejecting the Bible text) exist, in African Feminist Theology the whole Bible has remained central to the formulation of theology. However, in African Feminist Biblical Hermeneutics, patriarchy has been singled out as one of the tangents of oppression for women.

It can easily be accepted that the Old Testament was written in a patriarchal society, as there have never been any other societies in this world,[142] and since it was written in patriarchal societies it may surely reflect some structures and even values of such societies. But that is only part of the picture, and this part is of lesser importance.

If we accept the Bible (and with it the Old Testament) as divine revelation, it should be much more than a reflection of the society in which it was written. We therefore state: While the Old Testament does **reflect** to some extent the patriarchal society in which it was revealed, it does not **promote** patriarchy.

The Old Testament as God's Revelation

In order to support the thesis that the Old Testament does not promote patriarchy, we first have to state the premises of our theology:

- We believe that the whole Old Testament is the word of God.
- God revealed his will in the form of literature.
- This literature varies greatly, ranging from legal texts to praise poems and from history to prayer.

In order to perceive God's will for our times (and all times), his revelation in various genres of literature must be understood by doing justice to the qualities and intentions of each type of literature.

As divine revelation was given during the course of history in a "non-systematic" way, theologians must take into account all that is revealed, or as it used to be said, the "whole testimony of Scripture."

In assessing the whole testimony of Scripture, God's revelation for mankind must be seen in line with Salvation History.

---

[142] Here we need to note that a few Feminist scholars believe that the societies of the Near East were matriarchal well before biblical times. They point at the role of female gods and at social structures which would give women a larger role (as in today's matri*lineal* societies), but no convincing evidence for matri*archal* societies has been produced.

While the divine message, given at different times and in different literary forms may well differ in presentation, imagery and nuances, we believe that one text will not contradict another text.

For this chapter we will apply these principles to an Evangelical Feminist reading of the Old Testament. While we do this, these are the assumptions:

- The whole Old Testament is the word of God.
- Every text has its specific place in Salvation History.
- Each text must be interpreted in full recognition of its literary genre.
- Texts dealing with the same issue will not contradict each other.

As we look at the texts, we will try to provide answers to some claims that the Bible is patriarchal and oppressive to women. The Bible translation we use is the New International Version (NIV), unless otherwise stated,[143] and we will repeatedly refer to the principles of interpretation applied. We will follow the texts, looking at one genre at a time. When you follow our approach, make frequent reference to the Bible and do not only read the verse(s) mentioned, but also the surrounding text.

Old Testament Literary Genres

Before we deal with specific texts, we will list some of the literary genres[144] of the Old Testament, concentrating on those that are relevant for Feminist Theology.[145] Thus we will contextualize our interpretation to some of the claims that the Bible is patriarchal and oppressive to women.

Creation Stories

The Bible starts with this literary genre (Gen 1-11), which is often mistaken as history, because of the language in which it is couched. But creation stories are never records of history (which reporter could have been present at Creation?), but describe the proper order of society. This applies to all kinds

---

[143] The NIV is available in various editions. We recommend the NIV Study Bible, whose comments are very useful for the private reader and for the scholarly student alike. An electronic version of the NIV text can be downloaded from the internet.

[144] A literature genre is "a category of literary composition" (Wikipedia).

[145] This is not an attempt to give a comprehensive and proper classification of the various types of Old Testament literature.

of creation stories, and what makes the biblical story of creation different from those transmitted elsewhere is the divine authority attached to it, not the literary characteristics, which it shares with creation stories all over the world. Some of such stories from Malawi are reflected on in the following paragraphs.[146]

(1) The Horned Chameleon and the Origin of Life (Chewa). Here you find that Man expresses his authority by naming all the creatures (not himself, though, as the Horned Chameleon did it for him.) — In a similar way in the biblical (Second) Creation Story mankind's domination over the animal kingdom is expressed:

> Now the LORD God had formed out of the ground all the beasts of the field and all the birds of the air. He brought them to the man to see what he would name them; and whatever the man called each living creature, that was its name. So the man gave names to all the livestock, the birds of the air and all the beasts of the field (Gen 2:19-20).[147]

(2) Chameleon and the First Man and Woman (Yao): The (male) man makes fire, and the animals, in fear for their lives, flee into the forest.

(3) The Kaphirintiwa Myth (Chewa): Here there is more of the fire Man made: The Dog and the Goat ran to Man for protection, but the Elephant, the Lion and their companions ran away full of rage against Man.

Story (2) reflects the hostility between man and the wild animals, and story (3) explains that the domestic animals are living with man, subordinate to him as they need protection.

That the monkey lives in the bush and occasionally comes out to harvest from our fields is not an event in history, but a present day reality, and equally so is what is described in Genesis 1-3, with the only difference that Genesis 1-3 has been used by God to reveal his will.

(4) How the Men Took the Power from the Women (Kikuyu)

---

[146] These stories are put together in David Mphande, *Oral Literature and Moral Education among the Lakeside Tonga of Northern Malawi*, Mzuzu: Mzuni Press, 2014, pp. 35-38, who collected them from Matthew Schoffeleers and A.A. Roscoe, *Land of Fire. Oral Literature from Malawi*, Limbe: Montfort, 1985.

[147] These verses are from the second creation story of the Bible (Gen 2:4 - 2:25). The first creation story expresses the same truth with these words: "Rule over the fish of the sea and the birds of the air and over every living creature that moves on the ground (Gen 1:28).

That such myths from the beginning do not report history, but reflect present day reality is shown by a well known myth from Kenya.

> In the days of old, when all mankind was living in one village, the village was ruled by the women. The men resented this but did not have the power to effect a change. So they devised a plan: The men would all make their wives pregnant at the same time, and when the time came for the women to give birth, the men staged a revolt and took the power. And since then the women have lost their power and the men rule the village.[148]

Of course, no reporter could have been present, and indeed there was no need for such a presence, as the myth is not history but reflects (and sanctions) male dominance over women.

It is interesting to note that the biblical creation story equally uses mythical language on male dominance over women (Gen 3:16),[149] but it does *not* justify male dominance as a divinely sanctioned order, but *opposes* it as the result of human sin.

Prescriptive – Descriptive

In reading the Bible these two forms of texts must be clearly differentiated. Much of the Bible, where it tells history, is *descriptive*, and there is no immediate indication if what is described is a good thing or a bad thing. When God told Abraham to leave his home country and go elsewhere, this is *descriptive* of what happened, but not a *prescription* for all of us.

Sometimes the very position that the Genesis creation stories are prescriptive has been used by some theologians to promote oppression of women, for example in Gen 3 it is reported that Eve gave Adam the forbidden fruit, so she seduced him to sin. That then is generalized that women, even today, are a force to push men into sin. An Evangelical interpretation, based on the same understanding that Creation Stories are prescriptive, provides an explanation as to why the Creation Story affirms women's liberation.

---

[148] This story is based on Jomo Kenyatta, *Facing Mount Kenya*, 1938.
[149] "To the woman he said, 'I will greatly increase your pains in childbearing; with pain you will give birth to children. Your desire will be for your husband, and he will rule over you.'"

Wisdom Literature

Wisdom Literature has in common with the Creation Stories the fact that it is prescriptive, not descriptive. The Wisdom Literature is spread over various books in the Old Testament: Proverbs, Ecclesiastes, Song of Songs, Job and a number of Psalms. When assessing the role of women in the Wisdom Literature, we need to take into account that some proverbs, as it is usual with proverbs, are descriptive and not prescriptive.[150]

Historical Texts

When the Creation Stories come to their end with the story of the Great Flood (Gen 11), history begins with Abram and Sarai, and from then on much of the Old Testament is history, be it the experiences of the Patriarchs, of Israel in Egypt, in the Sinai Desert and in the Promised Land, the stories of the books of Kings and Chronicles that led to the Exile in Babylon and Ezra and Nehemiah after that.[151]

While the Creation Story (and much of the Wisdom Literature) is *prescriptive*, historical records are primarily *descriptive*. They tell us of women (and men) good and bad, of those men (and women) who kept God's law and those who broke it. What is recorded about women (as about men) is not necessarily approved by the holy text, and therefore a theological assessment is necessary in every case.

Legal Texts

Legal texts are very frequent in the books of Exodus, Leviticus, Numeri and Deuteronomy, and as they often speak about women, it is important for our study to understand their diversity in order to assess their relevance for us today.

In terms of literary structure, there is the differentiation between **apodictic law** and **case law**. The Ten Commandments are the most prominent examples of apodictic law: "You shall have no other gods before me" (Ex 20:3). Similarly structured is the command "Anyone who curses father or mother

---

[150] An example for a descriptive proverb is Prov 17:8 "A bribe is a charm to the one who gives it; wherever he turns, he succeeds." Cf Exodus 23:8.

[151] It must be noted, of course, that in books like Exodus, Kings, Chronicles and Nehemiah, not all texts are history, as Exodus contains many legal texts and Kings contains prayers and Chronicles and Nehemiah many lists and genealogies, etc.

must be put to death" (Ex 21:17); and there are many clear moral commands like "Do not mistreat an alien or oppress him" (Ex 22:30) and "Do not spread false reports" (Ex 23:1) or "Do not take the cloak of a widow as a pledge" (Dt 24:17).

The other type of legal literature is case law. This is a detailed example:

> ₂"If you buy a Hebrew servant, he is to serve you for six years. But in the seventh year, he shall go free, without paying anything.
>
> ₃If he comes alone, he is to go free alone; but if he has a wife when he comes, she is to go with him.
>
> ₄If his master gives him a wife and she bears him sons or daughters, the woman and her children shall belong to her master, and only the man shall go free.
>
> ₅"But if the servant declares, 'I love my master and my wife and children and do not want to go free,' ₆then his master must take him before the judges. He shall take him to the door or the doorpost and pierce his ear with an awl. Then he will be his servant for life. (Ex 21:2-6)

Another example concerning women is found in Ex 22:16-17:

> If a man seduces a virgin who is not pledged to be married and sleeps with her, he must pay the bride-price, and she shall be his wife.
>
> If her father absolutely refuses to give her to him, he must still pay the bride-price for virgins.

The Interpretation of Old Testament Laws

The laws of the Old Testament need to be seen in the context of Salvation History. There can be seen four different types of laws:

(1) The moral law of the Old Testament
(2) The case law of the Old Testament
(3) The ceremonial law of the Old Testament
(4) The purity laws of the Old Testament

Between these types of laws there is, of course, some overlap. But in general, the New Testament makes reference only to the moral law (1) of the Old Testament, and not to the case law (2) of the Old Testament.[152]

The ceremonial law (3) is fulfilled through Jesus Christ's sacrifice. Through His death, all the sacrifices (and the legal codes that went with them) are fulfilled in Jesus.[153]

The purity laws (4) are also reinterpreted by Jesus. Jesus explicitly declared all foods clean (Mk 7:19, cf Lev 11), and the Holy Spirit taught Peter the same lesson (Acts 10:9-23) and extended it to all the people who eat such food (the Gentiles). Further, the laws of uncleanliness are reinterpreted through Jesus' ministry of sanctification in the New Testament.[154]

Poetry

All of the Book of Psalms and much of the Wisdom Literature are written as poetry. The same is true of most prophetic texts. All poets make powerful use of imagery, and we do not expect these images to portray a physical reality, read for example Psalm 29:4-6:

> 4The voice of the Lord is powerful;
> the voice of the Lord is majestic.
> 5The voice of the Lord breaks the cedars;
> the Lord breaks in pieces the cedars of Lebanon.
> 6He makes Lebanon skip like a calf,
> Sirion [Mt Hermon] like a young wild ox.

When the prophet Isaiah announced the return of the exiled Israelites to their own land, he used similar poetic language (Is 40:3-4).

> 3A voice of one calling:
> "In the desert prepare the way for the Lord;
> make straight in the wilderness
> a highway for our God.
> 4Every valley shall be raised up,
> every mountain and hill made low;
> the rough ground shall become level,
> the rugged places a plain.

---

[152] Mt 19:2-11 and Mk 10:1-12 clearly show how Jesus refused to entangled in case law and therefore "jumped" to the Creation Story as God's permanent will.

[153] This point is argued extensively in Hebrews chapters 4-10.

[154] Here the laws on sexual emissions and bodily discharges are prominent: Leviticus 12-15.

Much of the prophetic literature is written in poetry, and so is most of the Wisdom Literature.

Praise Poems

A special (sub-)genre of poetry is the praise poem. Such poems are often addressed to rulers, heroes and other great men.[155] While they are not devoid of history and or reality, they are not detailed reflections of such. Quite a number of psalms can be seen as praise poems to Jahwe, the God of Israel, but for our study the praise poem for the "Wife of Noble Character" is the most prominent one (Prov 31:10-31).[156]

An Evangelical Feminist Interpretation of the Creation Story

In this section we point out how the story is used to oppress women and also how an Evangelical interpretation argues against that.

A Misconception

In Malawi, as in other places, it is often understood that the Bible teaches female subordination. When you ask for a reference, the Creation Story is often mentioned. If you ask for details, Genesis 2 is pointed out: God made man first, woman second. Therefore the man (all men) must rule and the woman (all women) must serve men (all men), not just the husband.

Like in so many cases here the Bible is abused to provide a holy support to attitudes far from holy. It is one of the cases where the biblical text is misused to support cultural attitudes, and where the Bible should speak, culture speaks instead.

An Evangelical interpretation deals with the misconception above in this way. In order to properly interpret the Creation Story, we must first read the story (stories) and then come to conclusions.

---

[155] They are recited at special occasions in a special atmosphere, as these lines show: "On being asked to address the people, King Mswati [of Swaziland] stood up, but said nothing for three minutes. As per tradition, those minutes were filled by the lofty tones of the royal poet as he recited the Swazi monarch's praise poem." (Boston Soko, *Zwangendaba and the Ngoni Myth,* Mzuzu: Mzuni Press [forthcoming]). The book also contains many details on the praise poem for Paramount Chief Mbelwa of the Ngoni.

[156] The poem is also an acrostic, each verse beginning with a successive letter of the Hebrew alphabet.

The Validity of the Creation Story

1. The Creation Story is part of God's revelation to humankind.

2. The Creation Story is foundational even for the New Testament.

3. The Creation Story is not history, but proclaims God's will for all times (and also describes the effects of sin).

4. Jesus identified the Creation Story as permanently valid, singling out specifically the female/male relationship.

5. Therefore we must see the Creation Story as **our story**, not as something gone by, as it is prescriptive.

The Importance of the Literary Character of the Creation Story

To repeat once more, the Creation Story describes our lives and God's will for them, not events at the dawn of world or human history. **This means that what the Creation Story teaches about *munthu*, is valid as God's will even today.**

This permanent validity applies to the teaching of this story, but not to its imagery or the assumed circumstances. *While the Creation Story is couched in historical terms, this is not the teaching.* If we read a Creation Story, we need to follow the story (which can be quite dramatic) to the end to derive the divine teaching from it. The literary character does not allow us to "jump out" of the story, pick an idea that suits us and run with it.[157]

Three Creation Stories

People often speak of the biblical Story of Creation. This is correct in a generic sense, but if we want to be precise, there are three stories of how God created humankind:

    (1) Genesis 1:26-31

    (2) Genesis 2:7 and 2:15-24

    (3) Genesis 5:1-2

The three stories are written differently and use different imagery, but they

---

[157] To pick out the (implied) sequence of creation (man first – woman second) and to interpret the story and with it the Bible on that basis is an *interpretation against the text*, which takes no note of this sequence.

all speak of the same thing, how God created (male and female) man [*munthu*].[158]

The first and third story of the creation of *munthu* (humankind) are quite similar, the second is very different.[159] While story no. 1 has a solemn style and a very obvious structure, story no. 2 is a free flowing story, full of surprises and excitement.[160] Two different stories indeed, and whoever put the two stories together as they are now, must have been aware of the obvious differences in style. Therefore, if we interpret them today, we must assume that, being part of the same Word of God, they may differ in style and imagery (as they obviously do), but that they will not promote contradictory teaching.

Equality in the 1st Creation Story

Wrong interpretations of words in the Creation Stories have been used to sanction women's oppression. In this section we provide an Evangelical position on the meaning of the word "Man" that promotes women's liberation.[161]

In the first creation story (Genesis 1:1-2:4) God creates everything, day after day. During the sixth day He creates man and woman. Both are equally

---

[158] This is in no way the same as the androgynic man idea, which claims that God created *munthu* in the beginning as having male and female characteristics in one person. For a detailed discussion see: Rosemary Radford Ruether, *Sexism and God-Talk: Towards a Feminist Theology*, London: SCM Press, 1983.

[159] Over the last 200 years or so, Old Testament scholars have developed a number of theories on the origin of the different Creation Stories. It is pointed out that the 1st story is more structured and more systematic, maybe of priestly origin, and that it, with its watery chaos and its downgrading of the sun and the moon from gods to lamps and time keepers (for the calendar) point to a Babylonian context, while the second story, where the original chaos is dry, may point to a context in Israel, where the desert is threatening from three sides. From such observations it has been concluded that the second Creation Story *maybe* dated around 1000 BC and the first Creation Story *maybe* 500 years later during the exile in Babylon. While the conclusions scholars draw from the text are not necessarily true beyond reasonable doubt, the differences in style and format are obvious.

[160] Rightly so! Why should man (*mwamuna*) not be excited about woman (*mkazi*)! Life would be terrible and boring for him without her!

[161] Many of the ideas here were first expressed in Janet Kholowa and Klaus Fiedler, *Pa Chiyambi Anawalenga Chimodzimodzi*, Blantyre: CLAIM-Kachere, 2002; translated as Janet Kholowa and Klaus Fiedler, *In the Beginning God Created them Equal*, Blantyre: CLAIM-Kachere, 2003.

human (*munthu*), and both are equally created in God's image. The story obviously assumes that they were created equal. Since our childhood days we believe that Adam was created first, and then Eve. But here we read nothing like that. We read that God created man (*munthu*), not that he created Adam. This misunderstanding could occur because in Hebrew the word for *munthu* (man) is *adam*, a word related to *adama*, the soil. In the whole Old Testament there is no one else called Adam. *Adam* does not mean an individual person, but all human beings, those created from the soil.[162] Those who translated the Bible into Chewa did well to translate *adam* by *munthu*, human being (*man*), which is a generic term. God did not only create the first man, but all men (male and female) are created by Him.

What is true of Adam is true of Eve. Eve is not an individual name. No-one else in the Bible had this name. God created mankind male and female. The words *male* and *female* are connected by the word "and.' There is no indication of first and second. The word "and" connects male and female equality.

If a feminist theologian is unhappy that in the Old Testament women are not well treated, she/he is not supported by the first Creation Story, where male and female *munthu* share equally in God's image, receive God's blessings equally and are equally his representatives on earth.[163]

If this is seen correctly, any theologian, Feminist or not, and any reader of the Bible, should expect that the second Creation Story teaches the same doctrine, not an opposing alternative.[164] Chapter 2 is not a continuation of

---

[162] This view differs from the position that "adam" is the proper name for the first male human being, as taught by Winston Kawale at Mzuzu University. However, the interpretation we put forward here is supported by Hilary Mijoga, "Gender Differentiation in the Bible: Created and Recognized," *Journal of Humanities* no. 13 (1999), pp. 87-113; reprinted in Jonathan Nkhoma, *Significance of the Dead Sea Scrolls and other Essays: Biblical and Early Christianity Studies from Malawi*, Mzuzu: Mzuni Press, 2014.

[163] In Islamic theology this is expressed by the concept that *munthu* is God's *khalifa* (representative) on earth.

[164] Neither should the third Creation Story teach a different message. It states: "When God created man, he made him in the likeness of God. He created them male and female and blessed them. And when they were created, he called them "man" [*munthu*].

the first Creation Story, but it is as complete as the first in itself. Just go along as we paraphrase and retell it:[165]

The second creation story tells us that the land was there first. The earth was dry and God created water and only then *munthu* was created. There is no indication if *munthu* was female or male. Having created *munthu*, God proceeds to create what *munthu* needs to live well. *Munthu* needs water to drink. So God makes the rain fall. *Munthu* needs food to eat, so God lets the soil grow the plants. *Munthu* also needs a good place to live, so God puts *munthu* into the Garden of Eden.

God gave *munthu* all that was needed, and he blessed them by giving them work, to look after the garden and to care for it (Gen 2:15). This story so far only speaks of *munthu*, it does not tell us if this *munthu* is male or female or both. Even in verse 18, when it tells us that *munthu* was alone, there is no indication if *munthu* is female or male. We are only told that *munthu* was alone and that God thought that that was not good.

God had created all that *munthu* needed: drink, food and a place to live. Now *munthu* needed company, which could not be found among the things created so far. So God tries another way. He creates the animals and birds. Each new creature God takes to *munthu* to be named. And *munthu* does right that, give them their names. When God showed *munthu* a big animal he called it "cow" (*ng'ombe*). God showed *munthu* a smaller animal, and *munthu* named it goat (*mbuzi*), and then one that runs fast, is clever and has long ears. *Munthu* named it *kalulu* (hare). God showed him a beautiful bird and *munthu* called it *nkhanga* (guinea-fowl). And so on the whole day. God brought the animals and birds He had created and *munthu* named them. A busy day. Was there none among the animals that could have been a help to *munthu*? Sure, the cow (*ng'ombe*) could have helped him plough the field and *mbuzi*, the goat, could have provided manure and both could have helped him with their milk. But *munthu* did not need things or animals to be his help. The whole day *munthu* worked hard naming the animals and the birds, but when night fell, *munthu* was very disappointed. He had worked the whole day, but no "help opposite-him" (fitting for him) was found. God had created the animals, all good in themselves, but not a *suitable* help for Man. *Munthu* was still alone, and God had to find another

---

[165] This dramatic retelling of the story should not in any way imply that God created the world through an experiment. This "retelling" is from Janet Kholowa and Klaus Fiedler, *In the Beginning God Created them Equal*, Blantyre: CLAIM-Kachere, 2000, pp. 22-24.

way, because, as he had said earlier, it was not good for *munthu* to be alone.[166]

With all the work *munthu* had done the whole day, *munthu* was very tired and God made him sleep soundly. While *munthu* was sleeping, God took a rib,[167] closed the place with flesh and formed the rib into another *munthu*. When a new day dawned, the first *munthu* woke up, expecting another hard day's work, naming another lot of animals. But he did not see any more of them, but instead was surprised to see another *munthu*, very much like him. Because of giving names all day, *munthu* searched for a name for that new creature as well, but could not find one. That new creature already had a name, his own name, *munthu*. The Bible expresses this with the words:

> "This is now bone of my bones and flesh of my flesh; she shall be called woman, for she was taken out of man" (Gen 2:23, NIV).

This new *munthu* was obviously the same, and then the first *munthu* recognized a small difference. *Munthu* recognized that he was a male *munthu*, and that this new person was a female *munthu*. This is difficult to express in most languages. In Chewa *munthu wamkazi/munthu wamwamuna* (female *munthu*/male *munthu*) is used. Even in English it is not as easy to express, though the words man/woman (female *munthu*/male *munthu*) both contain 'man.' But in the original Hebrew it is very clear. The male *munthu* is

---

[166] It is worthwhile to pause here for a moment and address another translation problem: The Hebrew word used here is *etser* (help), which occurs just over 20 times in the Old Testament. In almost all cases the "help" is God. See Ex 8:4 "My father's God was my helper;" Ps 33:20 "He is our help and our shield;" or Ps 28:7 "The Lord is my strength and shield, my hart trusts in him and I am helped;" or Ps 121:1-2: "I lift up my eyes to the hills—where does my help come from? My help comes from the Lord, the Maker of heaven and earth." (cf. Letha Scanzoni and Nancy Hardesty, *All we are Meant to be. A Biblical Approach to Women's Liberation*, Waco: Word Books, 1974, p. 26. *Etser* does not mean the little assistant, servant or housemaid, but the mighty helper; one could even speak of a saviour or redeemer. When Israel rebelled against God it sought *help* from Egypt, to which the prophet replies: "who go down to Egypt without consulting me, who look for *help* to Pharaoh's [useless] protection." – Contrary to the biblical evidence, where the help is from the stronger to the weaker, in common language it is usually understood to be the other way round: the little ones help the big people. This is clearly the meaning of *kumthangatira* in the Buku Lopatulika, but even the Buku Loyera's *kumthandiza* is often understood in the same way, not to rescue but to assist.

[167] In Hebrew, what is frequently translated *rib*, is expressed by the term "part of the man's side" (See NIV text note).

ish, the female *munthu* is *isha*. The word stem (*ish*) is the same, the difference is just the gender, expressed by the ending -a.

Many people think that there is inequality between women and men because the woman was created second. But the whole story emphasizes *equality*, not *difference*, let alone superiority. Firstly, if the sequence in the order of creation is considered as a reason for the man to be superior over the woman, then the animals are even more superior, as they were created a full day before either man or woman.

Secondly, the same expression as in Genesis 2:23 (bone of my bone and flesh of my flesh) is used elsewhere in the Bible, also to express equality. In Genesis 29:14 Laban says about Jacob:

> "You are my own flesh and blood."[168]

From ancient texts outside the Bible we know that "you are bone of my bone and flesh of my flesh" was a formula used at adoptions to express the equality between physical and adopted children.

Isn't this a fascinating and beautiful story? Gen 1:27 expresses the God given equality in abstract terms, but we may like Genesis 2 more, as it expresses the very same equality in a beautiful story. Before we move on to show how some of this beauty is destroyed by sin, a few more observations on this story.

God created the animals and *munthu* from the same substance, from soil. The woman was not created from soil, but from *munthu*. That is equality.[169]

We argue that the biblical texts *reflect* patriarchal culture but do not *promote* it. On this Gen 2:24 is actually very critical, as in patriarchal societies the **woman** leaves her home to join her husband in marriage, but Gen 2:24 says that the **man** will leave father and mother **and join his wife.**[170]

The Problem with the English Language

English is a beautiful and likable language, but one thing, at least, is unfortunate: That this beautiful language uses the same word for a male human

---

[168] The literal translation from Hebrew would read: "You are my bone and my flesh."
[169] There is a misinterpretation: "Since woman was taken out of man, she is inferior." If you take water out of water, it is still nothing but water.
[170] "For this reason a man will leave his father and mother and be united to his wife, and they will become one flesh."

being (*mwamuna*) and for all the human beings (*munthu*). That creates the impression that the male side of humankind is the dominant or better side, and it opens the way for endless misinterpretations. This language problem has helped to create the impression that God created the male man (*mwamuna*) first and then the woman. But the Bible tells us that God first created *munthu*, not *mwamuna*. And *adam* is not a male first name, but means "human being."

The Distortion of God's Creation (Genesis 3)

Another way how creation stories are used to promote women's oppression by men is the misinterpretation of the phrase that the man will rule over the woman. The interpretation, which advances man's superiority over woman, forgets that such a situation is part and parcel of the consequences of sin and must in no way be supported.

Equality between women and men was (**and still is**) God's good creation, but unfortunately, the devil is not happy with that (and many men and some women join him in that).

In reading Genesis 3 we must again remember that it does not talk of things that happened long ago, but it talks about us.[171] We must not blame Eve for her disobedience, as her sin is our sin, and with Adam the same is true.[172]

If we read Genesis 1-3 as part of the overall Creation Story, chapters 1 and 2 do not come before chapter 3 ("before and after the Fall"), but chapters 1 and 2 on the one side and chapter 3 on the other are **concurrent**, two realities **at the same time**.

In chapters 1 and 2 we read of the three great blessings God gave to *munthu*; and in chapter 3 we read how sin *distorts* these blessings. No, God did not take away the blessings at the end of Genesis 2. We still profit from them: (1) Sex, marriage and children (2) work ("to tend the garden") and (3) to rule over the animals and the world. God did not withdraw these blessings, but sin distorted them (and still distorts them).

God gave *munthu* the blessing of **work**, and the consequence of sin is not that work is withdrawn (such boredom would be terrible), but that the

---

[171] We thank Canon Hutchinson, Dogmatics teacher at Makerere, for this insight.
[172] Here we need to remember again that *adam* is not a personal name but a generic term, meaning *munthu*. Even Eve is not a name, it may mean "life", and the text speaks not of Eve, but of "the woman."

ground is cursed and will produce "thorns and thistles" (and we all know that experience).

The second blessing given was procreation. Yes, women still give birth to children, but giving birth is often painful and dangerous. All women who have given birth know that, and husbands who were present, have observed the same. And the pain of bearing children does not stop once the mother's wounds have healed, the pain continues all throughout her life. Pain in childbirth (and in bringing up children) is a consequence of sin, and therefore we must do everything to reduce such pain.[173]

The third blessing is to rule the animal kingdom. Here equally sin distorts God's good creation (Gen 3:16).

> "Your desire will be for your husband." – That is what God wanted and it is beautiful.
>
> "and he will rule over you." – That is the distortion brought about by sin.

Man was to rule over the animals and the rest of the world, not over his wife, let alone over all the women in this world.

In a theology class one (male) student rose up and said: "Yes, the Bible teaches that women are subordinate." He confirmed his answer with Genesis 3:16. But this is the verse where the Bible describes the consequences of sin, and to initiate sin is not good, neither here nor anywhere else in the world.

Some say that in Genesis 3 the woman was cursed. No, only the snake and the soil were cursed, but both the man and the woman, though not cursed, suffer the consequences of sin. Yes, sin is a reality, but we want to be found on Christ's side of redemption, and not on the side of sinful oppression. And here it makes no difference if we are theologians or just "ordinary" Christians. **We want to be on the side of life.**

A (Necessary) Clash with Culture

The wrong interpretation of the phrase "and he will rule over you" as implying superiority over women is fuelled by African culture. Therefore Feminist Theology demands not only a re-reading of the Bible (as done here), but also a re-reading of culture, as cultures can be oppressive for women, and

---

[173] Safe Motherhood campaigns in Malawi support such efforts.

African cultures are among the many oppressive cultures in this world. Here we provide some examples of such cultural oppression.

There is no room for a detailed discussion here, but proverbs and sayings offer some glimpses of cultural oppression (sinful culture). We will start with a wedding song.

| Wamkulu ndani m'banja? | Who is the boss of the family? |
| Wamkulu n'mwamuna! (2x) | The boss is the husband! (2x) |

Such is a husband's superiority by culture, but it is totally alien to the teaching of the Bible. Both husband and wife must be God's servants, but none is the servant of the other.

Another proverb that can not be found in the Bible is:

| Mwamuna ndi mwana | A man is a child[174] |

This implies that a man can well be irresponsible, and that, as he does foolish things (as men often do), he must not be held responsible, just like a little child that plays with fire and burns down the house.[175]

While this proverb is in Professor Chakanza's big collection, we found another one not included, but still part of the people's "wisdom."

| Mwamuna ndi mtonde, azinunkha | A man is a billy goat, he must stink |

Here, again, culture fights with the Bible. A billy goat is not content with one she goat, and he rules over them all.

When asking around, not all knew this proverb (but many did), but all women know its reality. This reality does not escape girls' initiation either. One of the teaching songs in such an initiation was recorded:

Tsegulire, tsegulire!	Open for me, open for me!
Ndakana, ndakana.	I have refused, I have refused.
Apanja, apanja	Those outside, those outside
Mulibe mwambo.	Have no behaviour.
Anyumba, anyumba	Those in the house, those in the house,
Mulibe mwambo.	You do not have behaviour. [176]

---

[174] J.C. Chakanza, *Wisdom of the People: 2000 Chinyanja Proverbs*, Blantyre: CLAIM-Kachere, 2000.

[175] There is no similar proverb in the biblical book of Proverbs.

Then, one *mlangizi* sang *kunkhani, kunkhani*,[177] and said: if a man sleeps outside, and comes very late, you should not refuse him entry into the house, do not leave him outside because an animal can kill and eat him. If this happens you will be sorry. So do not be jealous with your husband.[178]

More proverbs could be found and more tangents of oppression could be named, but what has been described here is enough evidence that sin is still invading the relationship between the sexes and that Feminist and other theologians have a lot to do to ensure that, if culture and the Bible clash, it is the Bible that wins.

An Evangelical Feminist Interpretation of the Role of Women in Wisdom Literature

Another reason why the Bible is blamed for being oppressive for women is that there is emphasis on theologies based on women who played a negative role (or are portrayed in such a role) in the Bible. Further that there is no attempt to search for a positive re-reading of such women to promote women's liberation. For an Evangelical Feminist reading of Wisdom Literature we start with the book of Proverbs. Our position is that there is no need for majoring on a theology of oppression for women, basing on women that played negative roles in the Bible, because there are far more women who played positive roles.

Thus, in the book of Proverbs the picture is mixed. Women are portrayed both negatively and positively as shown below.

The Immoral Women

Her portrait is clearly given in Proverbs 2:16-20.

> It [wisdom] will save you also from the adulteress,
> from the wayward wife with her seductive words,
> 17who has left the partner of her youth
> and ignored the covenant she made before God.

---

[176] Rachel NyaGondwe Fiedler, *Coming of Age: A Christianized Initiation among Women of Southern Malawi*, Zomba: Kachere, 2005, p. 64.

[177] "Kunkhani, kunkhani": The words have no direct meaning; they are a signal that instructions in prose will follow (after the song).

[178] Rachel NyaGondwe Fiedler, *Coming of Age: A Christianized Initiation among Women of Southern Malawi*, Zomba: Kachere, 2005, p. 64.

> 18For her house leads down to death
> and her paths to the spirits of the dead.
> 19None who go to her return
> or attain the paths of life.
> 20Thus you will walk in the ways of good men
> and keep to the paths of the righteous.

Besides this portrait, there are other references to the evil women.[179]

The Woman as a Nuisance

In several cases in this respect proverbs do not reflect any positive teaching, but show a reality that (unfortunately) is true. Here just two examples:

> Prov 11:22   Like a gold ring in a pig's snout
> is a beautiful woman who shows no discretion
>
> Prov 25:24   Better to live on a corner of the roof
> then share a house with a quarrelsome wife.

The Woman as a Blessing

The book of Proverbs does indeed portray some women as evil, but this is balanced by praise for those women who do right. Here again two examples:

> Prov 18:22   He who finds a wife finds what is good
> and receives favour from the LORD
> Prov 19:14   Houses and wealth are inherited from parents,
> but a prudent wife is from the LORD.

The Bible is also accused of being oppressive to women because of patriarchy promoted through the omission of women in some biblical texts. In Proverbs there are such examples:

The Proverbs are for the "Sons"

The book addresses all the teaching to a son, never to a daughter.[180] Though one may argue that what is useful teaching for sons is equally useful for their sisters, it is true that daughters are not addressed. Here we have a case where scripture reflects the patriarchal situation in which it was

---

[179] Examples are Prov 7:6-27; 22:14, 23:27.

[180] The word "daughter" occurs only once in the book, and it is not a compliment: "The leech has two daughters. 'Give! Give! they cry (Prov 30:15).

written. In this interpretation we argue that the word "sons" needs to be re-interpreted as including the daughters.

The Father as the Teacher

In the book of Proverbs the father is usually portrayed as a teacher, but twice the mother is included:

> Prov 1:8 Listen, my son, to your father's instruction
> and do not forsake your mother's teaching
> Prov 6:20 My son, keep your father's commands
> and do not forsake your mother's teaching.

Here we should assume that father and mother also taught their daughters, but again, they are not often mentioned together.

In addition to these references to father and mother as teachers, in the introduction to chapter 31, a mother is clearly portrayed as a teacher of wisdom for her son (King Lemuel),[181] and Prov 31:26 speaks of "faithful instruction" on the tongue of the Wife of Noble Character.[182]

An Evangelical position is that teaching at family level should not be restricted to women, but should include the men. The following section also attests to that.

Wisdom and Folly

While it can be argued that women are somewhat underrepresented in the family as a teaching and learning unit, it is different for the book of Proverbs, as here the main teacher is Wisdom, always portrayed as a woman.

> $_{20}$Wisdom calls aloud in the street,
>
> she raises her voice in the public squares;
>
> $_{21}$at the head of the noisy streets she cries out,
>
> in the gateways of the city she makes her speech: (Prov 1:20-21)

Wisdom was God's first creation, and in a way Wisdom is portrayed as a female side of God (8:22-31):

> $_{22}$"The Lord brought me forth as the first of his works,

---

[181] The mother warns him against the women, who can ruin kings, against alcohol, which can do it as well and she advises him to "speak up for those who cannot speak for themselves, for the rights of all who are destitute" (Prov 31:8).

[182] For more on this woman see the next section.

before his deeds of old;

23 I was appointed from eternity,

from the beginning, before the world began.

24 When there were no oceans, I was given birth,

when there were no springs abounding with water;

25 before the mountains were settled in place,

before the hills, I was given birth,

26 before he made the earth or its fields

or any of the dust of the world.

27 I was there when he set the heavens in place,

when he marked out the horizon on the face of the deep,

28 when he established the clouds above

and fixed securely the fountains of the deep,

29 when he gave the sea its boundary

so the waters would not overstep his command,

and when he marked out the foundations of the earth.

30 Then I was the craftsman at his side.

I was filled with delight day after day,

rejoicing always in his presence,

31 rejoicing in his whole world

and delighting in mankind.[183]

After being portrayed like that, chapter 9 gives the final invitation of Wisdom "from the highest point of the city" (9:2).

Another argument that the Bible is oppressive to women is based on the fact that the Bible presents women negatively. This is true for chapter 9:13-18, where there is another invitation: Folly calls, equally from the highest

---

[183] I heard these words read for the first time when I attended a Holy Communion service in a Brethren congregation, where they were understood as a direct reference to Jesus Christ. Here the NIV text note may be helpful: "A hymn describing wisdom's role in creation. Wisdom is here personified, as in 1:20-33; 3:15-18; 9:1-12. Therefore these verses should not be interpreted as a direct description of Christ. Yet they provide part of the background for the New Testament portrayal of Christ as the divine Word (Jn 1:1-3) and as the wisdom of God (1 Cor 1:24,30; Col 2:3). Here, wisdom is an attribute of God in creation."

point of the city (9:14), and equally portrayed as a woman. But while Wisdom offers life (9:6), Folly offers death (9:18).

Conclusion

If Feminist theologians look at the book of Proverbs with "gendered eyes," they may see a bit of patriarchal culture reflected in the omission of daughters as recipients of Wisdom's teaching, but as a whole women are given equal importance and maybe receive preferential treatment in the way Wisdom and Folly are portrayed as women, Wisdom even being portrayed as a divine attribute.

The fact that Folly is portrayed as a woman does not mean that women are worse human beings than men, because Wisdom is equally portrayed as a woman, and the teaching about both is addressed to the sons (including the daughters).

In our discussions so far we have left out Proverbs 31:10-31. This last chapter of the book of Proverbs has its own literary character.

A Praise Poem for Women

Some time ago we heard Prov 31:10-31 read on a Women's Sunday in a church as an exhortation for those who had recently married or were anticipating to do the same. The lady emphasized that "she gets up while it is still dark" (31:15) and that "her lamp does not go out at night" (31:18). Here she mistook a praise poem for practical advice, as verses 15 and 18, when applied in that way, would never allow her to sleep at all. This poem is not practical advice, but praise not just for one excellent woman, but for all of them.

How does the poem portray such excellent women? Yes, she is hard working. Some have decried that aspect as too demanding. That is correct if the poem is read as good practical advice for women, but that is not a problem in a praise poem, and in this praise poem several observations on the position of women as portrayed in the Bible are appropriate:

1. Her independence: She is the agent of all her activities; and husband, children and all the servants profit from that.

2. Her outside activities: "She considers a field and buys it; out of her earnings she plants a vineyard" (v. 16). In addition she is an independent trader (v. 24).

3. Her equality: "Her husband has full confidence in her" (v. 11) and as much she is respected, so is he (among the city elders, v. 23), while "her works bring her praise at the city gate" (v. 31).

Such an extraordinary woman can fit into a patriarchal society, but she is surely not an expression of patriarchal oppression.

We need to remember that the book of Proverbs as part of Wisdom Literature does not describe life as it is, but life as God wants it to be. And while it surely is not right to construct a timetable for working class women out of the text, it shows that there is strength in the wife's position and no dependency or subservience.

A woman like her fits well to Genesis 1 and 2, which equally portray God's will. Did not the man (having just discovered that he is a *male* man) say:

> This is now bone of my bones and flesh of my flesh (Gen 1:23).

And did not God say to the woman (as much as to the man):

> "Rule over the fish of the sea and the birds of the air
> and over every living creature that moves on the ground (Gen 1:28).

This shows that Proverbs, as part of the Wisdom Literature, shows the women as equal to men.

Ecclesiastes

In Ecclesiastes the woman is mentioned twice:

> I find more bitter than death
> the woman who is a snare,
> whose heart is a trap
> and whose hands are chains."
> The man who pleases God will escape her,
> but the sinner she will ensnare (Ecclesiastes 7:26).

While the Teacher's outlook on humans is generally pessimistic, it is more so on women.

> I found one upright man among a thousand,
> but not one upright woman among them all (Ecclesiastes 7:28).

The Song of Songs

A part of Wisdom Literature often overlooked is the Song of Songs. There have been several allegoric interpretations of this song, but nowadays it seems clear that it is a love song. The description of Love in Song of Songs 8:6-7 bears similarities to the descriptions of Wisdom in Proverbs 1-9 and so it can be seen as "wisdom's description of an amorous relationship."[184] Wisdom and Love can be seen as sisters, and Wisdom and Love may be seen as "two of God's choicest gifts."[185]

Just as the voice of wisdom (in Proverbs) is a woman's voice, so in the Song of Songs the voice of Love is a woman's voice.

> 6Place me like a seal over your heart,
> like a seal on your arm;
> for love is as strong as death,
> its jealousy unyielding as the grave.
> It burns like blazing fire,
> like a mighty flame.
> 7Many waters cannot quench love;
> rivers cannot wash it away.
> If one were to give
> all the wealth of his house for love,
> it would be utterly scorned.

In this book love and attraction are mutual, the female voice is leading, and no inequality shows. Here again a reference to the Creation Story may be appropriate: "For this reason a man will leave his father and mother and be united to his wife, and they will become one flesh. The man and his wife were both naked, and they felt no shame" (Gen 2:24-25).

An Evangelical Feminist Interpretation of the Legal Texts

We have seen so far that the texts of prescriptive character show no signs of promoting patriarchy, female oppression or subordination. This picture changes once we turn to the legal texts of the Old Testament.

---

[184] NIV Study Bible, Introduction to Song of Songs.
[185] Ibid.

Earlier in this book you find a distinction of various types of legal texts. They all reflect the culture of the day, patriarchal as it was, while in the apodictic law women were not mistreated.

Feminist theologians, including Evangelicals, have pointed out some of the laws that are oppressive to women. This section outlines some of them. [186]

The first are marriage laws on women. As an example, during marriage engagement, a bride was required to submit proof of her virginity at the time of her marriage, but not so the groom (Deut 22:13-21). According to this law in the Bible, if the girl was discovered not to have been a virgin, she was stoned to death (vv. 20, 21). Other marriage laws included: two months of isolation for uncleanness after giving birth to a girl child, but only one month when a boy child was born (Lev 12:2,5); Polygamy was also tolerated, for example Lamech had two wives (Gen 4:19). Solomon had a harem (1 Kings 11:1-3). Hence, some men had many wives plus concubines.[187]

Furthermore, the laws of inheritance favoured the male heir. Women were only recognized when there were no male children in the family like in the case of Zelophehad's daughters (Num 27:1-11; 36:1-13).

Divorce favoured men as in the text below:

> If a man marries a woman who becomes displeasing to him because he finds something indecent about her, and he writes her a certificate of divorce, gives it to her and sends her from his house,
>
> 2and if after she leaves his house she becomes the wife of another man,
>
> 3and her second husband dislikes her and writes her a certificate of divorce, gives it to her and sends her from his house, or if he dies,
>
> 4then her first husband, who divorced her, is not allowed to marry her again after she has been defiled. That would be detestable in the eyes of the Lord .Do not bring sin upon the land the Lord your God is giving you as an inheritance.

---

[186] Frank Chirwa, A Critical Examination of the Changing Role of Women in the Seventh-day Adventist Church in Malawi: A Historical, Theological and Socio-Cultural Analysis towards a Gender Inclusive Ministry, Mzuzu University, 2014.

[187] For a detailed assessment of the OT teaching on polygamy see the relevant chapter in Moses Mlenga, *Polygamy in Northern Malawi. A Christian Reassessment*, Mzuzu: Mzuni Press, 2016, pp. 45ff.

> ₅If a man has recently married, he must not be sent to war or have any other duty laid on him. For one year he is to be free to stay at home and bring happiness to the wife he has married.

The man is not *given* the right to divorce his wife, it is assumed that he has this right, and it is equally assumed that the wife has no such right.

An Evangelical Position on the Legal Texts

Firstly, it is clear that the texts are patriarchal as shown above. These Laws must be reinterpreted to promote women's liberation. For the apodictic laws, such as the Ten Commandments, they are equally valid for men as for women.[188]

An Evangelical Feminist Approach to Historical Texts

Feminist theologians sometimes criticize the Old Testament because of promoting representation of women that made negative contributions. However, this claim must be checked with the fact that there are examples of women that played positive roles and those that played negative roles. Some of the stories about women, and indeed the women stories in the Old Testament, are very different, ranging from the story of Queen Esther, a saviour of Israel like Moses,[189] via the story of Hannah, the first wife of a polygamous husband, and the 700 wives of King Solomon (1 Kings 11:1-13) to outright stories of terror like the rape of David's daughter Tamar (2 Sam 13) and the sacrifice of the virgin daughter of Jephthah (Judges 11:32-40).[190]

To come to terms with the variety of Old Testament women stories, let us remember three rules.

(1) *What is reported in the Old Testament is not necessarily approved.*

---

[188] In Jewish culture of those days as in much of Malawian culture these days, the law against adultery was largely seen as directed against women only. In Malawi that is expressed by the proverb "Mwamuna ndi mtonde, azinunkha—A man is a billy goat, he must stink"(behave like one).

[189] Lapani Nkhonjera, Esther as the New Moses: Deliverance Motifs in the Book of Esther, MA, University of Stellenbosch, 2015. – For a strictly Feminist interpretation see: Sarojini Nadar, "Power, Ideology and Interpretation/s: Womanist and Literary Perspectives on the Book of Esther as Resources for Gender-Social Transformation," PhD, University of KwaZulu Natal, 2003.

[190] Phyllis Trible, *Texts of Terror*, Philadelphia: Fortress Press, 1984.

For the rape of Dinah this is clearly stated and the consequences are clearly shown (2 Sam 13:23ff). The disapproval is not as clearly stated in the story of the virgin daughter of Jephthah, but there is no sign of any approval (Judges 11:40).

(2) The second rule is that *the Old Testament reflects the patriarchal culture it was written in, but it does not promote patriarchy.*

Therefore we should neither be astonished nor disturbed by the fact that Elkanah had two wives (1 Sam 1:2) and that some of the judges and kings had plenty of them. Nor should we be unduly disturbed by Naomi plotting a polygamous marriage for her daughter (in-law), nor by Mordecai who put his cousin Hadassah/Esther into the Persian king's harem (Esther 2:8).

Such things are indeed reflections of the patriarchal culture of those days. And though God may have brought good things out of such cultural practices (as was the case with Ruth and Esther), these cultural practices are not necessarily to be recommended, especially not today.

(3) *The third rule is that the whole Bible is the word of God.* As Evangelical Feminist theologians we accept all of sacred scripture, and we interpret every genre in it according to its own rules.

An Affirmative Visit

While it may be easy to find historical texts on women that are problematic for Feminist interpreters, there is a very positive text often overlooked: The visit of the Queen of Sheba to Solomon:

> When the queen of Sheba heard about the fame of Solomon and his relation to the name of he LORD, she came to test him with hard questions. Arriving at Jerusalem with a very great caravan—with camels carrying spices, large quantities of gold, and precious stones— she came to Solomon and talked with him about all that she had on her mind (1 Ki 10:1-2, NIV).

From an Evangelical Feminist point of view, we observe these things: (1) She is a queen in her own right. (2) No husband is ever mentioned. (3) She is fully equal to Solomon. (4) Jesus used her as an example to condemn the people of his own day who had not recognized that "one greater than Solomon" was in their midst (Mt 12:42; Lk 11:31).[191]

Polygamy

A difficult issue in a Feminist reading of the Old Testament is the topic of polygamy, and especially so if the Feminist theologian is in Africa at the same time. Here is an Evangelical Feminist position on this issue:

(1) One must understand the biblical teaching about polygamy

(2) One must apply it to a society where polygamy is not only common but also legal. Both tasks have been undertaken in depth by Moses Mlenga, whose arguments we follow in this section.[192]

Polygamy was never God's Intention

This comes out clearly in the Creation Story, which shows three divine blessings, right from the beginning.

- To rule the animal kingdom and all the world (Gen 1:28).
- To work (Gen 2:15)
- Sex and marriage (Gen 1:28; 2:24)

As the gift of sex and marriage is described in the Creation Story, there is no room for polygamy (Gen 1 and 2), and even in Genesis 3, which shows the misuse of God's original gifts, polygamy is neither mentioned nor implied.

The subsequent chapters Genesis 4-11 show the consequences of sin in stories of repeated and continuous decline.[193] Polygamy appears for the first time in one of these stories of decline, see Genesis 4:19:

---

[191] For good information on the Queen of Shaba and the possible circumstances of her journey, see the NIV Study Bible on this text. Her kingdom may have been in what today is called Yemen. The web contains much information on the Queen of Sheba and all the narratives that have developed around her. For a Jewish perspective see: Carole R. Fontaine, in "Queen of Sheba/Jewish Women's Archives."

[192] Moses Mlenga, *Polygamy in Northern Malawi. A Christian Reassessment*, Mzuzu: Mzuni Press, 2016.

[193] These chapters also show the continuity of God's grace, like in the stories of Cain and of the Flood, but that is not the issue here.

> Lamech married two women, one named Adah and the other Zillah.[194]

From Genesis 4 it can be argued that polygamy came in as one of the consequences of sin.[195]

Polygamy Tolerated

Although, polygamy is in the narrative sections of the Old Testament, there are three observations to apply:

(1) Polygamy is not condemned.

(2) Polygamy is not praised.

(3) Polygamy is often implicitly criticized by biblical narrators.

The conclusion from these observations is that God did not promote polygamy in the Old Testament, but that he tolerated it.

The same can be observed with the legal texts. Deuteronomy 24:1-5 does not explicitly mention polygamy, but fits well into it. The same applies to the Levirate law that a man whose brother has died must marry the brother's widow to produce children for his brother (Dt 25:5-10).

Here again polygamy is not explicitly mentioned, but the likelihood is high that the brother, who is to take care of his sister-in-law, is himself already married,[196] a probability that must also be assumed in the case of Ruth, David's great grandmother.[197]

While in these cases polygamy is implied, it is explicitly mentioned in another Deuteronomistic law:

---

[194] That Lamech married two wives is not explicitly criticized here, though it is part of the story of decline, which is emphasized by Lamech's cruel words, addressed to both of them:
"Adah and Zillah, listen to me;
wives of Lameck, hear my words.
I have killed a man for wounding me,
a young man for injuring me" (Gen 4:23).

[195] Feminist theologians can understand this, because polygamy is only possible on the promise of male/female inequality, which was and is not God's intention.

[196] Moses Mlenga, *Polygamy in Northern Malawi. A Christian Reassessment*, Mzuzu: Mzuni Press, 2016, p. 57.

[197] Ibid.

₁₅If a man has two wives, and he loves one but not the other, and both bear him sons but the firstborn is the son of the wife he does not love,

₁₆when he wills his property to his sons, he must not give the rights of the firstborn to the son of the wife he loves in preference to his actual firstborn, the son of the wife he does not love.

₁₇He must acknowledge the son of his unloved wife as the firstborn by giving him a double share of all he has. That son is the first sign of his father's strength. The right of the firstborn belongs to him.

In this law again polygamy is not promoted or recommended, but is simply assumed and the law, as many of the laws in Deuteronomy, is introduced to protect the weaker partner.

So the overall picture shown so far can be confirmed: Polygamy is not God's original (and everlasting) will, but it was tolerated, as is shown in both the narrative and the legal texts.

Women in Positions of Leadership in Israel

Some Feminist theologians claim that the Old testament promotes male leadership. An Evangelical position begins by admitting that every community needs both female and male leaders, and religious communities are no exception. The Old Testament makes it very clear that Israel is Jahwe's people and that he is therefore head and ruler of the nation. Jahwe arranged for three types of human leaders to represent him among his people: priest, kings and prophets. And although women were not engaged in all these leadership roles, they occupied some. The fact that women were not engaged in all the roles shows that the society then favoured male leaders.

Priests

The Old Testament nowhere explicitly states that a women can not be a priest, but all the regulations clearly imply that all priests must be male.

In the neighbouring Canaanite religion there were female priests as well as female gods, but in the religion of Jahwe there was no room for either of them.

The instructions in the Old Testament about the priesthood are part of the sacrificial code, and should be interpreted in the light of Jesus as the High

Priest[198] and that the New Testament proclaims the priesthood of all believers.[199]

Kings

The second office through which Jahwe wanted to exercise his authority over his people was that of the king. Here again we find an all male office.

Over the centuries Israel had only one queen, the usurper Athaliah (2 Chro 22:10-23:21), and she was overthrown and executed by the priest Jehoiada.

Though the Bible does not explicitly state that royal succession in Israel was from father to son, it is clear that in Israel kingship was seen as a male domain; but we must also note that there is no divine kingship in the times of the New Testament.

Prophets

Of the three offices of leadership of God's people in the Old Testament, those of priest and king were reserved for men, and both these offices were not continued into the New Testament. For both Testaments the situation is different for the third leadership office, that of the prophet. It was open to women in Old Testament times. In the New Testament the office of the prophet continued and there, too, it was open to men and women.

In the Old Testament we find two major variants of the prophetic office. In the times before the introduction of the kingship, it was more an office of direct leadership, while in the period of Israel's kingship it was more an office of correction, when the appointed office bearers, the kings, failed to fulfill their divine commission.[200]

---

[198] Hebrews 3-7.

[199] From this priesthood of all believers women are in no way excluded, in the same way as they are not excluded from the Great Commission. See Klaus Fiedler, *Baptists and the Ordination of Women*, Zomba: Lydia Print, 2008. If a theologian or a church equates the current day pastors with the priests of the Old Testament, then ordination of women priests is not that easy. If the current office of pastor is seen as part of the priesthood of all believers, ordination of women should not present a problem.

[200] A very spectacular case was when Nathan accused and convicted King David of the sins of adultery and murder (2 Sam 12:1-14; also Moses Mlenga, A Critical Examination of the Issue of Polygamy, p. 89). While in Nathan's case the king accepted correction and was forgiven, Jeremiah experienced the opposite all his life long. This rejection culminated when

In the whole Old Testament the majority of prophets are male, but there is no indication of any difference between female and male prophets. Some of the female prophets have been mentioned in the earlier paragraphs, but here we provide a little of their background. Again here we have female prophets that had positive contributions and those that did not.

Miriam

When Miriam was young she helped to save the life of her brother Moses, and during Moses' time as the leader of Israel in the wilderness, she was also recognized as a leader, and in Exodus 15:20 she is explicitly called a prophetess.[201]

Deborah, Judge and Prophet

Among the judges of Israel she is the only female one, but it is important to observe that she is not mentioned as an exception or as someone special. She is introduced with these simple words:

> Deborah, a prophetess, the wife of Lapidoth, was leading[202] Israel at that time (Judges 4:4).

The next verse shows that she ran an appeal court "under the Palm of Deborah" and that "the Israelites came to her to have their disputes decided" (Judges 4:5). One verse further down she is introduced as a political leader to free Israel from oppression.[203]

In her quality of a prophet she shows similarities to Samuel, equally a judge and a political leader and a prophet.

King Zedekiah rejected Jeremiah's direction which would have saved his life and Jerusalem from destruction by fire (Jer 38:14-28).

[201] Cf Frank Chirwa, A Critical Examination of the Changing Role of Women in the Seventh-day Adventist Church in Malawi: A Historical, Theological and Socio-Cultural Analysis towards a Gender Inclusive Ministry, PhD, Mzuzu University, 2014.

[202] The traditional translation here is "judged".

[203] Some traditional theologians, who dislike women as leaders, argue that God may indeed use women if men fail or are not available. This argument, though, is not supported by the text, which does not indicate that a male appeal judge could not be found or failed to perform.

Huldah

Perhaps the most influential female prophet in Israel was Huldah. Like Deborah she was married, and King Josiah inquired through her from God about the validity and importance of the Book of the Law. She answered the king's question in the affirmative and therefore she became crucial in the biggest religious reform in the period of the kings, under Josiah.[204]

Like in the story of Deborah, no specific mention is made that she was (only) a women. Neither is there any explanation why the king inquired from her and not from any other (probably male) prophet. For those who theorize that God may choose women when men fail or absent, the story of Huldah yields no argument, as she had at least two colleagues, Jeremiah and Zephaniah. Why did Josiah not call for Jeremiah? Maybe he was on leave, at home in Anathoth. But as Anathoth is only 5 km from Jerusalem, so Josiah could have easily recalled him... But we better stop speculating, as much as those who argue that God must have chosen Huldah because all the men (including Jeremiah and Zephaniah) failed should equally stop speculating.

Leaving aside all speculation: To be a prophet was an office open to men and women, simply depending on God's call, different from the offices of priest and kings, to which, from all we know, God did not intend to call women. But while the offices of king and priest were not continued in the church of the New Testament, the office of prophet was continued both in the male and in the female line, and while in the Old Testament the male side was numerically stronger, in the New Testament it was the opposite.

When, after centuries of silence, prophecy reappears, the first prophet mentioned is Anna, who welcomed the baby Jesus and who "spoke about the child to all who were looking forward to the redemption of Jerusalem." This shows that she did not only receive divine inspiration, but that she also had a leadership role for those who waited for "the redemption of Jerusalem." That seems to indicate that there was a kind of congregation (or maybe a fellowship) which recognized her as a leader.

In the Old Testament we know only three female prophets by name. Just as not all male prophets are named, we may assume that there were also other female prophets.

---

[204] 2 Kings 22-23.

An Evil Prophet (Female)

Besides the three, in the Old Testament one more prophet is named, Noadiah:

> Remember Tobiah and Sanballat, O my God, because of what they have done; remember also the prophetess Noadiah and the rest of the prophets who have been trying to intimidate me (Neh 6:14).

Just as with the other female prophets, nothing is made of the fact that she was a women.[205] The only thing that counts is that she was an evil prophet,[206] trying to intimidate Nehemiah together with her male colleagues, but since only her name is mentioned, she may well have been their leader.

The tradition of evil female prophets is also continued in the New Testament. One is mentioned by a "nickname," Jezebel. The name was taken from Jezebel, the evil wife of the evil king Ahab (1 Kings 16:30-31). The Jezebel of the New Testament was a member of the church in Thyatira, which got several compliments in Jesus' message for the church.[207] But there is one serious weakness: the church tolerates "that woman Jezebel, who calls herself a prophetess." Jesus' words do not condemn her for being a teacher in the church or a prophet, but that through her teaching *she promotes sexual immorality*.[208]

A Prophecy for Women

In addition to the female prophets named in the Old Testament, there is also a prediction of female prophets for the time of the New Covenant. The prophet Joel predicted the New Covenant, and Peter at Pentecost picked up the prophecy.

Joel (Joel 2:28-29)   **Peter** (Acts 2:17-18)

---

[205] This supports the assumption that female prophets were nothing extraordinary in those days.

[206] Those were not rare among male prophets. A shining example was the prophet Hananiah who predicted that the holy vessels of the temple (and with them the exiles) would return within two years from Babylon, to which Jeremiah's answer was: Not in two years, but in two generations (Jer 28-29).

[207] The church of Thyatira is complimented for "love and faith, service and perseverance" (Rev 2:19).

[208] This seems to indicate a Gnostic influence, based on the belief that matter is evil, a concept that could lead either to asceticism (see 1 Cor 7:1) or to licentiousness, as is the case here.

I will pour out my Spirit on all people	I will pour out my Spirit on all people.
Your sons and daughters will prophecy,	Your sons and daughters will prophecy,
Your old men will dream dreams,	your young men will see visions,
your young men will see visions.	your old men will dream dreams.
Even on my servants,	Even on my servants,
both men and women,	both men and women,
I will pour out my Spirit in those days.	I will pour out my Spirit in those days, and they will prophecy.

Here the continuity from the Old Testament to the New Testament is clear, and in both Testaments prophecy is equally female and male.

3.9 Conclusion: An Evangelical Feminist Reading of the Old Testament

Here we summarize the teaching of the chapter in 8 theses:

1. The Old Testament was written in a patriarchal society.

2. The Old Testament reflects in several ways the patriarchal society in which it was written.

3. Patriarchal tendencies can be seen in some of the narratives and in legal texts dealing with casuistic law (especially family laws and the laws of purity).

4. Such patriarchal tendencies must be reinterpreted in view of what is liberating to women and is in the spirit of Jesus Christ. Contrary to many popular perceptions, Genesis 2 expresses male/female equality as much as Genesis 1.

5. Genesis 3 declares male superiority as a consequence of sin. This sin must be overcome by redemption.

6. Jesus explicitly declared as permanently valid the teaching of Genesis 2.

7. The offices of priest and king were for men only, and they are not continued in the New Testament.

8. The leadership office of prophet was open to men and women, and in that form it has continued in the New Testament.

Chapter 4: An Evangelical Feminist Biblical Hermeneutic of the New Testament

For Christian theology both the Old Testament and the New Testament are divine revelation, but of different relevance: the Old Testament is preliminary, pointing ultimately to Jesus as the centre of Salvation History. And when he came, as anticipated in the Old Testament, he both fulfilled the Old Testament and re-interpreted it according to the Salvation message. One of the claims that the Bible is patriarchal is based on the idea that there are few women leaders in the Bible and that there are some verses that promote women's oppression. In this chapter we provide an Evangelical explanation to such a claim by providing evidence of women leaders in the New Testament. Since Paul is often accused of promoting women's oppression, we have a larger section in the chapter on Paul and women.

Jesus and Women

In terms of a Feminist reading of the gospels it is important to note that Jesus did not refer to the case law of the Old Testament when the opportunity arose,[209] affirming the earlier position that the divorce laws were patriarchal and oppressive to women. And he also provided an alternative interpretation of the Sabbath laws[210] and food taboos (Mk 7:19),[211] and the

---

[209] Here the most obvious case is when Jesus was asked by some Pharisee scholars on the interpretation of Deuteronomy 24:1-4. The followers of Hillel interpreted Dt 24:1 as allowing a man (only male men) to divorce his wife for any reason ("becomes displeasing to him"), while Shammai would only allow divorce for serious reasons ("finds something indecent about her"). Jesus did not take sides but referred to Gen 2:24 instead. And when challenged why, then, Moses had allowed divorce, he told the men that it was because of their hard hearts.

[210] Luke 6:1-5: One Sabbath Jesus was going through the grain fields, and his disciples began to pick some heads of grain, rub them in their hands and eat the kernels. 2Some of the Pharisees asked, "Why are you doing what is unlawful on the Sabbath?" 3Jesus answered them, "Have you never read what David did when he and his companions were hungry? 4He entered the house of God, and taking the consecrated bread, he ate what is lawful only for priests to eat. And he also gave some to his companions." 5Then Jesus said to them, "The Son of Man is Lord of the Sabbath."

[211] Mark 17:17-23: 17After he had left the crowd and entered the house, his disciples asked him about this parable. 18"Are you so dull?" he asked. "Don't you see that nothing that enters a man from the outside can make him 'unclean'? 19For it doesn't go into his heart but into his stomach, and then out of his body." (In saying this, Jesus declared all foods "clean.") 20He went on: "What comes out of a man is what makes him 'unclean.' 21For from within,

whole concept of ritual purity so prominent in the OT laws;[212] neither did Jesus refer to any of the stories in the Old Testament in any positive way which feminist readers find oppressive.[213] Jesus was also not in support of the Jewish tradition of polygamy,[214] and Jesus' main references to the Old Testament in terms of the roles of women and men point to Gen 1 and 2, which portray God's will then and now and for all times and which clearly portray women and men as equal.

Two Old Testament Prophecies

The first is quite direct, so we start with the less obvious one: the Second Isaiah predicted major changes in God's dealings with humankind. He predicted that the eunuchs would be admitted right into the Holy Temple (Isa 56:4-5),[215] that the foreigners would be welcome equally (Isa 56:3)[216] and that the Servant would be a light not only to Israel but to all the nations (Isa 56:7).[217] Jesus does not mention women explicitly, but we would not be astonished if God's re-evaluation of his dealings with humankind may (though not mentioned by the prophet) also include a re-interpretation of the role of women among God's people.

On this issue the prophet Joel is more explicit. He predicted for later days a new outpouring of the Divine Spirit. On the left side is the text of Joel 2:28-29, on the right side as quoted in Acts 2:17-18.

---

out of men's hearts, come evil thoughts, sexual immorality, theft, murder, adultery, 22greed, malice, deceit, lewdness, envy, slander, arrogance and folly. 23All these evils come from inside and make a man 'unclean.'

[212] Women's "impurities" are not explicitly mentioned here, but if the other impurities are removed, why should theirs be kept?

[213] Such stories could be the rape of Tamar (2 Sam 13), the murder of the Shechemites (Gen 34), or the sacrifice of Jephtah's daughter. Jesus does not refer to any of these stories.

[214] Moses Mlenga, *Polygamy in Northern Malawi. A Christian Reassessment*, Mzuzu: Mzuni Press, 2016, pp. 64-66.

[215] 4For this is what the Lord says: "To the eunuchs who keep my Sabbaths, who choose what pleases me and hold fast to my covenant-5to them I will give within my temple and its walls a memorial and a name better than sons and daughters; I will give them an everlasting name that will not be cut off.

[216] And Jesus quoted the prophet's words "My house will be called a house of prayer for all nations" (Mk 11:17 quoting Isaiah 56:7).

[217] 6He says: "It is too small a thing for you to be my servant to restore the tribes of Jacob and bring back those of Israel I have kept. I will also make you a light for the Gentiles, that you may bring my salvation to the ends of the earth."

₂₈"And afterward,	₁₇"'In the last days, God says,
I will pour out my Spirit on all people.	I will pour out my Spirit on all people.
Your sons and **daughters will prophesy**,	Your sons and **daughters will prophesy**,
your old men will dream dreams,	your young men will see visions,
your young men will see visions.	your old men will dream dreams.
₂₉Even on my servants,	₁₈Even on my servants,
both men and women,	**both men and women**,
I will pour out my Spirit in those days.	I will pour out my Spirit in those days,
	and they will prophesy.

This text relates to the New Covenant, which Jesus brought, and for which he sent the Holy Spirit in a way and in dimensions never heard of. To explain what had happened on Pentecost, Peter quoted the prophet at length. This gift of the Holy Spirit, the culmination of Jesus' ministry on earth, fulfilled also what the prophet Isaiah had prophesied that all nations would come to find salvation, and it included the gender equality, which Joel had predicted. This therefore became constitutive for the whole mission of the church: The Holy Spirit came on both women and men, and women and men were to drive the mission of the church.

Anna, the Prophetess

Just as we mentioned in chapter 3 of this book, women did not lead in all of the three religious offices in the Old Testament (Priests, Kings and Prophets)- Only one office was open to women, that of the Prophet, and it is also the only one that was continued into the New Testament. So it is not strange that Jesus was welcomed into this world by a female prophet, Anna, the daughter of Phanuel (Lk 2:36-37), and she spoke to "those who looked for the redemption of Jerusalem" (Lk 2:38).[218]

Jesus' Female Disciples

Among the disciples of Jesus, who followed him, there were women. Three are mentioned by name: Mary of Magdala (Mary Magdalene), Joanna (wife of Chuza, Herod's steward, and Susanna.

> After this, Jesus traveled about from one town and village to another, proclaiming the good news of the kingdom of God. The Twelve were with him, and also some women who had been cured of evil spirits and diseases: Mary (called Magdalene) from whom seven demons

---

[218] It looks that she did not talk to an ad hoc meeting, but to a *regular* group, like these days a fellowship.

had come out; Joanna the wife of Cuza, the manager of Herod's household; Susanna; and many others. These women were helping to support them out of their own means (Lk 8:1-3).

There were other women disciples, like Mary and Martha (John 11:1-43), who did not travel with Jesus. The text makes a clear distinction between the Twelve and the women, but all were following Jesus. It is clear that all the Twelve (most likely representing the New Israel with its 12 tribes) were male disciples. But neither Jesus nor the writers of the New Testament give any explanation for this choice.[219] In choosing female disciples Jesus differed from the Jewish Rabbis (and Jesus looked like one and was sometimes called "Rabbi") who would never accept female disciples.

Women Studying the Word of God

Jesus never taught in a school, either secular or religious, but he always taught, formally and informally. Never did he turn away any listener, male or female.

Jesus accepted the work of Martha to prepare food for all, but he rated Mary's interest in speaking to him and listening to his teaching as superior. "Mary has chosen what is better, and it will not be taken away from her" (Lk 10:42).

The Rabbis (Jewish Teachers) in Jesus' days did not allow even their own daughters to learn the Torah (the Word of God).[220] Jesus differs: He gives women free access to the Gospel (not *after* doing the house work, but even *before* and *instead*!)

Talking to Women

Jesus talked to women freely. The Rabbis were only to talk to women (outside their own household), when it was absolutely necessary. See John 4:27: "And at this point his disciples came and they marveled that he talked to a woman." He must also have talked a lot to Mary and Martha, who were

---

[219] Pope John Paul II in his encyclical letter Mulieris Dignitatem took Jesus' choice of (male) apostles as one reason that in the Roman Catholic Church only male men can be ordained priests. As non-Catholics we argue that this is an argument from silence, as Jesus dos not give any reason for his choice nor did any of the Twelve.

[220] For context and discussion see: Rabbi Yehuda Henkin, Talmud Study by Women, www.nishmat.net/torah/view.asp?id=44.

his friends (John 11). There was also Lazarus in the household, whom Jesus resurrected. But the two sisters were also his friends.

A Woman of Faith

Jesus praised the faith of a women, a Gentile for that: "'Woman, you have great faith! Your request has been granted.' And her daughter was healed from that very hour" (Mt 15:28). No such praise is recorded in rabbinical literature.

Jesus did not condemn women

Jesus protected women against male abuse and judgment. When a women caught red-handed in adultery (where was the man?) was brought to him, he did not judge her but pronounced forgiveness, freedom and a new life (John 8:11).[221] And when a woman, who was a "sinner," anointed his feet, he assured her that her faith had saved her and that she should go in peace (Lk 7:50).

Women ministered to him during his suffering

And when Jesus was anointed by another woman at Bethany, just before his death, he rebuked male complaints, called what she had done "a beautiful thing" and prophesied:

> "Wherever this gospel is preached throughout the world, what she has done will also be told, in memory of her" (Mt 26:13).

When Jesus was dying on the cross, John was the only male disciple there, but there were at least four of his female disciples who stayed with him to the end.

> Near the cross of Jesus stood his mother, his mother's sister, Mary the wife of Clopas, and Mary Magdalene (John 19:25).

Women were the first witnesses of the resurrection

Two women (Mary Magdalene and the other Mary) came first to Jesus' grave Mt 28:1-10. They did not expect the risen Jesus, but Jesus appeared

---

[221] "Woman, where are they? Has no one condemned you?" "No one, sir," she said. "Then neither do I condemn you," Jesus declared. "Go now and leave your life of sin."

to them before he met any of his male disciples/apostles. Jesus could easily have chosen to meet Peter or any other male apostle first.

Jesus told the women to tell "his Brethren" that he had risen (Mt 28:7). Jesus could easily have told any male disciple to do this, but he chose otherwise.

Women were among those that received the Holy Sprit at Pentecost

Jesus gave the disciples the command to stay in Jerusalem (Acts 1:4) and to wait for the Holy Spirit. This was obeyed by both women and men.

> These all continued with one accord in prayer and supplication, with the women and Mary the mother of Jesus, and with His brothers (Acts 1:14).

On the day of Pentecost "all of them were filled with the Holy Spirit and began to speak in other tongues as the Spirit enabled them" (Acts 1:4). Peter testifies to this when he quotes the prophet Joel in Acts 2:14-18.

Jesus' attitude to women is equally reflected by the Apostle Paul.

The Position of Women in some Passages of the Pauline Letters[222]

Introduction

In analyzing the role of women in the Pauline letters, we use a historical approach. This means that we will look at the historical evidence about women's role in the primitive church as provided in the Bible, concentrating on Paul, who has often been declared to have been an "enemy of women." Once the historical evidence is assembled and assessed, we will relate it to those verses, which belong to the realm of practical theology. To give prom-

---

[222] The ideas of this section were first presented as a paper at the Association of Theology Institutions in Southern and Central Africa (ATISCA) Conference in Harare, Zimbabwe in December 1998, which was then published as: Klaus Fiedler, "Gender Equality in the New Testament: The Case of St. Paul", *Malawi Journal of Biblical Studies*, no. 1, 2003, pp. 19-36. A result of this article is: Janet Kholowa and Klaus Fiedler, *Mtumwi Paulo ndi Udindo wa Amayi mu Mpingo*, Blantyre: CLAIM-Kachere, 2001. The most recent version is: Klaus Fiedler, "Gender Equality in the New Testament: The Case of St. Paul", in Klaus Fiedler, *Conflicted Power in Malawian Christianity: Essays Missionary and Evangelical from Malawi*, Mzuzu: Mzuni Press, 2015, pp. 160-177.

inence to the historical evidence is very much justified on Evangelical principles, since they take the primitive church not only as the beginning but also as the yardstick.[223] After that we want to relate the results to the systematic statement in Gal 3:28 and to current reality. In using this approach we were informed by a number of Evangelical missiologists of the second half of the nineteenth century.

In discussing the biblical evidence we follow the Evangelical approach to take all letters ascribed to Paul as having been written by him,[224] that the book of Acts accurately records history,[225] and that interference with the original text by later interpolators is most unlikely.[226]

Our approach is different from the frequent approach that starts from what may look like prescriptive ('legal') texts. This frequent approach is to search in the New Testament texts, and to relate them to the current issues as seen by the expositor. The legal framework gained in this way is almost exclusively a restrictive one for women in the church (or even in life as a whole). Once that legal foundation is established, those biblical verses which do not fit the restrictive frame can be overlooked or dealt with in some other way.

This approach has several problems: (1) it is an approach in systematic theology, but the texts used like 1 Cor 14:34 ("women must remain silent in the churches") and 2 Tim 2:12 ("I do not permit a woman to teach") may belong far more to practical theology, and Gal 3:28, the one text which is clearly a systematic statement, does not warrant any restrictions at all on women ("There is neither Jew nor Greek, slave nor free, male nor female,

---

[223] There is an interesting parallel to this attitude in Jesus' application of the creation story to current issues of marriages and divorce (Matt 19:4, "Haven't you read that at the beginning the Creator made them male and female..."). On the Genesis Story, see Janet Y. Kholowa and Klaus Fiedler, *In the Beginning God Created them Equal* (English Version), and *Pa Chiyambi Anawalenga Chimodzimodzi (Chichewa Version), Buku la Mvunguti*, Blantyre: CLAIM, 1999).

[224] This rules out the interpretation that, after all, Paul did not support the injunctions on female behavior in 1 Timothy.

[225] This rules out the view that the book of Acts does not reflect the reality of the primitive church, but just Luke's theology.

[226] This rules out the possibility of getting rid of the difficult text in 1 Corinthians 14 by seeing it as a later interpolation

for you are all one in Christ Jesus").[227] (2) This approach violates the Evangelical principle of Bible exposition, which demands that the *whole biblical evidence* be taken into account before coming to conclusions for today's behaviour, be it in church or outside. (3) This restrictive role ascribed to women can not be easily reconciled with Jesus' teaching and practice. Why then did he appear to women first after the resurrection?

Below is an analysis of the role of women in Pauline letters based on the historical approach.

Romans 16: How Paul appreciated women's ministry

This chapter of Romans is seen by many Bible readers as dull, containing names, names, names and greetings. But to the student of the primitive church it is a highly revealing chapter, and for those who follow Baptist ecclesiological premises it may even have some normative value.

It is first of all evident that Paul acknowledges women's role in general. Of the 26 persons he greets specifically, 10 are women. This is definitely more than courtesy in writing a letter. Some of the women are just mentioned (Julia, v. 15) or mentioned in relation to a male person (Nereus and his sister, v. 15). Two women (Rufus' mother, v. 13; Phoebe, v. 2) are mentioned in a typical female role ("who has been a mother to me, too"[228] and who "has been a great help[229] to many, including me").[230] The other women are mentioned in not obviously female roles: one had risked her life for him (Prisca, v. 3), another was in prison with him (Junias, v. 7), and the others are mentioned as "workers."

---

[227] This verse can be disposed of by relegating its injunctions of female/male equality to the realm of the spiritual. But that attempt was not successful for "neither slave nor free". For a recent discussion on gender in the Bible, see Hilary Mijoga, "Gender Differentiation in the Bible: Created and Recognized," *Journal of Humanities* no. 13 (1999), pp. 87-113; reprinted in Jonathan Nkhoma, *Significance of the Dead Sea Scrolls and other Essays: Biblical and Early Christianity Studies from Malawi*, Mzuzu: Mzuni Press, 2014, pp. 176-198.

[228] But even here it can not be excluded that she was a spiritual mother.

[229] The Greek word here is *prostatis*, which has, like the Hebrew word *etser*, a connotation of strength. *Prostasso* means to command, to order.

[230] Here the possibility can also not be excluded that Phoebe helped Paul not by cooking his meals and running errands for him but by preaching the Gospel and teaching the converts.

Paul acknowledges women as fellow missionaries

The most important of his female co-workers may have been Priscilla. Here, as often, Paul calls her with her shortened name, Prisca, and mentions her before her husband, to whom he accords the same title, "my fellow worker in Christ Jesus" (v. 3) (*synergous mou en Xristo Iesou*. The term is applied in the same chapter to Timothy (v. 21, *synergos mou*). It must have a strong meaning, since Timothy may be seen as the most prominent of Paul's fellow missionaries.

For other women's contribution, Paul uses verbal forms: Mary[231] "worked very hard for you" (*ekopiasen eis hymas*). The same is said in v. 12 of Tryphena and Tryphosa,[232] but this time the object they worked hard for is Christ (*ekopiasen en kyriō*). The same is said of Persis (v. 12).

The meaning of the word *kopian* is given as "work, work hard, labour; become tired, grow weary."[233] Paul uses the word in 1 Cor 4:12 ("We work hard with our own hands"), 1 Cor 15:10 ("No, I worked harder than all of them"), 1 Cor 16:16 ("submit to ... who joins in the work and labours at it"). Obviously, *kopian* refers for Paul primarily to spiritual work, so that he has to add "with our own hands" in 1 Cor. 4:12 (as in Eph 4:28), and the spiritual base meaning of the word is also seen in Paul's usage in Gal 4:11 (" I fear for you, that somehow I have wasted my efforts on you", similar in Phil 2:16).[234] It is obvious that Paul describes these women as doing spiritual work and as putting in a lot of effort. Sure, for Paul spiritual work may be very much down to earth ("serving" is seen as a spiritual gift), but if Paul had greeted (male) men in this way, we would have understood their hard work to include preaching, teaching and leadership, though not excluding serving at tables and cleaning up after a Gospel meeting. If that is so, there is no linguistic evidence in the text to treat female men (women) differently.

A case similar to Tryphena and Tryphosa is that of Euodia and Syntyche (Phi 4:2-3), only that Paul uses a different word to express that they were his co-workers, not that they worked hard, but that they "contended (*synēth-*

---

[231] There is no evidence to suggest that this Mary is identical to any Mary mentioned in the New Testament elsewhere.

[232] Their names suggest that they were sisters or even twins.

[233] Barclay M. Newman, *A Concise Greek-English Dictionary of the New Testament* (London: United Bible Societies, 1971).

[234] Other places where Paul uses *kopian* are: 1 Thess 5:12; 1 Tim 4:10; 5:17; 2 Tim 2: 6.

lēsan) at his side in the cause of the gospel", along with Clement and the rest of his fellow workers (*synergōn mou*). Here Paul obviously makes no differentiation between female and male co-workers, and as expositors we should not assume that the female co-workers did the serving and the male co-workers the leading.

In all cases, Paul does not speak of fellow missionaries, but of workers. But we think it is allowable to call them fellow missionaries since Paul saw himself first of all as a missionary. For most women he described as co-workers Paul gives no details, except for Junias.

Paul acknowledges a female deacon

If one reads Romans 16 carefully, the argument that the New Testament does not speak of women holding regular offices in the church, does not hold water. Paul describes Phoebe as *diakonos tēs ekklēsias tēs en Kegxreais*. The same word is used elsewhere in the New Testament for the deacons as office bearers of the church. This means that she was one, too. The word *diakonos* is of male gender, and as usual in Greek, that includes male and female persons.

Patriarchal bias is evident in many translations. The NIV, which tries to remain close to the Greek original, makes her to be a servant, and in a footnote says "or deaconess". The Greek text, though, gives no hint that her office was a female one, and if one translates the word as "deaconess", many readers will see the office as something specifically female.[235]

The current Chewa version (*Buku Lopatulika*) uses the same approach, making Phoebe a *mtumiki wamkazi*, whereas in 1 Tim 3:8 the word is simply translated as *atumiki*. The more recent and transitory translation of the New Testament (*Chipangano Chatsopano*) corrects this to a straight *mtumiki*, and this is also the text for the new version (*Buku Loyera*).

The German version which is seen to be closest to the original text, the *Elberfeld Version*, translated within the Brethren Movement, which restricts the women's role to full silence in the presence of men in the church, takes

---

[235] This is made easier by the fact that in Britain there developed a group of deaconesses in the last century, and in Germany the Diakonissen were a strong element in many Protestant churches, and many of them are there, still. Their motto was "my privilege is to serve", and most were trained and work as nurses. All these do not equate with the position of deacon in the church.

account of the fact that in Romans 12 and 1 Timothy 3 the same word is used, and being less clerical than other translations does not use the word deacon (*Diakon*), but the original servant (*Diener*) in both cases. But their bias still shows in translation: Phoebe is not *Diener*, but *Dienerin*, and she gets no footnote, while in 1 Timothy 3 a footnote tells the readers that the Greek really is "*Diakonen*" (deacons).

The list of biased translations could be extended,[236] but if one reads the texts without a bias, Paul just speaks of deacons, be they female or male. Or he just speaks of servants, be they male or female. But there is no justification to translate the same word differently in any case, unless there is a very good reason for doing so, and this we can not find.

Paul acknowledges a female teacher of theology

If Paul ever was of the opinion that women must not teach, then he had not yet developed this view when he wrote Romans, because Prisca (or more officially Priscilla) had been doing just that. Of her we read in Acts 18:26:

> When Priscilla and Aquila heard him [Apollos], they invited him to their home and explained to him the way of God more adequately.

Do we imagine that Luke wants to tell us that Aquila did all the teaching and Priscilla cooked *nsima* and *ndiwo*, and that Priscilla sat silently at the men's feet during whatever spare time she could find in between cooking meals? The text does not say that, and after all, Priscilla is mentioned first.[237]

She seems to have been a successful teacher. Apollos became a great theologian and preacher, at least in Paul's opinion. And Paul did not blame Phoebe for her success.

Paul acknowledges a female apostle

One of his more detailed comments Paul reserves for Andronicus and Junias, his co-workers who had suffered with him. Then he tells the Roman

---

[236] Like in the Swahili Union Version, where Fibi is *mhudumu* (servant), while then men in 1 Timothy 3 are *mashemasi*, which is a technical term describing an office.

[237] A way to get round Priscilla's theological teaching is to make her "*kukambirana*", to mean informal discussions, or to state that she did the teaching under her husband's authority.

church that they were "outstanding among the apostles", words not easy to deal with if you do not like women apostles.[238]

Translators and commentators found a number of ways round. The boldest were those who changed Junias into Junios, thus making her a (male) man. But for this there is only the faintest textual evidence, and in all secular literature available, Junias is always female.

The other solution is to understand "among the apostles" as meaning "in the opinion of the apostles". "The apostles" are then constituted as "The Twelve", a formally constituted body of a limited number of apostles. That is how readers often understand it today, but there is no real evidence that Paul did so, too. He understood himself to be an apostle (no. 13?), and other apostles are mentioned, like Barnabas. Paul also speaks of the church as being built on the "foundation of the apostles and prophets" (Eph 2:20). The fact that Paul mentions the apostles first makes it unlikely that the prophets are the Old Testament prophets and the apostles just the Twelve. There seems to be no problem for Paul to see Junias among the apostles.[239]

In this he is not alone, the famous preacher Chrysostomos shared that view. He wrote: "What great an honour must this woman have received to be called an apostle."[240] Chrysostomos was living in a patriarchal society, presiding over a diocese in a patriarchal church. Still he did not mind.

Paul acknowledges women prophets

There is no clearly defined structure of the churches in the New Testament, and as far as these structures are visible, they differ from place to place and from book to book. But it is clear that prophets played a major role in the early church. In Peter's first sermon, women prophets were included:

> Your sons and daughters will prophesy, your young men will see visions, your old men will dream dreams. Even on my servants, both men and women, I will pour out my Spirit in those days, and they will prophesy (Acts 2:17-18).

---

[238]

[239] For a thorough study of the meaning of apostleship see: Felix Nyika, Apostolic Office in Malawian Neocharismatic Churches: A Contextual, Biblical-Theological, and Historical Appraisal, PhD, University of Malawi, 2015.

[240] John Chrysostomos, *Homilies on the Acts of the Apostles and the Epistle to the Romans*, Philip Schaff (ed), Edinburgh: T&T Clark/Grand Rapids: Eerdmans, nd [1889], available as free download: NPNF1-11.

Paul obviously assumes the same Spirit's gender insensivity in 1 Cor 11:5. There he regulates how women prophets shall behave when delivering their message,[241] but does not question their right to public delivery.

The office of prophets is also mentioned in connection to Paul on his last journey to Jerusalem. At Caesarea the travelling company of missionaries stayed at the house of the Evangelist and Deacon Philip, who "had four unmarried daughters who prophesied" (Acts 21:9). If Paul had been unhappy to meet them, we think we can safely assume that Luke would not have recorded their presence in the way he did.

What about a woman church elder?

Paul may well have spoken of women deacons in 1 Tim 3:8,[242] but there is no evidence in the few words of his that have been preserved that he ever spoke of women elders. But how would he have spoken of Lydia? Just as his first convert and then hostess? We think he would also have considered her a church elder, if the nascent structures of that church had allowed such an office. The church met in her house, and when Paul and Silas had been freed from prison, they went to Lydia's house to discuss things with the brethren (a term that in Greek includes the sisters). Nothing detailed is said about Lydia's role, but if she had been a (male) man, we think she would be considered to have been the leading ruling elder of the Christian Church in Philippi.

The Evangelical missiologists of the 19th Century were keen readers of the Bible. In the New Testament they found that women played important roles, and even the study of the Old Testament confirmed this. Sure, God used men more frequently than women, but women had also been God's ministers: Miriam was a prophet, and so was Huldah. Both had male prophets around them: Moses and Jeremiah, and God called them nevertheless. Deborah likewise, she won the victory and judged Israel for many years, while Barrack was allowed to help her a bit in some specialized effort.

---

[241] What exactly his regulations were, is today open to mutually exclusive interpretations: Either he demanded that they cover their heads or he demanded that no women should be bothered about covering her head or not. See Thomas Schirrmacher, "Paul in Conflict with the Veil. An Alternative Interpretation of 1 Corinthians 11:2-16," Bonn: VTR, ²2007.

[242] The translation "their wives" seems to be a translators' view. The Greek text's simple "gynaikas hosautos" may well mean women deacons, which the NIV footnote acknowledges by offering "deaconesses" as an alternative translation to "their wives."

They also discovered that the "beautiful feet of those who bring good news on the mountains" belonged to women (Isa 52:7) and that the Old Testament part of salvation history came to an end with a woman prophet by the name of Anna.[243]

Paul's "Practical Theology" Texts about Women's Role

Having discovered all this, they concluded that women should preach the gospel and that women (married or single) must be missionaries in their own right. But with their deep love for and personal direct relationship to the Bible they had to find an answer to the two seemingly prohibitive texts in Paul's practical theology: Let women be quiet in church and don't allow them to teach.

Evangelical Understandings

Fredrick Franson's answer is very clear and stands for many similar answers: The evidence for women's preaching and so on is so clear, that the two texts must have another explanation. If we are not sure what this explanation is, we can be assured though, that they do not mean what they are widely supposed to mean, namely, that women should shut up. Maybe they were just local admonitions to solve local problems.

Another way used in the Holiness Movement to relate the historical evidence to the "different" Pauline injunctions is found in a theology of the Holy Spirit as a missionary spirit. Is it not God's aim that as many people as possible should find Christ and be saved? If the New Testament evidence shows clearly that God used women to achieve just that, the two difficult verses can not be given a meaning clearly contradicting the main thrust of the Gospel.

This line of argument is supported by a line of reasoning based on the obvious activity of the Holy Spirit. As history has shown, it is not always easy to identify certain historical events as God's action,[244] but one thing is certain:

---

[243] She seems to have had her own congregation: "she gave thanks to God and spoke about the child to all who were looking forward to the redemption of Israel" (Luke 2:38).

[244] In Germany, for example, many Christians, Evangelicals included, saw the coming to power of Adolf Hitler in 1933 as divine intervention to save the German nation (*Volk*) from Bolshevism, international (Jewish) capitalism and moral decline.

the conversion of sinners is God's action.[245] In the Holiness Movement there were many women evangelists, and had God not blessed their work with spiritual fruit? If that was the case, a few isolated verses of Scripture can not have been designed to stop that. Salvation, and therefore conversion, is the guiding principle of theological reflection, not the doubtful exposition of a few New Testament references.

The roots of this view go back at least to John Wesley. In his early years, even after he had been revived in his faith, he forbade women to speak in the Methodist meetings. But since it was revival time, the women did not really heed his injunction, and Wesley did not mind so much, either. He soon observed that some women did a good job as witnesses, and even as preachers. Then he did not stop them any longer, and finally he fully supported them. When he was asked how he could do that, he answered: "If God owns them in the conversion of sinners, who am I to hinder Him?"

Wesley's allusion to Peter's words explaining his motivation for the theological decision to admit Gentiles to the Christian Church directly through baptism and not as the Old Testament prescribed through circumcision (and proselyte baptism, and keeping the law of Moses) is a good summary of thought frequent in the Holiness Movement. Peter answered his ("conservative") critics:

> So if God gave the same gift as he gave us, who believed in the Lord Jesus Christ, who was I to think that I could oppose God? (Acts 11:17)

This way of reasoning was echoed by Amaro, a leading elder in the Evangelical Church of Guinea Bissao, the leading Protestant denomination in that country, founded by a woman. When asked about women preaching, he replied: "Maybe from the Bible that is not right." And then he added after a little hesitation: "But had it not been for a woman preaching, I would not have been saved." From this the conclusion can be drawn that it is better to be saved by a woman preaching than being lost for eternity for a man not preaching.

All these arguments find support in the basic Evangelical tenet that the whole testimony of Scripture must be used in any decision making process, and that any decision based on isolated verses may sound legally convincing, but even if it did so, it would not be true to the real evidence of Scrip-

---

[245] There will be joy in heaven even for one sinner converted, how much more joy will there be if many sinners are converted!

ture nor to the reality of the Holy Spirit working for the conversion of sinners.

Galatians 3:28 (The Magna Charta of Women)

If one follows the foregoing reasoning, Gal 3:28 falls easily into place. It is a statement made by Paul in a systematic context, and as such it must be accorded due prominence. The key to its interpretation may be the inclusion of slave and free. From the evidence of Paul's letters, it is clear that he accepted slavery, though he never commended it. In the great controversy over Christian slave holding, both sides appealed to Paul: The supporters to his real and realistic acceptance of slavery as a social institution, the opponents to his strong systematic statement. We know today that the opponents were right. Though a social reality, this reality can not be seen as good and commendable and must therefore be challenged from the systematic statement of Paul.

The same reasoning should be applied to the statement that there is neither male nor female. There may be room for accepting existing social restrictions and for giving advice within that framework (like Paul *may* have done in 1 Corinthians and 1 Timothy), but general conclusions can not be based on ancient pastoral adaptation to a given culture, but must be based on the authoritative (systematic) statements in scripture. In that process the unbiased study of the women's role in the early church in a historic way can help clarify what belongs to the systematic side of Paul's teaching and what belongs to the pastoral side. Just as much as slaves in their days were right in reading Gal 3:28 as a powerful critique of existing conditions, so women in the nineteenths century were—and today are—right in reading the same verse as a powerful critique of existing conditions in church and society. Though the early Evangelicals' fight for women's rights has now been overtaken by women's lib and other social movements, their insights can still be of quite some value for the church today.

Alternative Interpretations: Evangelical type

So far we have assumed that there was and is agreement over the interpretation of the very meaning of the difficult Pauline passages, though the application may strongly differ. This is a simplified view, in fact there are for each of them Evangelical interpretations which yield results contrary to what is widely accepted. These would support Franson's contention that there must be interpretations other than the restrictive ones, interpretations that match with the New Testament's theology of missions.[246]

Women must remain silent in the churches!

In traditional exegesis, 1 Cor 14:34 was often taken to mean that women must keep silent in church (*gynaikes en tais ekklēsiais sigatōsan*, in Latin the famous: *Mulieres in ecclesiis taceant*). Though this looks like a very general and therefore systematic statement, unbiased readers of the letter would soon see that the understanding that this verse forbids women to speak publicly in church is in conflict with Paul's own assumption of women publicly praying and prophesying recorded by Paul in 1 Cor 11:5.[247] Therefore the easiest explanation may be that Paul forbids women to "chatter" in church, an interpretation that gains strength from the fact that in the Jewish synagogues women would sit among themselves, and in Jewish synagogues there was a lot of chatting anyhow,[248] as some scholars argue, because not every part of the Jewish service needs the attention of everyone present.[249]

A woman who prays or prophesies must cover her head

Most Bible translations assume that this was what Paul wanted the women in the church of Corinth to do: Cover their heads. But possibly Paul told them exactly the opposite. Doubts about current translations arise because the word *exousia* in 1 Cor 1:10 is understood to mean veil, headscarf or any other piece of fabric to be put on a woman's head. But *exousia* elsewhere in

---

[246] He did not provide any of these interpretations, but was convinced that they would exist.

[247] The nicest explanation I found to get around this is that Paul, knowing that the Corinthians were difficult Christians, did not dare to tell them immediately what his real opinion was, and that he finally gathered the necessary strength for that when he had reached chapter 14: "Women must keep quiet! Basi."

[248] From this seems to have developed the German saying: *Ihr macht einen Lärm wie in der Judenschule* ("You make a noise like in a Jewish synagogue").

[249] At a marriage *mlandu* in a predominantly Muslim village in Southern Tanzania, the men were in charge and slightly in the majority, the women were sitting among themselves not exactly behind the men, but sideways, in a definitely subordinate place. Sometimes they talked among themselves, sometimes they went off with a child. Sometimes they contributed to (or interfered with) the proceedings, and sometimes the men even asked them for their opinion. Maybe there was some similarity between what happened in that village and the proceedings in a house church in Corinth?

the New Testament means authority and power.[250] Jesus taught like one having power (Matt 7:29) and he had authority on earth to forgive sins (Matt 9:6), and he gave his disciples authority to drive out evil spirits (Matt 10:1). The Jewish elders questioned Jesus by what authority he did what he did (Matt 11:23), and Jesus gives all who believe in him the authority to become children of God (John 1:12). In none of these verses has *exousia* been translated as "sign of authority", but just as authority. Why not translate in the same way when a women in involved: "Therefore the woman ought to have authority over her head", and therefore she can wear a hat, a turban, cut the hair short, curl it or straighten it, add braids to it or let it grow to her waist or tie it into a knot as my mother used to do. This interpretation fits well to what we know for sure about Paul: He appreciated highly the women's work for the Gospel.

If this was Paul's view, how do we reconcile earlier statements of his which seem to demand female submission, compulsory fabric etc? An answer would be a quotation. If Paul gave the direction that women should be left alone as far as head dress is concerned, the opposing view could have been quoted from the letter which he received and in which these questions were asked. Then Paul's own words would be vv. 2-3 and 10-16, and vv. 4-9 would be opinions he quotes and disapproves of.[251] Neither Thomas Schirrmacher nor we see this as the ultimate answer, with no queries permitted. But it is definitely a possible interpretation, with maybe less loose ends than other more common interpretations. The Evangelical missiologists did not foresee such a possible interpretation, but they made room in their theology where such an interpretation could find its place.

I do not allow a woman to teach!

This verse obviously conflicts with what we otherwise know about Paul. Did he change his mind as he grew older? Had women teachers disappointed him? Interesting thoughts, but speculations at best. Or maybe the author was not Paul? This is a view Evangelicals do not share. One way to under-

---

[250] The NIV tries to take account of this by making women "have a sign of authority on her head". The Swahili Union Version makes it very clear that the authority is not her's but over her: "*Kwa hiyo imampasa mwanamke awe na dalili ya kumilikiwa*" (sign of being ruled on her head).

[251] For a detailed discussion of this possibility including a review of exegetical literature on this issue see, Thomas Schirrmacher, *Paul's Battle against the Veil: An Alternative Interpretation of 1 Corinthians 11:2-16*, Bonn: VKW, 1993; ²2007.

stand that passage is that Paul, out of pastoral concern, gave instructions for a local church, which, though important at that time, may not be so for us today.

There was also the assumption that some local problem, the details of which we can not know today, caused Paul to advise as he did. Now some more details have been put to this thought. The key is the Greek word *authentein* in 1 Tim 2:12, which is usually translated "to have authority over". Does not even the English word show that the translation is correct? But, wait a moment. A German dictionary gives "to act independently" as the root meaning, rule over as the secondary meaning. The problem is that it occurs only once in the New Testament, and a solid exegetical rule states that one has to be careful in such cases.

A check of secular literature shows that *authentein* may mean: "To make sexual overtures". Then the text could read: "I do not want a woman to teach and to make sexual advances to men". Reading this interpretation for the first time, that looked quite crazy, why should Paul forbid what never would happen? But then there is the Book of Revelation, where Christ criticizes the church in Thyatira: "You tolerate that woman Jezebel, who calls herself a prophetess. By her teaching she misleads my servants into sexual immorality" (Rev 2:20). This means that the church of Thyatira would provide an example of a woman teacher who made advances to men and taught so. And she was probably not alone, since the Nikolaites seem to have held and practiced similar views (Rev 2:14-16).

Important for interpretation is that they all had a place within the churches, and that Christ does not criticize "Jezebel" for teaching as a woman but for combining that with explicit immorality.

It is difficult to prove that this understanding of Paul's injunction is the correct one, but the evidence seems to be strong that it is a possible interpretation. And therefore, if a text is open to such contradictory interpretations, today's church should not build a whole doctrine or practice on it.

Evangelical Missiology and Advances in Scholarship

It is important to note that the early evangelical missiologists did not build their case for women preachers on such interpretations favourable to their cause. Their decisions were much more fundamental: (1) take the historical evidence as a yardstick for today; (2) give priority to the Holy Spirit's activity of converting sinners; (3) leave seemingly contradicting practical apostolic advice aside. It may have either been a restricted advice for those times or further clarification may one day be found. (The last sections were such possible clarifications).

Possible Meaning for Africa

We are aware that a good part of this chapter was written from a Western European Evangelical perspective, but this is a contribution to the present efforts to redefine the possible limits of women's role in the churches in Africa. Many African Christians understand themselves as Evangelicals or share, without explicitly claiming the name, the same or similar views. For them these Evangelical assumptions can hopefully offer a way to increase participation of women in the life of the church without becoming unfaithful to Scripture and the Evangelical interpretation of it.

Chapter 5: Malawian Evangelical Feminist Hermeneutic

We have noted that African Feminist theology is very much variegated with patches of Evangelical theology as well as the more liberal theology that perceives human social relationships to be androcentric.[252] However, the Evangelical grassroots (from here on words, the name 'grassroots' will refer to Evangelical grassroots) women in Malawi mostly follow an Evangelical feminist interpretation that is mirrored by their culture. The grassroots interpretation shows that women have a tension between respecting their culture and at the same time respecting their evangelical tradition. This has meant that some interpretations show that grassroots women compromise their faith for the sake of respecting their culture. It is also true that these grassroots women's theologizing is changing, including more liberal aspects of African Feminist theologies.

In one way, these grassroots women seem to differ from more Liberal African Women Theologians in seeking transformation of their situations to live more fulfilled lives. These women show that they have little interest in dealing with issues of patriarchy in their daily Christian experience. On the other hand, these grassroots women are embracing glimpses of African Feminist Theologies in their life experiences. In this chapter we shed light on these mixed perceptions of grassroots liberation in Malawi with selected examples gleaned from experiences of grassroots women in the following aspects of life: through their marriage counselling sessions called *ulangizi*, bridal showers, *mwambo*, traditional initiation ceremonies, casual sexual relationships (grasshopper tradition), and ritual observances. We use story telling[253] and description of activities of women's experiences as approaches to unveiling liberation theologies of grassroots women in Malawi. Such an approach allows the grassroots Christian women to speak about their own theologies rather than the author speaking on their behalf. In these stories and descriptions of women's experiences, the women are carving out their own theologies that must be taken seriously.

---

[252] See Elisabeth Schüssler Fiorenza, *In Memory of Her. A Feminist Theological Reconstruction of Christian Origins*, New York: Crossroads, 1999 (1983).
[253] See Annalet van Schalkwyk, "Writing Southern African Women's Stories of Transformation – Some Methodological Aspects," *Journal of Constructive Theology* no. 6 (2), 2000, 21-37; Annalet van Schalkwyk, "Sister, we Bleed and we Sing: Women's Stories, Christian Mission and SHALOM in South Africa," PhD, UNISA, 1999.

A Malawian Evangelical Cultural Hermeneutics

African Feminist theologians argue that African culture is patriarchal and needs to be rid of elements that are oppressive to women. These patriarchal elements are present in matrilineal as well as patrilineal societies. In patrilineal societies, the husband and his brothers are in charge of a woman. This patriarchal reality is also called kyriarchy.[254] A kyriarchal arrangement is clear in that the father or the uncle is the ruler of the woman, her children (if any) and her property. Among Christian women in Southern Malawi, matrilineal communities are common. In both patrilineal and matrilineal communities a man is the leader in the home.[255] Liberation for these women is in most cases defined differently from how it is defined by the more liberal African Feminist thinking. For example, in most cases liberation for grassroots women is defined as economic and social security of family and marriage based on holding onto the male figure, be it husband, uncle or sexual partner. It is also defined in terms of how one has a sense of cultural identity with her family and kinship. This kind of liberation is shaped through the informal community and church based education programmes that are crucial in the formation of Christian women's well being. Such programmes usually sanction hegemonic social relationships where men are rulers and accord them a higher degree of dignity as opposed to women. This is in conflict with the majority voice of the African Women Theologians that subscribe to the idea of an egalitarian relationship between men and women. However, there are also small inroads of change into these perceptions among grassroots women in Malawi. These changes often tally with the desired goals of more liberal African Feminist thinking. On the other hand, there is no proof that these changes directly result from an interaction between African Feminist thinking and grassroots women's ideas. The changes that occur in these grassroots women's lives might have a broader origin that has not been dealt with in this book.

Preparing Girl and Boy Children for a Christian Marriage

Christian girls and boys in Malawi are groomed for Christian marriages through a variety of ceremonies. The first programme is called *ulangizi*. It is a programme aimed at preparing female and male children for marriage.

---

[254] "Kyriarchy" is a neologism coined by Elisabeth Schüssler Fiorenza.
[255] In patrilineal societies the father is dominant, in matrilineal societies the mother's brother is.

Among Christians in Southern Malawi there are two major programmes on how girls and boys[256] are prepared for marriage. The first one, which is usually done first, is through an initiation programme commonly referred to as *bwalo chinamwali* (if not organized by a church) or *ulangizi* (if organized by a church).[257] In this section, we tailor our discussions to girls' *bwalo* initiation programmes. The second is the one that takes place just before one gets a church wedding either at *chinkhoswe* ("engagement")[258] or a day before the wedding. Such *ulangizi* sessions are referred to as bridal showers and marriage send offs. At such occasions, usually women teach girls (the brides to be) and boys (the bridegrooms to be) regarding marriage. These sessions are available in all patrilineal and matrilineal societies of Malawi. There is another forum where marriage instruction takes place. This is called a marriage counselling session.[259] It is usually organized by churches and is open to all that are married either through a traditional marriage or a church wedding.[260] The Synod of Livingstonia for example has such marriage counselling programmes for men and women.[261] On the other hand,

---

[256] For initiation programmes for boys see: J.C. Chakanza, "The Unfinished Agenda: Puberty Rites and the Response of the Roman Catholic Church in Southern Malawi, 1901-1994" *Religion in Malawi* no. 5, 1995; Felix Chingota, "A Historical Account of the Attitude of Blantyre Synod of the Church of Central Africa Presbyterian towards Initiation Rites," *Religion in Malawi*, no. 5, 1995; Patrick Makondesa, "Christian Initiation Rites in Southern Malawi," MA module, Department of Theology and Religious Studies, University of Malawi, 1999.

[257] See Rachel NyaGondwe Fiedler, *Coming of Age: A Christianized Initiation among Women in Southern Malawi*, Kachere Series: Zomba, 2005, 91 pp.

[258] *Chinkhoswe* is sometimes indeed translated "engagement," and occasionally it means exactly that. But traditionally *chinkhoswe* was the wedding ceremony of the Chewa, and it is seen so even today by most who undergo it. For an argument to abolish church weddings in favour of a Christian *chinkhoswe* see: Klaus Fiedler, "For the Sake of Christian Marriage, Abolish Church Weddings," *Religion in Malawi*, no. 5, 1995, pp. 22-29.

[259] Towera Mwase, Marriage Instructions for Girls and Women in Mzuzu Churches, MA, Mzuzu University, 2012.

[260] For a discussion of traditional and church marriages, see Klaus Fiedler, "For the Sake of Christian Marriage Abolish Church Weddings," *Religion in Malawi*, no. 5 (1995), pp. 22-28, revised an reprinted in: Klaus Fiedler, *Conflicted Power in Malawian Christianity. Essays Missionary and Evangelical from Malawi*, Mzuzu: Mzuni Press, 2015, pp. 8-26.

[261] Mathews R. Gomezgani Phiri, A Study on the Pre-Marriage Counselling in the CCAP Synod of Livingstonia Ekwendeni Presbytery, BA, Mzuzu University, December 2009. Although the title suggests that the programme is for the unmarried, it is for married people. The preposition 'Pre' is used to mean that these married people have never undergone such a programme since they got married.

bwalo initiation programmes are common in all matrilineal societies and in the few patrilineal societies of Southern Malawi.

The body of knowledge provided to the girls and boys is largely androcentric. It is knowledge that is carefully selected by the instructors to serve the interests of men (a husband or a partner). This is against the Liberal voice in African Feminist theologies. In these programmes the messages are usually aimed at promoting male leadership in the home. The other knowledge regarding the welfare of the girl is largely omitted or cryptic. The goal of these sessions is to make them obedient to their husbands.

Initiation Ceremonies

The first organized contact to teachings that promote patriarchal relationships is through the (*bwalo*) traditional initiation ceremonies. The majority of Christians still sends their children to these ceremonies although churches discourage them to do so.[262] To avoid punishments from their churches, parents secretly send their children to the initiation programmes. Some do this by sending their children to have the initiation ceremonies away from where their churches are located. Initiation programmes for girls are patriarchal because the teachings and activities done at these programmes are androcentric. Girl children are subjected to patriarchal cultural practices and teachings that are oppressive to their well being as shown in the paragraphs below.

One of the oppressive practices is deploying a 'hyena' at the end of the girls' initiation to come to test whether the girls can dance well in bed.[263] Unfortunately, such a practice is often sanctioned by the parents of the girl. The hyena also known as the *fisi* (a man) is usually hired by the girl's mother's side, and he must come only once at night and must remain unknown. This practice is fading away not because women take such practices as unholy, but because of the threat this practice has through HIV/AIDS. As mothers are becoming increasingly aware of the health problem in the HIV era, the

---

[262] The Catholic Church disciplines those that attend such ceremonies. See J.C. Chakanza, "The Unfinished Agenda," *Religion in Malawi*, no. 5, 1995. Other churches also punish their members in one way or the other.

[263] See J.W.M. van Breugel, *Chewa Traditional Religion*, Blantyre: CLAIM-Kachere, 2001, pp. 197-195.

solution is found in substituting the *khundabwi*[264] medicine for the *fisi*.[265] There is evidence that there are now many girls' initiations without a *fisi*.

The other oppressive practice is that women must never ask the husband for sex and must accept a husband's immoral ways. These two practices are promoted through the following initiation songs: The first song promotes the idea of women accepting an immoral husband.

Tsegulire, tsegulire!	Open for me, open for me!
Ndakana, ndakana.	I have refused, I have refused.
Apanja, apanja	Those outside, those outside
Mulibe mwambo.	Have no behaviour.
Anyumba, anyumba	Those in the house, those in the house,
Mulibe mwambo.	You do not have behaviour.[266]

The interpretation of this song is that if a man sleeps outside, and comes very late, the wife should not refuse him entry into the house; she should not leave him outside because "an animal can kill and eat him." If this happens the woman would regret her action. The wife is further instructed not to be jealous of her husband's extramarital affairs. The second song dissuades a wife from asking her husband for sex.

Mwana mnyamata usagone 2x	Young man, do not sleep 2x
Utogona?	Are you sleeping?
Ona dina.	See my vagina.
Tandileke. 2x	Leave me alone.
Ndamwa mowa.	I drank beer.[267]

"The teaching is that even though a woman sometimes desires her husband, she should not request sex from him. She should wait till her husband desires her."[268]

---

[264] It is a herbal medicine usually provided by the chief which makes the girl child mature. See Molly Longwe, *Growing Up. A Chewa Girls Initiation,* Zomba: Kachere, 2006, p. 42.

[265] This has become a widespread practice now in the Chewa area around Lilongwe. The idea, advocated in the teaching of various churches, that neither the *fisi* nor the medicine are needed, has found less support. Ibid.

[266] Rachel NyaGondwe Fiedler, *Coming of Age. A Christianized Initiation among Women in Southern Malawi.* Zomba: Kachere, 2005, p. 82.

[267] Ibid., p. 74.

[268] The song itself is ambiguous, but the standard prose explanation leaves no ambiguity: "He should not sleep but see his wife's vagina and sleep with her. It teaches that sometimes it is a woman who desires the man, but sometimes the man is not interested. It teaches that

Redefining the majority of teachings and practices promoted by traditional initiation ceremonies has remained a problem to Christian Malawian women. This is because to go against such practices has negative social-economic consequences to the women as will be shown below. The only clear redefinition is as regards the hyena tradition. This is because there is a clearly defined remedy - *khundabwi*.[269] Further, the hyena has no financial gains for the women. It is therefore true that the hyena tradition seems to have been greatly reduced not only because of the threat it has to the spread of HIV/AIDS. If such was the case, then immoral practices that seem to be sanctioned by traditional initiation would have also disappeared. This dilemma points to the need of assessing approaches women use in re-imagining their traditional culture to achieve women's liberation. There are three approaches to this: The laissez faire approach, the rejectionist approach and the selective approach.

The Accommodation Approach

In the 21st century Malawi Christian world view, this approach seems to be frequently applied to teachings and practices relating to the moral life of grassroots Christian women and men in church and society. Regardless of counter teachings against immoral teachings and practices, there is little tangible morality change among the grassroots Christian women and men. Again, the social economic realities in which women and men are trapped seem to provide a major resistance to behaviour change. Thus, the more popular approach Christian women and men employ as regards immorality is an accommodation one. Unlike Christian women who are often caught up in immoral practices for economic gains, Christian men are caught in the same to satisfy their egoistic tendencies.[270] It is a means to portray their masculinity over women. The men also have the means to achieve their egoistic tendencies because they are economically empowered.[271] They also

---

a woman should not request a man for sex; the man should desire sex by himself (Rachel NyaGondwe Fiedler, *Coming of Age. A Christianized Initiation among Women in Southern Malawi*, Zomba: Kachere, 2005, p. 74).

[269] See Molly Longwe, *Growing Up. A Chewa Girls' Initiation*, Zomba: Kachere, 2006, p. 42.

[270] Proverbs such as "Mwamuna ndi tonde azinunkha" (The man is a billy goat. He must stink [behave like one]) promote this behaviour. This proverb is well known, but it is not contained in the large collection of Chewa proverbs: J.C. Chakanza, *Wisdom of the People. 2000 Chinyanja Proverbs*, Blantyre: CLAIM-Kachere, 2000.

[271] For an inquiry into Malawian concepts of masculinity see: Norwegian Church Aid, *Masculinity, Alcoholism and HIV/AIDS in Malawi*, Mzuzu: Luviri Press, 2016.

have the environment in which to harness their immoral behaviours. It is interesting to note that African Feminist theologians rarely address this male cultural orientation.

The Rejectionist Approach

This approach to culture was promoted by some missionaries that brought the church to Africa.[272] This was the same in Malawi. Missionaries who employed such an approach were the Southern Baptist missionaries that brought Baptist Convention churches to Malawi in the 1960s. In the beginning, grassroots Baptist Convention women were expected to choose between following their traditional culture or the Baptist church. This was visible when Mrs Blanche Wester began the first congregation in the Jali area of Zomba.[273] One of the conditions for membership was to stop getting involved in traditional dances. However, even though they managed to temporarily discourage women from participating in initiation programmes, that often demeaned women's dignity, they robbed women of cultural elements that were useful to their dignity. Cultural teachings about respecting elders were compromised.[274] The other church that deployed a similar approach is the Dutch Reformed Church Mission (DRCM). Isabel Apawo Phiri quotes Mrs Stegman's paper presented at a conference of missionary women to reflect on the reasons for opposing initiation programmes in this way:

> There are many things in the ceremonies which were in conflict with demands of Christianity. Emphasis was that a 'pagan girl' was accom-

---

[272] Very often, though not always, initiation ceremonies were rejected. In other cases they were ignored, and sometimes they were actively Christianized. In the Leipzig Lutheran Mission on the slopes of Kilimanjaro, Bruno Gutmann, the veteran missionary there, strongly supported the right to circumcision (including for girls), while opposition to (male and equally female) circumcision came from a group of educated Christians, mostly teachers (Klaus Fiedler, *The Gospel Takes Root on Kilimanjaro. A History of the Evangelical Lutheran Church of Old Moshi-Mbokomu 1885-1940*, Zomba: Kachere, 2006, pp. 16-17, 43-46.) For an extended discussion of various attitudes to circumcision in East Africa see: Klaus Fiedler, "Bishop Lucas' Christianization of Traditional Rites, the Kikuyu Female Circumcision Controversy and the 'Cultural Approach' of Conservative German Missionaries in Tanzania" in Noel Q. King and Klaus Fiedler (eds), *Robin Lamburn – From a Missionary's Notebook: The Yao of Tunduru and other Essays*, Saarbrücken, 1991, pp. 207-217.

[273] Rachel NyaGondwe Banda [Fiedler], Women *of Bible and Culture. Baptist Convention Women in Southern Malawi*, pp. 31, 42, 49.

[274] Missionaries coined their own teachings by introducing the Ulangizi Booklet (*Buku la Alangizi*, Lilongwe: Baptist Publications, nd).

panied by much cruelty and degradation. Therefore in order to rescue Christian girls, the church thought of banning *chinamwali*.[275]

Although the pioneers of this rejection approach were some of the early missionaries, it is also common among Evangelical movements of the 21st century. Just as missionaries failed to provide an adequate alternative solution to the 'evils' of traditional culture, Evangelical churches have also failed to provide such solutions through spiritual warfare.[276] There is little evidence that Evangelical solutions have reduced the immoral behaviours that traditional culture is promoting. Thus, the problems of immorality are for Christian women and men of all Christian movements. It seems that behaviour change as regards immorality is not an issue that can be dealt with by spiritual weapons alone but material ones also. Economic and social empowerment of women must accompany spiritual reform programmes to provide a comprehensive answer to this problem. However, there is also no evidence that economic empowerment reduces immorality among women although there are many HIV and Aids projects that use this approach to reduce the prevalence of infection among women.[277]

The Selective Approach

In this approach, grassroots women disagree with the view that all culture is evil. They uphold the fact that certain elements of culture must be kept and others discouraged. However, what guides their choice of what must be kept and what must be removed seems to be based on what is useful for their daily survival. Thus although immorality is dangerous in the era of HIV and AIDS, women continue to be involved in immorality for their socio-economic survival.[278] Underlining the above approaches is the desire to

---

[275] See Isabel Apawo Phiri, *Women, Presbyterianism and Patriarchy. Religious Experiences of Chewa Women in Central Malawi*, p. 62.

[276] Spiritual warfare seems to be effective only to areas such as witchcraft and not in solving problems of immorality. Rhodian Munyenyembe's work shows how Charismatic movements have excelled in dealing with witchcraft. See Rhodian Munyenyembe, "Christianity and Socio-Cultural Issues. An Evaluation of the Charismatic Movement's Contribution towards the Contextualization of the Gospel in Malawi," MA, University of Malawi, 2006, p. 90.

[277] Chimwemwe Kalalo found out in her research that not all women opt for extramarital affairs for economic gain. See Chimwemwe Kalalo, *Women's Sexual and Reproductive Health, HIV and AIDS and the Anglican Church in Southern Malawi*, Mzuzu: Mzuni Press, 2016.

[278] The Circle puts issues of economic empowerment at the centre of their theologies. For example see: Sophia Chirongoma, "Women, Poverty, and HIV in Zimbabwe. An Exploration

inculturate traditional initiation programmes into those that are acceptable to the theologies of particular churches. Below is an example of such attempts of inculturation.

Inculturation of the Traditional Initiation

Churches in Malawi have a long history of inculturating traditional initiation programmes into forms that are palatable to their faithful.[279] In the experience of Baptist women in Malawi the women resisted earlier attempts by missionaries to Christianize initiation. They only sanctioned Christianized programmes when the locals became satisfied that such modifications would not jeopardize their children's ethnic identities. When the missionaries devised a way of instructing children by using a booklet, hence booklet *chinamwali*, the local women did not patronize it for a long time. They felt that the essence of what makes them women in this matrilineal society was sacrificed in the name of Christianizing the rite.[280] Unlike the *bwalo chinamwali*, it excluded drama, singing, dancing, and clapping of hands among other things. The initiates on the other hand were given a challenge to become Christians. For the local Baptist women this was a shock. It was not only that they were forbidden to participate in traditional initiation but that the alternative was not local. The booklet rendered the initiation ceremony dry and dull (and very short).[281] It also created a feeling that they would miss out on certain central teachings that identified them as women in this matrilineal society.

It is interesting that the Baptist women whom the missionary women consulted in the formulation of the booklet *chinamwali* were all not from the Zomba region. Mary Galatiya, the first Baptist Convention pastor's wife in

---

of Inequalities in Health Care," in Isabel Apawo Phiri, Sarojini Nadar (eds), *African Women, Religion, and Health. Essays in Honour of Mercy Amba Oduyoye*, Pietermaritzburg: Cluster, 2006, pp 173-186. Latin America Feminism also puts this element at the core of their theologizing. See Mary Judith Press, "Feminist Christians in Latin America," in *Voices from the Third World Women*, vol. viii, no. 3, p. 56.

[279] Many churches have inculturated traditional initiation rites; Isabel Phiri describes these for the Chewa of Nkhoma Synod (Isabel Apawo Phiri, *Women, Presbyterianism and Patriarchy. Religious Experiences of Chewa Women in Central Malawi*, Blantyre: CLAIM-Kachere, ²2000, pp. 62-68; Molly Longwe for the Baptist Convention congregations in the same area (Molly Longwe, *Growing Up. A Chewa Girls Initiation*, Zomba: Kachere, 2006, pp. 71-81).

[280] See *Buku la Alangizi*, Lilongwe: Baptist Publications, nd.

[281] Molly Longwe, *Growing Up. A Chewa Girls Initiation*, Zomba: Kachere, 2006, p. 97f.

Malawi was part of this group. She is a South African and had lived many years in South Africa. Agnes Njolomole Phiri came from the central region, was probably more aligned to the effectiveness of the *chilangizo* in Nkhoma Synod, which had its own *ulangizi* booklet.[282] The fact that the booklet was constructed without any relationship to the *bwalo chinamwali* reduced its credibility. This is probably why there are only two churches we know in the Zomba area that have ever held the booklet initiation.[283] The fact that the authors did not explain to instructors the dangers of going to *bwalo* initiation, assumed that African children were a tabula rasa as regards initiation ceremonies.

It is clear that Baptist women in this culture found the booklet *chinamwali* inadequate. Their rejection of the booklet was not in relation to whether it was patriarchal or not. What strengthened their identity was liberating. This is shown in that women in this region did not use it even though the church did have women holding the position of an instructor (*mlangizi*). Most of those that held such posts were pastors' wives.[284] This meant that during this time when there was only this booklet initiation, local women in this church mainly participated in *bwalo chinamwali* that reinforced their cultural identity.

In recent years, the booklet *chinamwali* has died a natural death in Southern Malawi. Instead the local women have developed their own initiation ceremony called *chinamwali cha pa tchalitchi* (church initiation). This *chinamwali* is very popular among Baptist Convention women in the South East Region because of its closeness to *bwalo chinamwali*. Chinamwali is well documented.[285] Since then there have been changes and adaptations to different shapes without losing the flavour of the traditional initiation ceremony. Just as the *bwalo chinamwali*, this church *chinamwali* still deploys dance, drama, songs, hand clapping, and sometimes traditional medicines and rituals as an approach of instruction for the women. This is what

---

[282] For many details of *chilangizo* in Nkhoma Synod, see Isabel Apawo Phiri, *Women, Presbyterianism and Patriarchy. Religious Experience of Chewa Women in Nkhoma Synod*, Blantyre: CLAIM-Kachere, ²2000, pp. 62-68).

[283] There are well over a hundred Baptist congregations in the wider Zomba area.

[284] See Rachel Banda, "Liberation through Baptist Polity and Doctrine. A Reflection on the Lives of Women in the History of Women in the Baptist Convention of Malawi," MA, University of Malawi, 2001.

[285] See Rachel Banda, "Liberation through Baptist Polity and Doctrine," pp. 234-273, later published as: Rachel NyaGondwe Fiedler, *Coming of Age: A Christianized Initiation among Women in Southern Malawi*, Zomba: Kachere, 2005, ²2007.

is more accepted by Christian women in this region than the initiation programme organized by missionaries.

One of the reasons why this church initiation is well accepted by the women is that although it is different from the traditional one, it has important components that reinforce these women's cultural identity. The instructor in this church initiation takes time to tell the girls some of the passwords to tell others who might want to know whether they were properly initiated. From the reactions of the group, those that took their children to church initiation were really contented. There was no *chitekwe*[286] and she did not encourage much dancing for the initiation ceremony of the girls, but the girls knew all they needed to know that constituted their cultural identity.

The women use a selective approach in analyzing culture; however, it is not the questions raised by the wider Feminist Theological movement that inform their choices. It is not clear whether they see patriarchy, androcentrism and patriarchal hegemonic relationships between men and women as guiding their quest for liberation. It is clear that economic and social security, marriage security and cultural identity inform their selection.

Evangelical Feminist Hermeneutics of Agony: Torn between Purity and Impurity

Even though Evangelical theology is often linked to pure theology because of its reliance on the Bible, it is clear that Evangelical theology is sometimes prone to compromising its gospel. This is exemplified in the *Kachiwala* Tradition. In this type of marriage relationship a woman stays married only occasionally, usually at night, to a man without the knowledge of either the society or the wife to this man. Such a marriage exists especially among single women (mostly divorced or widowed).[287] A critical analysis of this tradition shows that this form of immoral behaviour does not directly originate from the traditional initiation teachings. At initiation programmes, men are encouraged to be immoral while women are discouraged from being immoral. Girls are clearly dissuaded from engaging in immoral behaviour through the following song.

Mtsikana woyendayenda, ee!	The movious girl, eeh!
Mwana wafera panjira.	The child has died on the way.
Anafera panjira.	She died on the way.

---

[286] *Chitekwe* is an ad hoc and informal dance performed before the real rite begins.
[287] See Rachel NyaGondwe Fiedler, "Kachiwala Tradition," unpublished.

Mwana wachigololo	The fornicious child
Anafera panjira.	Died on the road.[288]

Through this song, women are traditionally taught that immorality is deadly. This song accompanies a drama where a little girl is faked to have died because she was immoral and was never afraid of sleeping with the older men.[289] The song and drama further teaches girls to abstain from sex outside marriage. The only place for extra marital sex for women in traditional teaching is related to the hyena tradition, to widowhood cleansing and avoidance of *tsempho*.[290] The *kachiwala* immorality seems to be a new phenomenon to these women and men. It also has a new approach. Rather than promoting men's immorality alone, it also promotes women's immorality. This new face to immorality seems to address a particular societal problem that revolved after the genesis of traditional initiations. They are a new phenomenon of an emerging new culture.[291] An example of emerging teachings in the context of the new culture is expressed in this song.

Usandiyang'ane	Do not look at me
Mwamuna wako	Your husband
Samagona ndi ine	Does not sleep with me
Mwamuna wako	Your husband
Anali kwathu	Was at my place
Andigulira Gesha ndi mafuta,	He bought me Geisha [bathing soap] and [cooking] oil
Atakaneneyo ndi wabodza	The one who will report this is a liar

In both songs, grassroots Christian women do not condemn women's immorality because sex is a means for women's economic liberation. It does

---

[288] Rachel NyaGondwe Fiedler, *Coming of Age*, p. 73.

[289] The *alangizi* interprets the drama in this way: "The girl that you see lying dead on the road has died because of promiscuity. She had sex with a man and because she was young, she died and was dumped on the road" (Rachel NyaGondwe Fiedler, *Coming of Age*, p. 73).

[290] For a thorough discussion of all the taboos and customs related to *tsempho* and the *mdulo* complex see chapter 6 of J.W.M. van Breugel, *Chewa Traditional Religion,* Blantyre: CLAIM-Kachere, 2001.

[291] For comprehensive orientation on cultural change read Rhodian Munyenyembe, "Christianity and Socio-Cultural Issues. An Evaluation of the Charismatic Movement's Contribution towards the Contextualization of the Gospel in Malawi," MA, University of Malawi, 2006; published as: Rhodian Munyenyembe, *Christianity and Socio-cultural Issues. The Charismatic Movement and Contextualization of the Gospel in Malawi*, Zomba: Kachere; Mzuzu: Mzuni Press, 2011.

not matter whether it is a sexual relationship that is outside marriage. Both songs talk about a woman having extramarital relations with someone's husband. Promiscuity that earns them material security is one of such ways of survival. The *kachiwala* practice is also supported by the belief that single women occasionally need sex for them to have "Vitamin K" to keep their health.[292] Such promiscuity is organized to the greater extent by women but supported by patriarchal structures that omit women in programmes of financial security. In both cases women conscientize each other not to question the woman the husband has an affair with. The women should, if anything, deal with their unfaithful husbands and not the woman in question. The wife does not confront the husband or if she does, chooses not to divorce him because she does not have material security to survive on her own. Patriarchy therefore promotes this behaviour.

In the second song, women sensitize each other against revealing each others' extramarital affairs even if one may know the man involved. Because the women are impoverished, they feel entitled to earn their economic gains through such a relationship. This again explains why women do not tell their women friends about the extramarital relations that their husbands might be having. It explains the fact that immorality is a well protected phenomenon in our culture because of poverty promoted by patriarchal decisions at grassroots level and beyond. This means that the spread of HIV/AIDS in Africa is also a poverty issue and not only a moral one.[293]

The view that promotes immorality of women to achieve economic success is alien to traditional teaching. In traditional initiation sex is viewed as a tool for economic prosperity only in the context of marriage. This is shown in this song below. It teaches women to treat their bodies carefully when married because their vagina is capital for material gain.

Namu idyani,	In here, eat,
Namu idyani,	In here, eat,
Muli malata [zigayo, nyumba etc][294]	There are iron sheets [grinding mills, houses etc]

---

[292] See Rachel NyaGondwe Banda [Fiedler], *Women of Bible and Culture*, p. 185. Some people ascribed Liddah Kalako's death to the lack of Vitamin K.

[293] Sophia Chirongoma shows this in her research. See Sophia Chirongoma, "Women, Poverty, and HIV in Zimbabwe. An Exploration of Inequalities in Health Care," in Isabel Apawo Phiri and Sarojini Nadar (eds), *African Women, Religion, and Health. Essays in Honour of Mercy Amba Ewudziwa Oduyoye*, pp. 173-186.

[294] These words are substituted with various material goods in various stanzas.

A rich married woman might have attained her riches through her vagina. It is not a song that teaches women to use their bodies for economic gain outside marriage. The disadvantage of this teaching, however, is that such teachings socialize men into an attitude of treating their wives as sex objects. Further, women that are not in a monandrous relationship might seek other sexual partners for material gain.

The Pulling Factors of Kachiwala Practices

The first reason why this tradition thrives among Christians is that it provides economic advantages. The main reason why women's economic empowerment could be an answer to dealing with immorality among Christian women and men is that money determines the demand and supply of sexual promiscuity among Christian women and men. There is a high demand from grassroots women for extra marital relations from men because women lack economic empowerment. This economic empowerment can easily be supplied by men who usually have the lead in economic empowerment. Although the same experiences might be present among women of other religions, these discussions are based on experiences of Christian women in Malawi.

The second reason is that the Christian message of abstinence and being faithful in marriage promoted by the churches is overcome by the traditional mindset of the believers. Christians in this portray that they are not completely distanced from their other anti Christian cultural teachings. Christians may also be crying for a theology of the church that deals with both the soul and the body. In this case, the church should help in some way in empowering her members economically as well as spiritually.

The third reason is failure to condemn Christian men that are perpetrators of this behaviour. Christian women fail to condemn their immoral husbands for fear of being censored by their churches and loosing material benefits. Since the Bible condemns extramarital relations, a Christian woman who reveals to the church that her husband is promiscuous faces rejection within her church community. If the husband is a pastor, he might loose his position. For the sake of maintaining her husband's monogamous marriage, a woman allows him to maintain an outside relationship with a woman she knows. Socially, since the marriage will remain monogamous in the sight of the society, the woman is well accepted in her church.

The fourth reason is that Christian men are still being controlled by wrong notions of masculinity that promote immorality and control of women. The men are also controlled by wrong concepts about women. These also may have their origins in the traditional culture. One of such wrong perceptions about women is that women are sex objects.

An Example of a Kachiwala Marriage

A mother of one child from a rural village in Zomba lives with a man for material security. She lost her parents to HIV/AIDS in 2003. Being the first-born she was left with four siblings to care for. Since she never went to school and could not find regular employment, she decided to accept this occasional marriage to a man who at that time had two wives. The man is able to buy maize for her and even buys school related items for her siblings. She goes to a Baptist church and has only one child from this marriage. This is the first marriage she has ever had.[295]

It is interesting that women sometimes encourage each other to have such a marriage. In a Baptist association meeting that took place in Southern Malawi, we had a group discussion with widows alone. When we inquired about how frequently such marriages occur, the women agreed that it is the only way they can provide for the needs of their children.[296] In fact, the women did not see the *kachiwala* tradition as evil; it was just a means of coping with the loss of a husband.[297] As if this was not enough, It was alarming to see that one of the widows had the strength to even tell the group as to how she attracts grasshoppers to herself.[298]

Hazards of the Kachiwala Tradition

It is obvious that *kachiwala* "marriages" are potential carriers of HIV/AIDS; however, group interviews with women generally show that this threat is

---

[295] I learnt of her story when I was counselling her in her spiritual life, 2005.
[296] Widows group, Domasi Baptist Association, August 2004.
[297] See Chimwemwe Kalalo, "Women's Sexual and Reproductive Health in the Context of HIV/AIDS," p. 64.
[298] The woman said "There is a day when this man met me on the road and requested me that he come home at night. Since I was not well supplied with household items I decided to take him in. I went home and cleared my house. I made tea ready and put it in the bedroom and put on my nice clothes I usually have."

not taken seriously.[299] Some of the responses of one group of twelve illustrate this. Two women explained that HIV/AIDS should not be feared. The basis of this understanding rested on their literalistic interpretation of the Bible, arguing that HIV/AIDS was already prophesied in the Bible, that it would come in the end times. One of the two women passionately encouraged her fellow women not to be afraid because either her or them one day will catch the disease, as it is prophesied in the Bible. To this, a third woman explained that it is only through prayer that, if she gets the virus, she would not get sick quickly. A fourth lady echoed this and said, "This is why some women stay on for years with the disease while the others die quickly, because of prayers."[300]

A fifth woman explained that HIV/AIDS should not be feared because it came for human beings, not for dogs or rocks. She continued to say that, for this reason, everyone should be prepared to get infected because it is a disease that has come for them as people.[301] From this it is clear that grassroots women take a victim's approach to liberation. This is different from African Feminist thinking which advocates that women should change their status for the better.

Cultural Practices and Immorality

Among Christian women and men of Malawi, observance of cultural practices still persists. Most of such cultural practices have been ably dealt with by many scholars.[302] In this section, we point out only three practices that specifically influence Christian women in Southern Malawi.

Widowhood Cleansing and Immorality

For a long time in Africa, singlehood has been a condition that is frowned upon. Every woman is expected to get a husband and keep him as much as she can. When a woman is single after marriage through divorce or death of her spouse, the society makes sure that she gets the message that she is incomplete without a male partner. This androcentric perception is a basis

---

[299] Chimwemwe Kalalo made very similar observations in her research: "Women's Sexual and Reproductive Health in the Context of HIV/AIDS," p. 78.

[300] Group interview through participatory investigation, 12 Baptist Convention women in Jali, Zomba June 2005.

[301] Ibid. It is interesting that there was no woman who argued against these views in the group. This is a fatalistic viewpoint.

[302] See J.W.M. van Breugel, *Chewa Traditional Religion,* Blantyre: CLAIM-Kachere, 2001.

of the so many attempts women use to keep a husband in the relationship. Some of these attempts have been described in the earlier paragraphs. In this section, we highlight one way women are asked to use to keep a new husband after the death of a husband. This practice is patriarchal because it serves men.[303]

On the 16th of June 2001, a certain widow went into the rural areas of Zomba to do research and when she told a Baptist pastor's wife in that area about her pending re-marriage, she responded by this statement.

> If you want him not to die as your first husband did, you must sleep with another man before marrying him so that this other man must cleanse you of the impurities of your late husband. If you have ever slept with a man after the death of your husband, then you are already safe and your new husband will be safe.[304]

This was echoed by two other women, also from the Baptist Church. One of them hailed from Jali area while the other came from the periphery of Zomba municipality. They both worship in one of the urban churches. These said "the tradition of sleeping with another man before remarriage is *kuchotsa fumbi*." It is clear that this tradition is sustained by patriarchy. It serves the many men that would be involved in cleansing widows including those that are infected.

The man who does it is called a "*fisi*." He is a "*fisi*" because he comes at night just like hyenas do. The woman is not supposed to recognize him. A relative of the woman such as a grandmother usually arranges for this "*fisi*." Sometimes, the widow is told the same night the "*fisi*" comes, without prior agreement with the widow. In certain cases, the widow agrees with the "*fisi*" and just informs the relatives about his coming.

One of the two respondents also explained that the "*fisi*" is also needed when a couple has lost a child or when the husband was having extramarital affairs before he can resume sexual relations with his wife who traditionally refrains from marital relations with her husband as a mourning ritual.

---

[303] For a literary reaction to the problem see: Steve Chimombo, *The Hyena Wears Darkness*, Zomba: WASI Publications, 2006.

[304] Name of pastor's wife withheld. - Chimwemwe Kalalo records her very similar experience (Chimwemwe Kalalo, *Women's Sexual and Reproductive Health, HIV and AIDS and the Anglican Church in Southern Malawi*, Mzuzu: Mzuni Press, 2017).

In this case, where the husband has been unfaithful, he is considered to be "hot" while the wife is considered to be "cold", and "hot" and "cold" cannot mix. It is then the duty of the husband to look for a *fisi*, usually his friend, to sleep with his wife so that she is rendered safe for him to have sex with. This request goes with a confession to the *fisi*: "Sindinachite bwino kunyumba kwanga" (I have not done well at my home.) He then begs the friend to "put things right" in his home by sleeping with his wife.[305]

Abstinence after Delivery

Another cultural practice that promotes immorality among men and women in Southern Malawi is "abstinence after delivery" (*kudika*). The practice promotes immorality in that during this avoidance period a man may enjoy sexual relationships outside marriage and still keep the wife. The woman on the other hand is not allowed to have sexual partners outside marriage. The initiation into *kudika* takes place after the child is born, preferably during the time the woman completes her period of seclusion (*chikuta*), which usually lasts as long as the child's umbilical cord takes to fall off, around seven days on average.

At one mock initiation, all the 42 women that participated agreed that they taught or have seen their friends teaching about 6 months abstinence from sex after delivery. One woman also told ways of how she could help her husband deal with his emotions during this time of sexual avoidance. She encouraged her friends to assist the husband to have non-penetrative sex by folding one of her legs so that he can discharge through the fold. There is no teaching on how the woman should relieve her own sexual emotions. The other teaching given is that the woman should always have a cloth tied around her waist covering her vagina for the 6 months period. This is to help her to prevent the husband from having sex with her. The other reason is to prevent the child from having a "split head" (*liwombo*).[306] This teaching is harmful because it encourages a husband to be involved in extramarital affairs, since to some masturbation is not an option. This practice in turn breeds HIV/AIDS, as a husband may seek sex with other women during that period.

---

[305] These rules are part of the *mdulo* complex. For details see: Joseph DeGabriele, "When Pills don't Work - African Illnesses, Misfortune and Mdulo, *Religion in Malawi*, no. 9, 1999, pp. 9-23.

[306] Open fontanelles.

Six Months Abstinence

Only a small percentage of women at the mock initiation were reluctant to ignore the avoidance tradition (*kudika*). These strongly believed that the woman would harm the man since she will not be pure before 6 months. They even lobbied for a 4 months avoidance period as the minimum period of abstinence. When this idea was conveyed to the group, one lady shared her experience of how she never followed this rule of abstinence except when she was menstruating. She argued that regardless of the fact that she did not follow the practice, her children are grown up and her husband is still alive.

Following this testimony was a discussion that women follow the tradition less because they receive a different message from the hospitals. After delivery, medical people tell women that after the 6 weeks post natal check up they are free to resume marital relations, if the doctor certifies their health.[307] Many women resume sex earlier than the traditionally prescribed period. The approach they use in redefining culture here is what is liberating to them or not. Since the medical position is liberating to the women and men, they choose to follow it.

Bridal Showers and Marriage Send Offs

The other occasions where such patriarchal hegemonic relationships are shaped is at the Bridal Shower and Marriage Send Off. A bridal shower is a pre-wedding session that takes place usually a week before the wedding. At this session only women are invited to attend. The session is largely for the bride; however, the bridegroom may also be invited at the time when "communication" and "budgeting" are being treated. These two topics require the bridegroom to be present because they involve both the bride and the bridegroom. At a "send off," both the bride and the bridegroom are asked to attend. Both men and women attend this session.[308] There is more sympathy for a send off than a bridal shower among those that would like to transform patriarchal relationships, however, observations of what happens at a "send off" show that presence and participation of men at this function cements oppression of women rather than their liberation. The

---

[307] Chimwemwe Kalalo, *Women's Sexual and Reproductive Health, HIV and AIDS and the Anglican Church in Southern Malawi,* Mzuzu: Mzuni Press, 2016.

[308] A send off is not much different from a bridal shower except that the audience is both men and women.

women are often controlled by the voices of the men calling the women to be submissive and subscribe to ideologies that support men rather than women.[309] The women that are often very vocal at promoting women's liberation at the 'bridal shower,' become apologetic and often succumb to patriarchal ideologies at a marriage send off. The main reason for such behaviour among women is that women do not want to risk their reputation as faithful Christian women among men some of whom are leaders of their particular churches. Thus both at bridal showers and marriage send offs, women face patriarchal oppression because the instructors are reluctant to go against the perceived official teachings of the church.[310] It is true that those invited and giving instructions at the bridal shower are not from one church, but the leader of these sessions is often the leader in the church of which the bride and bridegroom are members. As such, this leader feels obliged to make sure that the teachings at these sessions are somehow in line with what her church would sanction.+++

Mwambo[311] *Sessions*

The second occasion when women are drilled in support of patriarchal relationships is during *mwambo*. The women are not alone at this occasion. This is the time when the men *alangizi* participate. In some churches, they allow only couples that themselves had a church wedding to take part in instructing the newly wed couple. For the five couples that we referred to at the beginning of this section, indeed both men and women instructed the couple. With this membership that is gender balanced one would think that there would also be a balanced engendered teaching given to the couple. But to the contrary, women's oppression is promoted. This is clear from the analysis of wedding instructions presented in this section.

A group of instructors were selected by the church to carry out *ulangizi*. With all of them the church did not demand a church wedding or a

---

[309] This I personally observed at two send off sessions that took place in Zomba. At both sessions, the men preached and were much more prominent in giving advice than the women.

[310] At one bridal shower, a woman vehemently warned the leader of the bridal shower against reinterpreting the woman's role in the bedroom, because she argued that it would be against the Women's Guild values. The other woman retorted and argued for a reinterpretation of the practice and claimed that she was not afraid of being disciplined by her Women's Guild.

[311] *Mwambo* means custom, but here it refers to marriage instructions given just after the wedding.

"blessed" wedding[312] to participate in the instructions.[313] The central area of concern at this function is to prepare the couple to have a good relationship with each other, with in-laws and their own family. However, this "good relationship" seems to be based on the woman adhering to patriarchal teachings. The woman even at this function is reminded of her primary responsibility to serve her husband.

At marriage related ceremonies like bridal showers, marriage send offs, *mwambo*, the following are the key teachings given to women. The teachings clearly promote male dominance in marriage, although currently some changes are occurring.

Mwamuna ndi Pamimba

One common patriarchal instruction to the woman is transmitted in a proverbial saying, *mwamuna ndi pamimba* (a husband is his stomach).[314] The teaching is androcentric. This proverb appeals to the woman to look well after her husband. It shapes the women to occupy household roles of providing for her husband and children (if any). Such an instruction is often linked to the teaching that a woman should not complain if a husband is not much at home. Thus the woman resigns from seeking assertive roles and places much emphasis on cooking and caring for her family to keep her husband. With this patriarchal ideology, women groom their girl children to learn skills of raising their families such as cooking and looking after future husbands. Such a perception has also contributed to the lag in the numbers of girls accessing higher education. This has led to the fact that the man is advantaged over and above a woman in terms of economic progress. Access to education has opened opportunities for paid jobs to men and not to women who do not have the required education. When the uneducated girl marries such a privileged man, she often suffers from domestic violence,

---

[312] A blessed wedding (*ukwati wodalitsa*) is, of course, also a church wedding, but it is ranked lower than a "proper" church wedding (*ukwati woyera* - "holy wedding"), which must take place somewhat early in or even at the beginning of a marriage.

[313] In the Baptist Convention, church weddings are encouraged but are not a must for someone to serve in leadership positions. Some pastors in this church are not even married in church (Rachel NyaGondwe Banda [Fiedler], *Women of Bible and Culture*, pp. 172-176.)

[314] In the most comprehensive collection of Chewa proverbs (J.C. Chakanza, *Wisdom of the People. 2000 Chinyanja Proverbs*, Blantyre: CLAIM-Kachere, 2000), this proverb is no. 1052 "*Mwamuna mpamimba, nkhope siisintha.* – For the man it's the belly, the face does not change." The meaning attached to the proverb is: "A man works better on a full stomach. This is mainly expressed for ladies" (p. 225).

because the man knows that the girl's survival rests on his economic security. In this setting, often men use their economic empowerment to oppress women (wives) both physically and psychologically. The women become helpless to leave an abusive marriage for fear that they may not survive economically without their husbands. Women who have paid employment outside the home are detracted from being competent in their profession as they spend much time caring for home and husband. However, to these Christian grassroots women liberation is keeping the home and the man at home. That is more important than their own economic advancement.

Mwamuna ndi Wamkulu Mbanja

Another proverbial teaching at such functions that has shaped patriarchal imbalances of power between men and women in Malawi is "*Mwamuna ndi wamkulu mbanja*" (The husband is the boss in a marriage).[315] This is often used at such a function probably because it resonates well with literalistic interpretations of Ephesians 5:22-23 quoted below: "Wives, submit to your husbands as to the Lord. For the husband is the head of the wife as Christ is the head of the church, his body, of which he is the Saviour" (NIV). Such interpretations emphasize a woman's submission to her husband and forget the opening phrase in Ephesians 5:21, which demands submission of husband and wife to each other. The verse reads, "Submit to one another out of reverence for Christ" (NIV).[316]

The *alangizi* therefore feel obliged to highlight this proverbial teaching so that they please the men who represent the official statement of the church concerning a marriage. In this official teaching, the man is the head of any family.[317] *Mwamuna ndi wamkulu mbanja* is not only said in a proverb but it is often sung during the wedding and at this function. The song begins with a question: "*Wamkulu ndani mbanja?*" and this is quickly followed by an answer, "*Wamkulu ndi mwamuna.*" Such a perception renders women powerless. The women are often told not to follow those women that profess not to follow a husband's idea. They argue that those that ad-

---

[315] In one family, the husband has a girlfriend known to his wife. The husband has openly run this relationship and has even told the wife that he does not love her any more, but the wife has continued to stay in this relationship hoping that one day things will change.

[316] Translators and interpreters who want to get away form the implication for husbands make verse 22 to be the final statement of the section "Living as Children of Light," starting in 4:17 as in the NIV.

[317] Pastor's wife's talk, bridal shower, 1.10.2006.

vise women such practice in actual fact do not really do it to their husbands at home. Contrary to their teaching, they respect their husbands and that is the basis for a strong marriage. In African Feminist thinking, the concept of 'headship of man over woman' has often been critiqued. It is also a concept that is viewed to promote HIV and Aids infection of women by their husbands.[318] It is also true that this concept of headship of a man over a woman is also slowly being challenged by grassroots Christian women.

This teaching is being reread by the women at the bridal shower and even during the wedding. The song: *Wamkulu ndani mbanja? Wamkulu ndi mwamuna* expresses this. This teaching has at some occasion been changed to: *Wamkulu ndani mbanja? Wamkulu ndi Yesu* (The leader in marriage is Jesus). This new teaching calls for both the bride and the bridegroom to respect each other in marriage but even more to respect Jesus Christ. Again this redefinition tallies with African Feminist thinking on the position of women in marriage. However, it is an urban phenomenon that we have not come across among rural women in Southern Malawi. These hints at the possibilities of bridal showers and marriage send off ceremonies as channels through which feminism can be promoted to local women in Malawi. These urban women as they visit rural areas might become a useful channel in making ground work for feminism in the rural areas.

Banja Nkupirira

The lady is often encouraged to stay in the marriage even if she might face troubles there. The bride is told not to pack her possessions and go to her parents' home once there is trouble in her marriage. This teaching is hard to resist among Christian women because it is also sanctioned by the church, especially in the marriage vow "till death do us part."

An example here is a lady who is married to a Baptist leader in the Southern region. She has lived in an abusive marriage for several years but has refused to leave the husband because to her, marriage is to be endured. In another case, the woman boasts of the fact that she endured hardship in her marriage because she is now enjoying the riches of her children after the husband died. Unfortunately, she is infected because the husband died of HIV/AIDS. Such experience illustrates that the meaning of liberation for these grassroots women is constructed differently from women in the Wid-

---

[318] See Isabel Apawo Phiri, "A Theological Analysis of the Voices of Teenage Girls on Men's Role in the Fight against HIV/AIDS," *Journal of Theology for Southern Africa*, 2004, p. 20.

er Feminist Theological Movement. These women's liberation is based on how much they are able to endure suffering and gain future rewards. This eschatological liberation is also (wrongly) cemented from the book of James that promotes perseverance among Christians to refine their character and gain eternal glory (James 1:3-12). However, there are also glimpses of change among grassroots Christian women in this orientation of *'Banja nkupirira'*. Some women have chosen to leave an abusive husband.[319] However, in all the cases where women have divorced their husbands, the women had the means of economic survival.

Women are slowly rereading the teaching (*banja nkupirira*) by changing it to the new slogan *banja ndi kunjoya* (marriage is enjoyment). This reinterpretation tallies well with the African Feminists' advancement of women's dignity in marriage. However, this rereading seems common among urban Christian women who are exposed to winds of Feminism through media or interaction with other women that are attuned to such liberation movements. The women in the urban settings also have financial securities that rural women do not have and so they are more flexible to shake off patriarchal oppression. The teaching on *banja ndi kunjoya* implies that a woman should make choices to leave an abusive husband. However, it is rare for an instructor at either a bridal shower or marriage send off to explicitly advise the bride on divorcing her husband. Among rural women, it is rare to hear of a woman that has divorced her husband because of suffering abuse, especially in the case of a wealthy husband. The new reinterpretation of *banja ndi kunjoya* as opposed to *banja ndi kupirira* makes sense mostly among urban and economically empowered women.

Bedroom Instructions

The other venue where women and men receive marriage instructions is through bedroom instructions. This discussion of theologies at bedroom instruction is based on an empirical study of Christian women in Malawi. However, the hub of the information is based on the five weddings observed in Zomba District between 2002 and 2006. To counteract the limitation of one method, we also read books on marriage and conducted interviews. Among the five weddings observed only one of them had bedroom instructions at the end of a combined *chinkhoswe* and wedding. The couple

---

[319] In a Baptist Church in Lilongwe, a pastor's wife divorced a promiscuous husband. A Presbyterian woman with some leadership roles in her church also divorced her promiscuous husband.

chose to combine both wedding and *chinkhoswe* to reduce costs. Three couples underwent bedroom instructions a day before their wedding. These were getting married for the first time. One couple had bedroom instructions at the *chinkhoswe* as well as at the wedding. This happened because they had a "blessed wedding."[320] Before then only one of the four couples had received bedroom instructions at the *chinkhoswe*.

In a typical bedroom instruction ceremony, a selected group of women are usually left alone to give instructions to the girl in seclusion. The women are called *alangizi*. Their number ranges on average between two and five. These are women that are culturally qualified to do this work in this women's context. The instructions are carried out verbally accompanied by drama, singing and the introduction of equipment to use in the bedroom. The girl is taught to serve the husband. In liberal African Feminist understanding this is about women organizing their own oppression. However, for the majority of Christian women in Malawi, this is about how a woman can achieve a more fulfilled life in marriage. The woman being counselled is presented with a long piece of cloth, two pairs of safety pins, small pieces of cloth, a razor blade, a bottle of Vaseline, a pail, a basin, beads of assorted colours (red, black and white beads must always be among them because of specific meanings in them), a teapot or flask and two teacups. These are all presented one at a time with instructions attached to them. Patriarchal dominance is usually promoted in these women's transformation, the very problem, liberal African Feminist theology seeks to address. Here we just mention uses of a few items presented to the newly weds.

A Teapot or Flask and Two Teacups

For the Christian woman in Africa, the nutritional needs of a man are central to her everyday chores. The girl is advised to prepare tea for the husband before the night and keep it in her flask. If she does not have a flask, she must make tea for the husband in the night (this is where she needs a teapot). Many girls in the village can not afford a flask, so they cook at night. The girl is told to serve her husband this tea after they have made love to each other. The girl must do that because, apparently, the husband has used too much energy during lovemaking, and that must be replaced.

---

[320] See Klaus Fiedler, "For the Sake of Christian Marriage Abolish Church Weddings," *Religion in Malawi* no. 5, 1995, pp. 22-29; revised in Klaus Fiedler, *Conflicted Power in Malawian Christianity: Essays Missionary and Evangelical from Malawi*, Mzuzu: Mzuni Press, 2015, pp. 6-21.

There is no consideration that the woman has also lost energy, especially since she is taught to dance as much as she can during lovemaking.[321] She therefore must serve him tea after each occasion. The woman must also take tea at each occasion, hence the two teacups, but the focus is the man. There is no advice that the man should make tea for the woman in the bedroom.

Beads of Assorted Colours

The woman is portrayed as an object to entice a husband towards sex. The woman is taught to wear beads which her husband can play with during lovemaking. These beads together with all the equipment stated above are bought by an aunt or a grandmother or any elderly relative who is entrusted with this activity in her family and brought to where the bedroom instructions are taking place. This relative accompanies the *alangizi* during the bedroom instructions and provides the *alangizi* with the equipment. The beads have a special importance during lovemaking. The girl is told how to put them on around her waist. In most cases, the girl already knows, because all along she has been wearing beads for decorative purposes. At the bedroom instructions, the beads have a deeper meaning. The first meaning is that of regulating sexual activities between her and her husband. The *alangizi* firmly advise the girl how to tell the husband when it is safe to have sex with her or not, using red, black and white beads in this way: The girl is told to display red beads at a special place, usually on a wall in her bedroom, when she is menstruating. These red beads are a warning to the husband that she is menstruating and that it is not safe for him to have sexual relations with her. The girl is firmly told not to let the husband have sex with her during this time. She is warned that if they make love to each other during this time, the husband would suffer from *kanyela*, a deadly slimming disease.[322] When the girl's menstrual fluids turn blackish, she should remove the red beads from the wall and replace them with black beads. This, though, is not a safe period either for the husband to have marital relations with his wife. It is only a sign to the husband that he should get set for marital relations with his wife because soon it will be safe to resume sex. It is usually within 24 hours that the wife's black menstrual fluids stop.

---

[321] This is a major teaching in all girls' initiations.

[322] The song about this runs: "*Chinyela, chinyela chitha amuna. Akazi natsala.* – *Chinyela, chinyela* finishes (kills) the men. Women remaining" (Rachel NyaGondwe Fiedler, *Coming of Age. A Christianized Initiation among Women in Southern Malawi*, Zomba: Kachere, 2005, p. 86.] – *Chinyela* is the local version of the more widespread *kanyela/kanyera*.

This is the end of menstruation and the girl removes the black beads and replaces them with white beads. It is now safe for the husband to resume sex with his wife. According to Liberal Feminist interpretation this is probably one of the rare opportunities where a woman can use this teaching to liberate herself, at least temporarily, from an abusive sexual relationship.[323]

The second importance of beads is to provide pleasure during lovemaking. The girl is told that before going to bed, she must wear beads around her waist for the husband to play with before and during lovemaking. The girl is told that the beads give pleasure to her husband as well as to her. Her husband's playing with the beads also arouses sexual feelings in her to be ready for marital relations. Some women indeed put on beads all the time, day and night, but some put them on only during the night. Among those that put on beads at night, some do not put them on every night but just occasionally. The girl is often instructed to put on beads occasionally. Occasional usage provides extra pleasure to the husband since they are not always there. When he sees them occasionally, it is something special and she becomes more attractive to him.

Reinterpreting Bedroom Instructions

The above bedroom instructions originate from traditional culture. However, Christian women in Malawi have made little attempt to reinterpret the instructions. These women seem not to consider a patriarchal marriage arrangement as oppressive to women. Unlike liberal African Feminist women, these Christian women seem to enjoy this patriarchal hegemonic relationship enhanced by the teachings of their female elders (*alangizi*). Even in the case where the boy marrying the girl attends the instructions, the presence of the boy does not change the content of the instructions. The *alangizi* have continued to promote their traditional patriarchal education within their teaching on Christian marriage as described above. In the event that a prospective bridegroom attends the bedroom instructions, the *alangizi* inform the boy the reason why he is asked to be present at these instructions. The reason for his presence is firstly that he will not be surprised at the things that the wife will do in the bedroom. Secondly, that the girl is accountable to the man concerning the instructions that she has received. Although the boy is present at the bedroom instructions, there is no man

---

[323] Fulata Moyo, "Red Beads," Malaka-le Theologies: Women, Religion and Health, A Circle of Concerned African Women Theologians Pan-African Conference, Kempton Park, South Africa, July 10-15, 2005.

among the *alangizi*. The men are meant to instruct the boy without the presence of the girl and other women. This practice cements the idea that men ought not to be accountable to their spouses about sexual matters.

In addition to the instructions above, at each of the five bedroom instructions, the *alangizi* asked the girl to stand and dance the sexual dance in their presence in case she was not attuned to this dance. The boy is not asked to dance because it is assumed that he knows it all or that he does not need to dance since the woman will dance for him. This is not even seen as sexism against the girl in the eyes of grassroots women or the girl. Even if the girl did, she has no power to reject what has been asked of her. She dances so that she is not a black sheep in the community having dishonoured the elder women. At all the occasions, the girls made an impressive dance before the *alangizi* and the boy. This shows that girls are taught about this dance earlier than their wedding day. Some of them have learned the dance at the initiation camp, and those that do not attend initiation ceremonies, are taught by the elder women individually before the wedding day.[324] For a grassroots Christian woman, being able to dance for a man during lovemaking is liberation. She defines liberation as marriage security, which is presumably achieved by following these bedroom instructions well.[325] This is contrary to liberal African Feminist theologies that perceive such teachings as oppressive to women.

Reasons for Lack of Reinterpretation

The lack of reinterpretation of traditional teachings about marriage by Christian women in Malawi is firstly due to the fact that patriarchy in the African culture has a long history and is well internalized by women who teach marriage instructions. Secondly, Christian women value marriage and are willing to keep these teachings that are understood to contribute to solid Christian marriages. The *alangizi* are those that have learnt these teachings over a period of time. They feel they must be faithful to the teaching of their elders even though at times they may realize dangers embedded in them. Even though these *alangizi* may be exposed to the church teaching that orients them to equality between men and women, the fact that churches also promote the teaching of the man being head over the woman, may encourage these women to continue with their patriarchal teachings. This notion makes the church *alangizi* uneasy to reinterpret any

---

[324] See Rachel NyaGondwe Banda [Fiedler], *Women of Bible and Culture*, p. 183.
[325] Equally seen as a marriage security is the elongation of the labia minora.

of the instructions. Further, an attempt to reinterpret this tradition would be costly to the church in that the elders of the girl would not send their girl children to the bedroom instructions conducted by the church. This is because even parents support these patriarchal teachings and they believe that disregarding them would be a threat to their child's survival. The third reason is that the *alangizi* do not have the kind of theological training to reinterpret this tradition in the light of what is oppressive in it or not. Unlike women in the African Feminist Movement and those from the Wider Feminist Theological Movements, they are not aware of the fact that these teachings are oppressive to women. The women have less contact with women from other countries that may orient them to such kind of Feminist Theological approaches. They probably are not literate enough to read African Feminist books that would orient them to liberal African Feminist transformative resources. Much of what they teach is as learned from and passed on to them by the elders.

A dualist understanding among African women concerning the body and the soul also contributes to patriarchal understanding of marriage by Christian women in Malawi. The church has a dualistic understanding about marriage. Things related to the body are not for the church but those that belong to the spirit. In this case, the bedroom instructions are for the body and must be taken care of by those responsible for this area. In this case it is the elders (*alangizi*) who care for the body. The women therefore uncritically apply traditional teachings about marriage to Christian marriages. The church, because it is usually ruled by men, is also patriarchal and may also like this kind of patriarchal advocacy the elders are engaged in. The church has therefore left it to culture and medical experts to deal with this area of sexual relationships in marriage. The absence of men at bedroom instructions is connected to this. Since men are custodians of the spiritual side of marriage as leaders of churches, it is not proper for them to attend such functions of the body. Their presence at such functions would suggest that the church is also for the body. However, the introduction of 'marriage send offs'[326] by women is bringing change to this earlier concept. It can be argued therefore that women are redefining this dualistic approach to marriage practiced by the church and proposing a new church model that would view the body and the spiritual side of marriage as one. However, for these women, to ably fulfil this agenda, they require adequate theological

---

[326] At marriage send offs, both men and women are involved in teaching *mwambo* (marriage instructions) to the bride and bridegroom

orientation as well as the stamina to present theologies that address the role of the bride and bridegroom in carving out an egalitarian relationship in marriage. This would be the starting point of their liberation in the light of African Feminist theologies.

A Malawian Evangelical Feminist Biblical Hermeneutics

One avenue through which African Feminist theologians seek to achieve women's liberation in church and society is through Biblical reinterpretation. In this section, we seek to show how an Evangelical interpretation of scriptures by grassroots women enhances their liberation. Further, we seek to investigate a possible relationship to the African Feminist biblical reinterpretation. For the purposes of this section, we limit our discussion to a biblical reinterpretation that takes place among the grassroots Baptist Convention women of Southern Malawi. We have chosen two areas where Bible reinterpretation is taking place: Permanent marriage and forgiveness in marriage. We have chosen these two areas because of their bearing on HIV and AIDS. We have used story telling in analyzing models of biblical reinterpretation used by these women. Through their stories, these women show how they interpret the Bible. Further, we have also used Contextual Bible Studies for the same purposes.

Rereading "Until Death Do Us Part"

As regards the above sacramental vow, grassroots Baptist women articulate two kinds of interpretation: The first one is that marriage should be permanent even with an immoral partner. The other equally weighty view is that the woman should divorce the unfaithful partner. An explanation given for this choice was that bringing HIV/AIDS into the family is to bring death and so divorce in the event of unfaithfulness fulfils the sacramental exhortation "Until Death Do Us Part." The two views testify to the reality that even in a single denomination there can be multiple biblical interpretations.

Divorcing an Immoral Partner

An example of this Evangelical Biblical Hermeneutics is portrayed by this story: In an Umodzi meeting at Zomba Baptist Church a woman stood up explaining why she had left her first husband. Her husband was in the habit of drinking and coming home late. For a long time she did not suspect him to be unfaithful to her. However, one night he did not come the whole night and only in the early morning did he appear with not even underwear in his hands. He knocked at the door and the wife went to look and was astonished to see her husband at the door naked. Even though he pleaded for pardon from the wife, the wife refused to remain married to him, as she felt that this was too dangerous in the era of HIV/AIDS. In this experience, the woman defined her own liberation as having good health as opposed to having a permanent marriage.

Keeping an Immoral Partner

In a second story, the lady decided to keep her husband who was involved in adultery for three times. He got infected and became very sick but the wife did not disown him. This shows that there is a possibility of keeping an unfaithful partner in marriage. Further, the story affirms that God forgives a sinner. However, the woman sacrificed her health by holding to this kind of interpretation. Further, this story encourages a theology of church solidarity for the suffering: in this case, even those that die of AIDS as a result of sexual infidelity. It is a theology that discourages stigmatization and discrimination and brings healing to the infected community. This story shows that women do not always take material gains as a form of liberation. In this case, receiving spiritual rewards was liberation to these women.

The first biblical interpretation that seeks to preserve life is the more dominant in African Feminist thinking. The second interpretation that promotes spiritual liberation above women's dignity and health is rarely if ever articulated.

However, in the above discussions, it is clear that there is a relationship between African Feminist theology and grassroots Christian women's theologies of Liberation. Often grassroots theologies are not in tandem with African Feminist thinking. However, there is a clear testimony that ideas of African Feminist Theologians are sometimes being expressed by grassroots Christian women. This testifies against the assumption that African Feminist thinking is only for elitist African women. Grassroots women might benefit from an exposure to African Feminist theologies.

A Malawian Evangelical Feminist Relational Hermeneutics

In Malawi, the issue of power balance between men and women is real. The first area concerns equal access to theological training and consecutive employment for those that have received such training. It is clear that although women are slowly getting access to theological training and employment, they have a long way to catch up with men.

The place that has the fewest women as compared to men is that of the ordained ministry. Slowly, some churches are ordaining women. The first church to ordain women was Assemblies of God and even now there are more ordained women in Pentecostal and Charismatic churches than in mainline churches.[327] Many churches are still not ordaining women. Among these, some have started discussing the possibility of ordaining women, others have not. Women are least represented in this area because this engagement is linked to administering the sacraments. There are cultural and theological reasons that are used to deter women from participating in such a role. One such reason is that women are unclean due to the issue of blood during menstruation and child birth. There is ignorance that seminal fluids also make men unclean according to the Levitical laws.[328] Some men are aware of this fact but have chosen to cast a blind eye on it.

Women are a little more represented as lecturers at secular universities and theological colleges than as ordained ministers. This is because less emphasis is placed on ordination for one to be a lecturer. However, because few women have received higher theological training, the number of women lecturers is smaller than that of men. At Chancellor College of the University of Malawi, two out of six lecturers are women. At Mzuzu University, one out of seven lectures is a woman. This trend is similar at theological colleges.

Other women are involved in development work. They are involved in the caring ministry such as orphan care projects. However, there are more women than men in this area when the particular development work is done on a voluntary basis. Women seem to be more willing to work as vol-

---

[327] In the CCAP Livingstonia Synod women are deterred from becoming pastors as they, different from men, will only be approved to go for theological training if they are married (Joyce Mlenga, Women in Holy Ministry in the CCAP Synod of Livingstonia: The Case of Livingstonia and Ekwendeni Congregations, PhD Module, Department of Theology and Religious Studies, Mzuzu University, 2008).

[328] Leviticus 15:16-18 shows an example.

unteers than men. This is because women theologians at times do not have the privileges of working in paid employment. Thus when development projects attract funding, often leadership roles are given to men.

The other area where women are disadvantaged is in the case when they have equal opportunities to work but women's work is not rewarded. A classical example is the experience of pastors and pastors' wives in Malawi. Often, churches pay pastors and not pastors' wives, regardless that a pastor's wife works with the women of that church.

In addition, pastors' wives receive less training compared to pastors. Even though pastors' wives work with women, they also have the same spiritual needs. The women would benefit greatly from the services of a pastor's wife who has adequate training.[329]

On the whole, women in Malawi are a long way from achieving equality with men in the area of leadership roles in the church and society.

Integrating African Feminist Theologies

It is clear that though there are glimpses of African Feminist thinking being expressed by the grassroots, there are also conflicts between African Feminist theologies of liberation and grassroots theologies. To resolve such conflicts, a dialogical pastoral approach must be deployed if African Feminist theologies are to influence grassroots women's liberation. The following are some of the avenues through which African Feminist thinking can be disseminated to the grassroots women in Malawi.

Identifying Structures

There is need for a cautious effort to discover structures within church and society through which African Feminist theologies can be integrated. One must firstly analyze particular structures and investigate whether it is possible to integrate African Feminist teaching through them. These should be structures that allow some flexibility but also where women are given access to teach. It is even more effective if an African Feminist woman has access to such structures.

---

[329] See: Molly Longwe, "A Paradox in a Theology of Freedom and Equality: The Experiences of Pastors' Wives (Amayi Busa) in the Baptist Convention of Malawi (BACOMA)," PhD, University of KwaZulu Natal, 2010.

Women Structures

Women in churches in Malawi are active in educating young girls and fellow women. The key forums for women are the women's organizations. In the Baptist Convention it is called Umodzi wa Amayi.[330] This organization has weekly meetings for women at the congregational level but also joint meetings with other congregations either at associational, regional or national level. At such meetings women have much flexibility to teach each other principles of Christian living ranging from topics that are more solemn to those that are very relaxing and interactive. The Bible is taught at these sessions and in fact rarely do women use written manuals. They have much freedom to use what they have developed personally. The fact that earlier teaching manuals are less accessible in the churches because of high costs of publishing is a blessing in disguise to the women because they can develop their own materials. This is where biblical reinterpretation can take place. If women leaders of the Umodzi are taught a biblical hermeneutics that aims at transforming gender inequalities, they can easily incorporate this in their teachings. An example here would be to develop Bible study materials that centre on women stories in the Bible with an interpretative tool that enhances women.

Public Church Structures

Churches in Malawi run Sunday services at which sermons are an important means of transmitting message to the people. This structure can also be used to integrate African Feminist messages. One way to do this is to include women stories or passages on women as texts for preaching. The liturgy of the Sunday service can also be used to transmit African Feminist theologies especially in churches where there are opportunities to share one's experience. In some Charismatic and Pentecostal churches this is regularly possible, but also in many Baptist churches. Such churches usually have an open time for the congregation to share testimonies. This is a good time when some of the women's experiences can be shared. Many churches also have youth and adult Sunday Schools that can be important structures to transmit African Feminist theology. It is not always possible to use these public structures of the church to transmit African Feminist theologies that touch on sensitive issues of women. The Sunday pulpit, even Sunday School, is traditionally viewed as not the place to transmit sexuality is-

---

[330] See Rachel NyaGondwe Banda [Fiedler], *Women of Bible and Culture: Baptist Convention Women in Southern Malawi,* Zomba: Kachere, 2005.

sues. For sexuality issues, the church uses other more accommodating structures.

Public Society Structures

It is a common perception among church members in Malawi that the church's mandate is to take care of the issues of the spirit in a human being, while society must take care of cultural issues. In the Baptist Convention in Southern Malawi, there is an emerging perception in one congregation that the church must not initiate girls but the girls' elders in her society must initiate the girls.[331] If this perception grows into a fact, the future of the church initiation programme recorded in this chapter is dim. The perception is based on the idea that the church must train its members about God but that society should teach girls about traditional culture. The elders and the society at large conduct this teaching at the *bwalo* initiation. Whereas the church initiation is private, the *bwalo* initiation is public. For such a society, integration of African Feminist theology at a society level must take place through the *bwalo* initiation programme. The challenge for the church to use this structure is that some African Feminist theologians might not see this as a safe place to integrate African Feminist Theologies. They might fear the danger of their church not sanctioning this practice, because most churches in Malawi discourage their members to participate in such occasions. For African Feminist Theologians to penetrate this structure, they need to train traditional leaders in African Feminist Theologies so that they in turn can use them in training girl children at the *bwalo* initiation.

The society has other programmes that are not church based. These also can be used as a medium for integrating African Feminist Theologies. The National Initiative for Civic Education (NICE), for example, could be such a medium. This means that African Feminist Theology should not target church structures only but also non church structures. For this to be successful, African Feminist theology must continue to adapt itself to the issues of the day. An example here is the production of an HIV/AIDS booklet that distils African Feminist theology to the grassroots understanding.[332] These booklets have been utilized by church based communities as well as outside the church.

---

[331] Focus Group Discussion, 7.10.2006.
[332] See Rachel NyaGondwe Fiedler, *Be Careful. Aids is Real*, Zomba: Lydia Print, 2006; in Chewa: *Chenjerani. Matenda a Edzi Alikodi*, Zomba: Lydia Print, 2006, 24 pp.; in Tumbuka: *Tichenjere! Edzi Yiriko Nadi*, Zomba: Lydia Print, 2007.

Chapter 6: Conclusion

This book has provided a historical development of Feminist Theologies and shown that their Hermeneutics are informed by the context within which they developed. We have also shown that African Feminist Hermeneutics are varied and require a variety of approaches in the interpretation of culture, the Bible and power relations to realize women's liberation.

We have shown also that a Feminist interpretation is nothing new to the Bible, as all the genres testify, from creation stories to praise poetry. Our Feminist interpretation has been guided by a wholistic interpretation of the Bible, rather than by an interpretation based on isolated texts.

It has also been guided by the nature and the mission of God the Father, the Son and the Holy Spirit to the world. God created women and men equally in his image, and Jesus affirmed the position of women. In spite of this fundamental truth, culture and patriarchal interpretations have often clouded the liberative essence of the Bible.

This book has also shown the continuous conflict between the biblical message of female male equality with some elements of the cultures of the day, but inasmuch as some elements of today's cultures can be oppressive, the book has shown that some of these elements are becoming increasingly dislodged under pressure from Christian and non-Christian ideas. The power dynamics that have defined women as being inferior to men have been challenged and need to be challenged further by the Gospel.

Altogether this book has provided a detailed analysis of how an Evangelical Feminist Hermeneutic can be utilized in promoting women's liberation. This book has also shown that, inasmuch as Feminist Movements are (sometimes) seen as an adulteration of the Christian faith, this fear may not be necessary as Evangelical Feminist Theologies uphold the full sacredness of Scripture and the full Evangelical faith.

The Evangelical Feminist Hermeneutic in this book is not the only possible one; therefore this book opens up a dialogue. So this book can be an inspiration to other scholars to present their approach in a systematic way. As Evangelical as this interpretation is, it is not shared by all Evangelicals.

Bibliography

Published Materials

Ackermann, Denise, "Claiming our Footprints. Introductory Reflections," in Denise Ackermann, Eliza Getman et al (eds), *Claiming Our Footprints. South African Women Reflect on Context, Identity and Spirituality*, Matieland: EFSA Institute of Theological and Interdisciplinary Research, 2000.

Ackermann, Denise, "Tamar's Cry: Re-reading an Ancient Text in the Midst of HIV/Aids Pandemic," in Musa W. Dube and Musimbi Kanyoro, *Grant Me Justice, HIV/Aids and Gender Readings of the Bible*, Pietermaritzburg: Cluster, 2004, p. 27-34.

Ackermann, Denise, Eliza Getman et al (eds), *Claiming our Footprints. South African Women Reflect on Context, Identity and Spirituality*, Matieland: EFSA Institute of Theological and Interdisciplinary Research, 2000.

Ackermann, Denise, Eliza Getman, Hantie Kotzé, Judy Tobler (eds), *Claiming Our Footprints. South African Women Reflect on Context, Identity and Spirituality*, Matieland: EFSA Institute of Theological and Interdisciplinary Research, 2000.

Ackermann, Denise, J.A. Draper and E. Mashinini (eds), *Women Hold up Half the Sky. Women in the Church in Southern Africa*, Pietermaritzburg: Cluster, 1991.

Akintunde, Dorcas Olubanke, "The Attitude: A Model for Contemporary Churches in the Face of HIV/Aids in Africa," in Isabel Apawo Phiri, Beverly Haddad, Madipoane Masenya (ng'wana Mphahlele), *African Women, HIV/Aids and Faith Communities*, Pietermaritzburg: Cluster 2003, pp. 94-110.

Akintunde, Dorcas Olubanke, *African Culture and the Quest for Women's Rights*, Sefɛr: Ibadan, 2001.

Anderson, Cheryl Barbara, "Lessons on Healing from Naaman (2 Kings 5:1-27): An African American Perspective," in Isabel Apawo Phiri (ed), *African Women, HIV/Aids, and Faith Communities*, Pietermaritzburg: Cluster 2003, pp. 23-24.

Banda, Rachel NyaGondwe [Fiedler], *Women of Bible and Culture: Baptist Convention Women in Southern Malawi*, Zomba: Kachere, 2005.

Becher, Jeanne (ed), *Women, Religion and Sexuality. Studies on the Impact of Religious Teachings on Women*, Geneva: WCC, 1991.

Boff, Leonardo and Virgil Elizondo (eds), *Concilium. Theologies of the Third World. Convergences and Differences*, Edinburgh: Page Brothers, 1988.

Bosch, H.M. van den, "African Theology: Is it Relevant for Global Christianity? *NGTT*, 2009, pp. 530-537.

Breugel, J.W.M. van, *Chewa Traditional Religion*, Blantyre: CLAIM-Kachere, 2001.

Bruce, Patricia Frances, "The Mother's Cow: a Study of Old Testament References to Virginity in the Context of HIV/Aids in South Africa" in Isabel Apawo Phiri et al, *African Women, HIV/Aids and Faith Communities*, Pietermaritzburg: Cluster, 2003.

Buku la Alangizi, Lilongwe: Baptist Publications, nd.

Cannon, Ketie Geneva, "The Emergence of Black Feminist Consciousness," in Letty Russel (ed), "Feminist Interpretations of the Bible," in Letty M. Russel, *Feminist Interpretations of the Bible*, London/New York: Basil Blackwell, 1985.

Chakanza, J.C., "The Unfinished Agenda: Puberty Rites and the Response of the Roman Catholic Church in Southern Malawi, 1901-1994," *Religion in Malawi*, no. 5, 1995.

Chakanza, J.C., *Wisdom of the People, 2000 Chinyanja Proverbs*, Blantyre: CLAIM-Kachere, 2000.

Chingota, Felix, "A Historical Account of the Attitude of Blantyre Synod of the Church of Central Africa Presbyterian towards Initiation Rites," *Religion in Malawi*, no. 5, 1995.

Chirongoma, Sophia, "Women, Poverty, and HIV in Zimbabwe. An Exploration of Inequalities in Health Care," in Isabel Apawo Phiri and Sarojini Nadar (eds), *African Women, Religion, and Health. Essays in Honour of Mercy Amba Oduyoye*, Pietermaritzburg: Cluster, 2006, pp. 173-186.

Cochrane, James R. et al (eds), "Overcoming Violence against Women and Children," Special Issue, Nov. 2002, *Journal of Theology for Southern Africa*.

Denis, Philippe, "Sexuality and Aids in South Africa," *Journal of Theology for Southern Africa*, March 2003.

Dickson, Kwesi A., *Theology in Africa*, London: Darton, Longman and Todd; Maryknoll: Orbis, 1984.

Douglas, Kelly Brown, *Sexuality and the Black Church. A Womanist Perspective*, Maryknoll: Orbis, 1999.

Dube, Musa W. (ed), *Other Ways of Reading. African Women and the Bible*, Atlanta/Geneva: Society of Biblical Literature/WCC, 2001.

Dube, Musa W. and Musimbi Kanyoro (eds), *Grant Me Justice. HIV/Aids and Gender Re-readings of the Bible*, Pietermaritzburg: Cluster, 2004.

Dube, Musa W., "Grant Me Justice: Towards Gender Sensitive Multi-Sectoral HIV/Aids Readings of the Bible." In Musa W. Dube and Musimbi Kanyoro, *Grant me Justice. HIV/Aids and Gender Readings of the Bible*, Pietermaritzburg: Cluster, 2004, pp. 16-21.

Dube, Musa W., "Preaching to the Converted: Unsettling the Christian Church. A Theological View: A Scriptural Injunction," *Ministerial Formation*, Geneva: World Council of Churches, April, 2001, pp. 38-50.

Dube, Musa W., *Postcolonial Feminist Interpretation of the Bible*, St Louis: Chalice Press, 2000.

Edet, Rosemary and Margaret A. Umeagudosu (eds), *Life, Women and Culture: Theological Reflections: Proceeding of the National Conference of a Circle of African Women Theologians*, Nigeria: MUA Printers 1990.

Fabella, Virginia (ed), *Asia's Struggle for Full Humanity*, Maryknoll: Orbis, 1980.

Fabella, Virginia and Sergio Torres (eds), *Irruption of the Third World. Challenge to Theology*, Maryknoll: Orbis, 1983.

Fiedler, Klaus, "Bishop Lucas' Christianization of Traditional Rites, the Kikuyu Female Circumcision Controversy and the 'Cultural Approach' of Conservative German Missionaries in Tanzania" in Noel Q. King and Klaus Fiedler (eds), *Robin Lamburn – From a Missionary's Notebook: The Yao of Tunduru and other Essays*, Saarbrücken, 1991, pp. 207-217.

Fiedler, Klaus, "For the Sake of Christian Marriage Abolish Church Weddings," *Religion in Malawi*, no. 5 (1995), pp. 22-28. Revised in: Klaus Fiedler, *Conflicted Power in Malawian Christianity. Essays Missionary and Evangelical from Malawi*, Mzuzu: Mzuni Press, 2015, pp. 6-21.

Fiedler, Klaus, *Baptists and the Ordination of Women*, Zomba: Lydia Print, 2008.

Fiedler, Klaus, *Conflicted Power in Malawian Christianity. Essays Missionary and Evangelical from Malawi*, Mzuzu: Mzuni Press, 2015.

Fiedler, Klaus, *Missions as the Theology of the Church. An Argument from Malawi*, Mzuzu: Mzuni Press, 2015.

Fiedler, Klaus, *The Gospel Takes Root on Kilimanjaro. A History of the Evangelical Lutheran Church of Old Moshi-Mbokomu 1885-1940*, Zomba: Kachere, 2006.

Fiedler, Klaus, *The Story of Faith Missions. From Hudson Taylor to Present Day Africa*, Oxford et al: Regnum, 1994.

Fiedler, Rachel NyaGondwe, "Against the Flow: Stories of Women Pastors in the Baptist Convention in Malawi," in Isabel Apawo Phiri, Devarakshanam Betty Govinden et al, *Her Stories. Hidden Stories of Women of Faith in Africa*, Pietermaritzburg: Cluster, 2002, pp. 181-201.

Fiedler, Rachel NyaGondwe, "Pastors' Wives and Patriarchy: Experiences of Church Women in Malawi," *Religion in Malawi*, 13, 2006, pp. 23-27.

Fiedler, Rachel NyaGondwe, "Theological Education for Women in Malawi", *Studia Historiae Ecclesiasticae*, vol. 35, 2009, Supplement, pp. 119-134.

Fiedler, Rachel NyaGondwe, *Be Careful. AIDS is Real*, Zomba: Lydia Print, 2006.

Fiedler, Rachel NyaGondwe, *Chenjerani. Matenda a Edzi Alikodi*, Zomba: Lydia Print, 2006.

Fiedler, Rachel NyaGondwe, *Coming of Age. A Christianized Initiation among Women in Southern Malawi*. Zomba: Kachere, 2005, ²2007.

Fiedler, Rachel NyaGondwe, *Tichenjere! Edzi Yiriko Nadi*, Zomba: Lydia Print, 2006.

Fiorenza, Elisabeth Schüssler, *Bread Not Stone. The Challenge of Feminist Biblical Interpretation*, Boston: Beacon Press, 1999 (1984).

Fiorenza, Elisabeth Schüssler, *In Memory of Her. A Feminist Theological Reconstruction of Christian Origins*, New York: Crossroads, 1999 (1983).

Fiorenza, Elisabeth Schüssler, *The Power of Naming. A Concilium Reader in Feminist Liberation Theology*, Maryknoll: Orbis, 1996.

Franzosa, Susan Douglas and Karen A. Mazza, *Integrating Women's Studies into the Curriculum*, West Port: Greenwood Press, 1984.

Getman, Eliza Jane, "Ground Cover" in Denise Ackermann et al (eds), *Claiming Our Footprints. South African Women Reflect on Context, Identity and Spirituality*, Matieland: EFSA Institute of Theological and Interdisciplinary Research, 2000, pp. 62-67.

Getui, Mary and Hazel Ayanga (eds), *Conflicts in Africa: A Women Response*: Nairobi: Circle, 2002.

Getui, Mary N., "Women's Priesthood in Relation to Nature", in Musimbi Kanyoro and Nyambura Njoroge (eds), *Groaning in Faith: African Women in the Household of God*, Nairobi: Acton, 1996, pp. 31-39.

Getui, Mary, "Africa, Church and Theology: Do they Need Each Other?" *Ministerial Formation*, January 1999.

Gnanadason, Aruna, *No Longer Silent: The Church and Violence against Women*, Geneva: WCC, 1993.

Goba, Bonganjalo, "Emerging Theological Perspectives in South Africa," in Virginia Fabella, M.M. and Sergio Torres, (eds), *Irruption of the Third World Challenge to Theology*, New York: Orbis Books 1983, pp. 19ff.

Govinden, Devarakshanam Betty, "'The Mother of African Freedom' – The Contribution of Charlotte Maxeke to the Struggle for Freedom in South Africa," in Isabel Apawo Phiri, Devarakshanam Betty Govinden and Sarojini Nadar (eds), *Herstories. Hidden Histories of Women of Faith in Africa*, Pietermaritzburg: Cluster, 2002, pp. 304-326.

Gutierrez, Gustavo, "The Meaning of the Term Liberation" in Deane William Fern, *Third World Liberation Theologies. A Reader*, New York: Orbis Books, 1986.

Haddad, Beverly Gail, "Gender Violence and HIV/AIDS: A Deadly Silence in the Church," *Journal of Theology in Southern Africa*, 11.2003, pp. 93-106.

Isherwood, Lisa and Dorothea McEwan, *An A to Z of Feminist Theology*, Sheffield Academic Press, 1996.

Isichei, Elisabeth, *A History of Christianity in Africa: From Antiquity to the Present*. Melksham: Cromwell Press, 1995.

James, Rhodah Ada, "The Scope of Women's Positions in the Church, " in Mercy Amba Oduyoye and Musimbi Kanyoro (eds), *Talitha Qumi. Proceedings of the Convocation of African Women Theologians 1989*, Accra-North: Sam-Woode, 2001, pp. 192-200.

Kabanda, Peggy Mulambya, "Single Women Parents in Africa," in Mercy Amba Oduyoye, and Musimbi Kanyoro (eds), *Talitha Qumi, Proceedings of the Convocation of African Women Theologians 1989*, Accra-North: Sam-Woode, 2001, pp. 183-191.

Kalu, Ogbu U., "Daughters of Ethiopia Constructing a Feminist Discourse in Ebony Strokes," in Isabel Apawo Phiri and Sarojini Nadar (eds), *Women, Religion and Health, Essays in Honour of Mercy Amba Ewudziwa Oduyoye*, Pietermaritzburg: Cluster, 2006.

Kanyoro, Musimbi and Nyambura Njoroge (eds), *Groaning in Faith: African Women in the Household of God*, Nairobi: Acton, 1996.

Kanyoro, Musimbi, "Beads and Strands: Threading More Beads in the Story of the Circle," in Isabel Apawo Phiri, Devarakshanam Betty Govinden, and Sarojini Nadar (eds), *Her-stories: Hidden Histories of Women of Faith in Africa*, Pietermaritzburg: Cluster 2002, pp. 15-38.

Kanyoro, Musimbi, *Introductions in Feminist Theology: Feminist Cultural Hermeneutics. An African Perspective*, Sheffield Academic Press, 2000.

Kapuma, Gertrude Aopesyaga, "'Troubled but not Destroyed': Women of Faith Reclaim their Rights," in Isabel Apawo Phiri, Devarakshanam Betty Govinden and Sarojini Nadar (eds), *Her-stories. Hidden Histories of Women of Faith in Africa*, Pietermaritzburg: Cluster, 2002, pp. 348-369.

Kholowa, Janet and Klaus Fiedler, *In the Beginning God Created them Equal*, Blantyre: CLAIM-Kachere, 2000.

Kholowa, Janet and Klaus Fiedler, *Mtumwi Paulo ndi Udindo wa Amayi Mumpingo* [The Apostle Paul and the Authority of Women in the Church], Blantyre: CLAIM-Kachere, 2001.

Kholowa, Janet and Klaus Fiedler, *Pa Chiyambi Anawalenga Chimodzimodzi* [In the Beginning God Created them Equal], Blantyre: CLAIM-Kachere, 1999.

Kok, Bregje de, *Christianity and African Traditional Religion: Two Realities of a Different Kind*, Zomba: Kachere, 2004.

Lancaster, Sarah Heaner, *Women and the Authority of Scripture: A Narrative Approach*, Harrisburg: Trinity Press, 2002.

Landman, Christina (ed), *Digging up our Foremothers. Stories of Women in Africa*, Pretoria: UNISA, 1996.

Landman, Christina, "A Land Flowing with Milk and Honey", Musimbi Kanyoro and Nyambura Njoroge (eds), *Groaning in Faith: African Women in the Household of God*, Nairobi: Acton, 1996, pp. 99-111.

Lengermann, Madoo, Patricia and Jill Niebrugge-Brantley, *Contemporary Feminist Theory, Sociological Theory*, Singapore: McGraw Hill, 1992.

Longwe, Hany, *Christians by Grace – Baptists by Choice. A History of the Baptist Convention of Malawi*, Zomba: Kachere, 2010.

Maluleke, Tinyiko S., "Half a Century of African Christian Theologies: Elements of the Emerging Agenda for the Twenty-first Century", Journal of Theology for Southern Africa, 1997, 99, pp. 4-23

Manda, Christine, "A Testimony against Polygamy," in Mercy Amba Oduyoye and Musimbi Kanyoro (eds), *Talita Qumi. Proceedings of the Convocation of African Women Theologians 1989*, Accra-North: Sam-Woode, 2001, pp. 152-154.

Mijoga, Hilary, *Separate but Same Gospel. Preaching in African Instituted Churches in Southern Malawi*, Blantyre: CLAIM-Kachere, 2000.

Mijoga, Hilary, "Gender Differentiation in the Bible: Created and Recognized" in *Journal of Humanities*, no. 13, UNIMA, 1999. Reprinted in Jonathan Nkhoma, *The Significance of the Dead Sea Scrolls and other Essays. Biblical and Early Christianity Studies from Malawi*, Mzuzu: Mzuni Press, 2013, pp. 174-198.

Mkwambisi, David, Joshua Valeta, Edgar Lungu, Macdonald Gomani, *Masculinity, Alcoholism and HIV/AIDS in Malawi*, Zomba: Kachere, 2010.

Moosa, Najma, "The Flying Hadji," in Denise Ackermann et al (eds), *Claiming Our Footprints. South African Women Reflect on Context, Identity and Spirituality*, Matieland: EFSA Institute of Theological and Interdisciplinary Research, 2000, p. 98ff.

Mosala, Itumeleng J., *Biblical Hermeneutics and Black Theology in South Africa*, Grand Rapids: Eerdmans, 1989.

Mouton, Elna, "After the Locusts: Letters from a Landscape of Faith," in Denise Ackermann et al (eds), *Claiming Our Footprints. South African Women Reflect on Context, Identity and Spirituality*, Matieland: EFSA Institute of Theological and Interdisciplinary Research, 2000.

Muilenburg, J., "Form Criticism and Beyond;" *FBL* 88 (1969).

Mulambya, Peggy, "Single Women Parents in Africa," in Mercy Amba Oduyoye and Musimbi Kanyoro (eds), *Talitha Qumi. Proceedings of the Convocation of African Women Theologians 1989*, Accra-North: Sam-Woode, 2001, pp. 192-198.

Mwachukwu, Daisy, "The Context of African Women's Life," in Mercy Amba Oduyoye and Musimbi Kanyoro (eds), *Proceedings of the Convocation of African Women Theologians 1989, Accra-North*: Sam-Woode, 2001, pp. 118-121.

Mwaura, Philomena Njeri, "Nigerian Pentecostal Missionary Enterprise in Kenya", Ogbu Kalu, Chima Jacob Koriah, G. Ugo Nwokeji and Obiama Nnaemeta (eds), Religion, History and Politics in Nigeria, University Press of America, 2005.

Mwaura, Philomena Njeri, "Stigmatization and Discrimination of HIV/AIDS Women in Kenya: A Violation of Human Rights and its Theological Implications", Exchange, vol 37, 2008, pp. 35-51

Mwaura, Philomena Njeri, "The Anthropological Dimension of a Patient's Treatment: a Response to Prof. Bernard Ugeux", International Review of Mission, vol 95, pp. 136-142.

Mwaura, Philomena Njeri, "Women's Healing Roles in Traditional Gikuyu Society", in Musimbi Kanyoro and Nyambura Njoroge (eds), Groaning in Faith: African Women in the Household of God, Nairobi: Acton, 1996, pp. 253-269

Nadar, Sarojini, "Barak God: Women, HIV/Aids and a Theology of Suffering" in Musa W. Dube and Musimbi Kanyoro (eds), Grant Me Justice. HIV/Aids and Gender Readings of the Bible, Pietermaritzburg: Cluster, 2004.

Nadar, Sarojini, "Emerging from Muddy Waters. For the Man in My Life - My Inspiration to Soar," in Denise Ackermann, Eliza Getman et al (eds), Claiming Our Footprints. South African Women Reflect on Context, Identity and Spirituality, Matieland: EFSA Institute of Theological and Interdisciplinary Research, 2000, pp. 15-31.

Ndyabahika, Grace N., "Women's Place in Creation," in Musimbi Kanyoro and Nyambura Njoroge (eds), Groaning in Faith: African Women in the Household of God, Nairobi: Acton, 1996, pp. 23-30.

Njoroge, Nyambura and Irja Askola (eds), There were also Women Looking from Afar, Geneva: World Alliance of Reformed Churches, 1998.

Njoroge, Nyambura and Musa W. Dube (eds), Talitha Cumi! Theologies of African Women, Pietermaritzburg: Cluster 2001.

Njoroge, Nyambura, Kiama kia Ngo: An African Christian Feminist Ethic of Resistance and Transformation, Legon Theological Studies: Legon 2000.

Nkhoma, Anthony, Women in Search of Identity. The Case of Women's Ordination in Zambezi Evangelical Church, Zomba: Kachere, 2005.

Oduyoye, Mercy Amba (ed), Transforming Power: Women in the Household of God. Proceedings of the Pan-African Conference of the Circle of Concerned African Women Theologians, Accra-North: Sam Woode, 1997.

Oduyoye, Mercy Amba and Elizabeth Amoah (eds), People of Faith and the Challenge of HIV/AIDS, Ibadan: Sefεr, 2004.

Oduyoye, Mercy Amba and Musimbi Kanyoro (eds), Proceedings of the Convocation of African Women Theologians 1989, Accra-North: Sam-Woode, 2001.

Oduyoye, Mercy Amba and Musimbi Kanyoro (eds), Talitha Qumi, Proceedings of the Convocation of African Women Theologians 1989, Accra-North: Sam-Woode, 2001.

Oduyoye, Mercy Amba and Musimbi Kanyoro (eds), *The Will to Arise: Women, Tradition, and the Church in Africa*, Maryknoll: Orbis, 1992.

Oduyoye, Mercy Amba, "Women Theologians and the Early Church. An Examination of Historiography," *Voices from the Third World Women, Colombo*: EATWOT, 1885, vol. viii 3, pp. 70-72.

Oduyoye, Mercy Amba, *And Women, where do they Come in?* Lagos: Methodist Church Nigeria Literature Bureau, 1977.

Oduyoye, Mercy Amba, *Daughters of Anowa. African Women and Patriarchy*, Maryknoll: Orbis 1995.

Oduyoye, Mercy Amba, *Hearing and Knowing: Theological Reflections on Christianity in Africa*, New York: Orbis, 1986.

Oduyoye, Mercy Amba, *Introducing African Women's Theology*, Sheffield Academic Press, 2001.

Ogundipe, Chief (Mrs) G.T., *The Ordination of Women*, Lagos: Methodist Church Nigeria Literature Bureau, 1977.

Ott, Martin, *African Theology in Images*, Zomba: Kachere, 2000.

Parrat, John (ed), *A Reader in Christian Theology*, London: SPCK 1987.

Parsons, Susan Frank, *The Cambridge Companion to Feminist Theology*, Cambridge University Press, 2002.

Pemberton, Carrie, *Circle Thinking: African Women Theologians in Dialogue with the West*, Leiden: Brill, 2003.

Phiri, Isabel Apawo and Sarojini Nadar (eds), *African Women, Religion, and Health: Essays in Honour of Mercy Amba Ewudziwa Oduyoye*, Pietermaritzburg: Cluster 2006.

Phiri, Isabel Apawo and Sarojini Nadar (eds), *On Being Church: African Women's Voices and Visions*, Geneva: World Council of Churches, 2005.

Phiri, Isabel Apawo and Sarojini Nadar, *African Women's Voices and Visions*, Geneva: World Council of Churches, 2005.

Phiri, Isabel Apawo, "A Convocation of African Women in Theology, Trinity College, Legon, Accra, Ghana 24-30th September, 1989," *Religion in Malawi*, no. 3, 1991, pp. 39-41.

Phiri, Isabel Apawo, "A Theological Analysis of the Voices of Teenage Girls on Men's Role in the Fight against HIV/AIDS," *Journal of Theology for Southern Africa*, 2004, pp. 20ff.

Phiri, Isabel Apawo, "A Theological Analysis of the Voices of Teen Age Girls on Men's Role in the Fight against HIV/AIDS in KwaZulu-Natal, South Africa," in Steve de Gruchy et al, Special Issue, *The Agency of the Oppressed Discourse: Consciousness, Liberation and Survival in Theological Perspective*. 120, November 2004.

Phiri, Isabel Apawo, "African Women of Faith Speak out in an HIV/AIDS Era" in Isabel Apawo Phiri, Beverly Haddad and Madipoane Masenya (ng'wana Mphahlele) (eds), *African Women, HIV/AIDS and Faith Communities*, Pietermaritzburg: Cluster 2003, pp. 6ff.

Phiri, Isabel Apawo, "Department of Religious Studies 1973-1988," *Religion in Malawi*, no. 2, 1988.

Phiri, Isabel Apawo, "Healing from the Traumas of Crime in South Africa: Interaction of African Religion with Christianity as Perceived by African Female Traditional Healers," *The Lutheran Federation*, 2005.

Phiri, Isabel Apawo, "HIV/AIDS Review," Volume 56, no. 4, October 2004.

Phiri, Isabel Apawo, "HIV/AIDS. An African Theological Response in Mission," *Ecumenical Review*, vol. 56, no. 4, 2004.

Phiri, Isabel Apawo, "Marching, Suspended and Stoned: Christian Women in Malawi 1995," in Kenneth R. Ross (ed), *God, People and Power in Malawi: Democratization in Theological Perspective*, Blantyre: CLAIM-Kachere, 1996, pp. 63-105.

Phiri, Isabel Apawo, "Stand up and be Counted. Identity, Spirituality and Theological Education in my Faith Journey," in Denise Ackermann et al (eds), *Claiming Our Footprints. South African Women Reflect on Context, Identity and Spirituality*, Matieland: EFSA Institute of Theological and Interdisciplinary Research, 2000.

Phiri, Isabel Apawo, "The Church as Healing Community: Voices and Visions from Chilobwe Healing Centre," in Isabel Apawo Phiri and Sarojini Nadar (eds), *On Being Church: African Women's Voices and Visions*, World Council of Churches, 2005, pp. 13-27.

Phiri, Isabel Apawo, "Transformation in South African Universities: The Case of Female Academics in Leadership Positions in Theological Institutions," in Roswitha Gerloff (ed), *Mission is Crossing Frontiers*, Pietermaritzburg: Cluster, 2003.

Phiri, Isabel Apawo, "Women in Theological Education in Malawi," *Religion in Malawi*, no. 2, 1988, pp. 24-28.

Phiri, Isabel Apawo, "African Women's Theologies in the New Millennium," *Agenda* 61, 2004.

Phiri, Isabel Apawo, Betty Devarakshanam and Sarojini Nadar (eds), *Her-stories. Hidden Histories of Women of Faith in Africa*, Pietermaritzburg: Cluster, 2002.

Phiri, Isabel Apawo, Beverly Haddad et al, *African Women, HIV/Aids and Faith Communities*, Pietermaritzburg: Cluster, 2003.

Phiri, Isabel Apawo, Beverly Haddad, Madipoane Masenya (ng'wana Mphahlele) (eds), *African Women, HIV/Aids and Faith Communities*, Pietermaritzburg: Cluster, 2003.

Phiri, Isabel Apawo, Devarakshanam Betty Govinden and Sarojini Nadar (eds), *Her-stories. Hidden Histories of Women of Faith in Africa*, Pietermaritzburg: Cluster, 2002.

Phiri, Isabel Apawo, *Women, Presbyterianism and Patriarchy. Religious Experiences of Chewa Women in Central Malawi*, Blantyre: CLAIM-Kachere, ²2000 (1996); Zomba: Kachere, ³2007.

Press, Mary Judith, "Feminist Christians in Latin America," in *Voices from the Third World Women*, vol. viii, no. 3, pp. 56ff.

Ramazanoglu, Caroline, "Feminism and Liberation," in Linda McDowell and Rosemary Pringle (eds), *Defining Women. Social Institutions and Gender Divisions*, Cambridge: Blackwell, 1992.

Reinharz, Shulamit, *Feminist Methods in Social Research*, New York: Oxford University Press, 1992.

"Report of the EATWOT Women's Commission Conference, St. Lucia Park, Harare, Zimbabwe, 21st – 25th June 1999", in Philomena N. Mwaura and Lilian D. Chirairo, *Theology in the Context of Globalization. African Women's Response*, Nairobi: EATWOT Women's Commission, 2005, pp. 96-106.

Ross, Kenneth R., "The Theology of Hope," in Kenneth R. Ross, *Gospel Ferment in Malawi: Theological Essays*, Mambo-Kachere, 1995, pp. 65-80.

Ross, Kenneth R., "Theology and Religious Studies at the University of Malawi 1993-1998," *Religion in Malawi*, no. 9, 1999, pp. 3-9.

Ruether, Rosemary Radford, *Sexism and God-Talk: Towards a Feminist Theology*, Boston: Beacon Press, 1999.

Russell, Letty M., *The Future of Partnership*, Philadelphia: Westminster, 1979.

Salinas-Hultman, Rosa, "Hispanics, Catholics and Women in the 'Americas.' Possibilities of the Hispanic American Women's Perspective," University of Linköping, nd.

Scanzoni, Letha and Nancy Hardesty, *All we are Meant to Be. A Biblical Approach to Women's Liberation*, Waco: Word Books, 1974

Schalkwyk, Annalet van, "The Story of Anne Hope: A White Woman's Contribution towards South African Liberation," in Isabel Apawo Phiri, Devarakshanam Betty Govinden and Sarojini Nadar (eds), *Her-stories. Hidden Histories of Women of Faith in Africa*, Pietermaritzburg: Cluster, 2002, pp. 279-304.

Schalkwyk, Annalet van, "Writing Southern African Women's Stories of Transformation – Some Methodological Aspects," *Journal of Constructive Theology*, no. 6 (2), 2000, pp. 21-37.

Schreiter, Roberts J., *Constructing Local Theologies*, Suffolk: SCM Press, 1985.

Shaw, Mark, *The Kingdom of God in Africa: A Short History of African Christianity*, Grand Rapids, 1996.

Shisanya, Constance Ambasa, "Professor Hannah Wangeci Kinoti: Your Seeds are Germinating in Kenya," in Isabel Apawo Phiri, Devarakshanam Betty Govinden and Sarojini Nadar (eds), *Her–stories: Hidden Stories of Women of Faith in Africa*, Pietermaritzburg: Cluster, 2002, pp. 327-345.

Sundkler, Bengt and Christopher Steed, *A History of the Church in Africa*, Cambridge University Press, 2000.

Trible, Phyllis, "Depatriarchalizing in Biblical Interpretation", *JAAR* 41 (1973), p. 36.

Walker, Alice, *In Search of Our Mothers' Gardens. Womanist Prose*, New York: Harcourt, Brace, Jovanovich, 1983.

Wamue, Grace and Mary Getui (eds), *Violence against Women: Reflection by Kenyan Woman Theologians*, Nairobi: Acton, 1996.

Unpublished

Banda, Rachel [Fiedler], "Liberation through Baptist Polity and Doctrine. A Reflection on the Lives of Women in the History of Women in the Baptist Convention of Malawi," MA, University of Malawi, 2001.

Beatrice Okeyere-Manu, "Sacrificing Health for Well Being: Sex Work as a Livelihood Option for the Poor Women in Pietermaritzburg," Malaka-le Theologies 2005.

Fiedler, Rachel NyaGondwe, "*Kachiwala* Tradition," unpublished.

Getman, Eliza Jane, "Giving Birth to God Our Mother: Nurturing a Theology of Birth as Creative Power," Malaka-le Theologies 2005.

Getui, Mary, "Masanta: Traditional Healer among Abagushii of Western Kenya," Malaka-le Theologies, 2005.

Haddad, Beverly Gail, "The Mothers' Union in South Africa. Untold Stories of Faith Survival and Resistance," PhD, University of KwaZulu Natal, 2000.

Kalalo, Chimwemwe, "Women's Sexual and Reproductive Health in the Context of HIV/Aids: The Involvement of the Anglican Church in the Upper Shire Diocese in Southern Malawi," MA, University of Malawi, 2006.

Kanyoro, Musimbi, "Revisiting the History of the Circle," paper presented at a conference on Biographies of Women, Kempton Park, 2003.

Katumbi, Chimwemwe Harawa, "The Interaction between Christianity and Traditional Medicine in the Livingstonia Synod," MA, University of Malawi, 2003.

Kinoti, Hannah Wangeci, "Aspects of Gikuyu Traditional Morality," PhD, University of Nairobi, 1983.

Kishindo, Monica, "A Survey of Likoma Island from Early Times to 1935," Final Year History Paper 1969/70, University of Malawi.

Labeodan, Helen Adekunbi, "Women Reproductive Health in Nigeria, A Theo-Philosophical Approach," Malaka-le Theologies 2005.

List, Institute of Women in Religion and Culture, accessed 15.9.2003.

Longwe, Hany, "Democratization of the Christian Faith: The Influence of the Baptist Doctrine of 'Priesthood of All Believers' on the History of the Baptist Convention of Malawi (BACOMA)," PhD, University of Malawi, 2008.

Longwe, Molly, "From *Chinamwali* to *Chilangizo*: The Christianisation of Pre-Christian Chewa Initiation Rites in the Baptist Convention of Malawi," MTh, University of KwaZulu Natal, 2003.

Molly Longwe, "A Paradox in a Theology of Freedom and Equality: The Experiences of Pastors' Wives (Amayi Busa) in the Baptist Convention of Malawi (BACOMA)," PhD, University of KwaZulu Natal, 2010

Makondesa, Patrick, "Christian Initiation Rites in Southern Malawi," MA module, Department of Theology and Religious Studies, University of Malawi, 1999.

Masenya, Madipoane, "The Bible as a 'Sword' and a 'Tool for Healing'," Malaka-le Theologies, 2005.

Memo from WCC to Musimbi Kanyoro from Mercy Amba Oduyoye, nd.

Mlenga, Joyce, Women in Holy Ministry in the CCAP Synod of Livingstonia: The Case of Livingstonia and Ekwendeni Congregations, PhD Module, Department of Theology and Religious Studies, Mzuzu University, 2008.

Moyo, Fulata, "Red Beads," Malaka-le Theologies: Women, Religion and Health, A Circle of Concerned African Women Theologians Pan-African Conference, Kempton Park, South Africa, July 10-15, 2005.

Moyo, Fulata, "Women, Sexuality Envisioned as Embodied Interconnected Spirituality and Sexual Education in Southern Malawi. A Quest for Women's Sexual Empowerment in the HIV/Aids Context – The Case of *Kukhonzera Chinkhoswe Chachikhristu* (KCC) among Mang'anja and Yao Christians of T/A Mwambo in Rural Zomba," PhD, University of KwaZulu Natal, 2009.

Munyenyembe, Rhodian, "Christianity and Socio-Cultural Issues. An Evaluation of the Charismatic Movement's Contribution towards the Contextualization of the Gospel in Malawi," MA, University of Malawi, 2006.

Mwaura, Philomena Njeri, "Perceptions of Women's Health and Rights in Neo-Pentecostal and Charismatic Churches in Kenya," Malaka-le Theologies, 2005.

Nadar, Sarojini, "Power, Ideology and Interpretation/s: Womanist and Literary Perspectives on the Book of Esther as Resources for Gender-Social Transformation," PhD, University of KwaZulu Natal, 2003.

Nana Adwoa, The Helper's Ministry; A letter to my Grand Children, Circle meeting 17-21 January 2002.

Nkhoma, Anthony, "Women in Search of Identity. The Case of Women's Ordination in Zambezi Evangelical Church," BA, University of Malawi, 2005.

Nyika, Felix, Apostolic Office in Malawian Neocharismatic Churches: A Contextual, Biblical-Theological, and Historical Appraisal, PhD, University of Malawi, 2015.

Phiri, Isabel Apawo, Oral Presentation, Malawi Circle, 13.7.2006.

Phiri, Mathews R., "A Study on the Pre-Marriage Counselling in the CCAP Synod of Livingstonia Ekwendeni Presbytery," BA, Mzuzu University, Dec 2009.

Pillay, Miranda N., "Luke 7:36–50: This Woman? Towards a Theology of Gender Equality in the Context of HIV/Aids," Malaka-le Theologies, 2005.

Provisional Addis Ababa Circle Report, accessed 6.3.2006.

Public Seminar, Circle Meeting, Lydia Foundation Building, Zomba, 13.7.2006.

Schalkwyk, Annalet van, "Sister, we Bleed and we Sing: Women's Stories, Christian Mission and SHALOM in South Africa," PhD, UNISA, 1999.

Tribute to the Very Rev Charles K. Yamoah in a Brief Biography of the Very Rev Charles Kwa Yamoah BD (London) in Souvenir Programme for the Home Call of the Very Rev Charles Kwa Yamoah (B.D. London), January 23, 1987.

Umeagudosu, Margaret A., "'Act of God?' The Experience of Women Living with Vesico Vagina Fistula (VVF) among Women in Northern Nigeria," Malaka-le Theologies 2005.

Yila, Othniel Mintang, "The Place of Women in the Church Ministry as Shown in 1 Timothy 2:9-15," June 1998, MA Thesis, Nairobi International School of Theology

Yinda, Hélène and Kä Mana, Pour la Nouvelle Théologie des Femmes Africaines. Repenser la difference sexuelle, promouvoir les droits des femmes et libérer leurs energies créatives, Yaoundé: Editions CLE-CIPRE, 2001. Another title is

Yinda, Hélène, Cercle des Théologiennnes Africaines Engagées: Femmes Africaines. Le Pouvoir de Transformer le Monde, Yaoundé: Editions Sherpa, 2002.

Oral Sources

Focus Group Discussion, 7.10.2006.

Focus Group Presentation, 2002 Circle Conference, Johannesburg, South Africa.

Focus Group, Isabel Phiri and Fulata Moyo, Malaka-le Theologies, 14.7.2005.

Focus Group, Rev Peggy Mulambya Kabonde and Lilian Siwila, Malaka-le Theologies, 14.7.2005.

Group interview through participatory investigation, 12 Baptist convention women in Jali, Zomba, June 2005.

Interview Bishop Patrick Kalilombe, Postgraduate Colloquium 2003, Department of Theology and Religious Studies, University of Malawi.

Interview Circle woman from Uganda, Kempton Park, 12.7.2005.
Interview Circle women in ministerial formation, Addis Ababa, 2002.
Interview Constance Ambasa Shisanya, Circle meeting, 13.7.2005.
Interview Denise Ackermann, Cape Town, May 2002.
Interview Isabel Apawo Phiri, Kempton Park, 14.7.2005.
Interview Joyce Boham, 16.9.2005.
Interview Mary Getui, The Institute of Religion and Culture, Ghana, 2005, 14.9.2005.
Interview Mary Mumo, Nairobi International School of Theology, 8.2005.
Interview member of Namibia Circle, Kempton Park, 14.7.2005.
Interview Mercy Amba Oduyoye, Institute of Women in Religion and Culture, 14.9.2005.
Interview Mercy Amba Oduyoye, Kempton Park, 13.10.2003.
Interview Mercy Amba Oduyoye, The Institute of Women in Religion and Culture, Accra, 14.9.2005.
Interview Miranda N. Pillay, Kempton Park, South Africa, 14.7.2005.
Interview Modupe Dube, Sept 2005.
Interview Musa Dube, 2005.
Interview Philomena Njeri Mwaura, Kempton Park, South Africa, 15.7.2005.
Interview Prof Elna Mouton, Stellenbosch University, International Office, 2002.
Interview Prof. Noel Q. King, Ndangopuma, Zomba, Nov 2002.
Interview Sr Annie Nasimiyu, 14.7.2005, Kempton Park.
Interview Sr Annie Nasimiyu, Circle Conference, Kempton Park, 13.7.2005.
Interview Sr Annie Nasimiyu, Kempton Park, 12.7.2005.
Interview Sr Teresa, Kempton Park, 12.7.2005.
Interview, Nyambura Njoroge, Addis Ababa, 2002.
Oral presentation, Addis Ababa, 4-9.8.2002.
Oral presentation, Mercy Amba Oduyoye and Brigalia Bam, Pan African Conference, Institute of Women in Religion and Culture, Accra, Trinity College, 12.9.2005.
Oral presentation, Rev Afo Blay, Pan African Conference, 12.9.2005.
Pastor's wife's talk, bridal shower 1.10.2006.
Personal observation, Institute of Women in Religion and Culture Meeting, Ghana 12.-16.9.2005.
Public Seminar, Circle Meeting, Lydia Foundation Building, Zomba, 13.7.2006.
Widows group, Domasi Baptist Association, August 2004.

Correspondence and other Archival Sources

1996 Institute of African Women in Religion and Culture History, accessed 14.9.2005.

Acknowledgement Letter, Anne Harding Col Territorial President of Women's Ministry, to Mercy Amba Oduyoye, 9.9.2003.

Assessment Grade Reports 1993, Chancellor College, accessed 2001.

Assessment Grade Reports 1994, Chancellor College, accessed 2001.

Assessment Grade Reports 1995/96, Chancellor College, accessed 2001.

Assessment Grade Reports, 1967-1997, Chancellor College, accessed 2001.

Assessment Record, University of Malawi, Chancellor College, 1992, accessed 2001.

Circle Newsletter no. 6, April 2006, p. 2.

Circle Newsletter no. 9, 2006, p. 3.

Circle of Concerned African Women Theologians, Process of Creating Biennial Institutes of African Women in Religion and Culture, nd, no author, The Institute, Ghana.

Circular Letter, Mercy Amba Oduyoye to Persons Invited to the 2003 Institute of Women in Religion and Culture Meeting, 8.9.2003.

Circular Letter, Mercy Amba Oduyoye, 2003 Correspondence File, accessed 15.9.2005.

Conference Programme Document, 18-23 July, Nigeria/Lagos.

Conference Programme, The Circle of Concerned African Women Theologians Biennial Institutes Project, Session Zonal Conferences (West Africa), 18-23 July 1993 Lagos/Nigeria.

Elna Mouton, "'From Woundedness Towards Healing'. Rhetoric or Pastoral-Theological Vision?" 14th National Conference: Southern African Association for Pastoral Work, Cape Town, 12-14 May 2003.

Graduates of the University of Malawi 1992-1993, accessed 2001.

International Arrivals, Institute Correspondence, 8.9.2003.

Joyce Boham, Circular Letter to Circle members, 6.11.2001.

Letter by John Pobee to Elizabeth Amoah, 10.9.1993.

Letter by Mercy Amba Oduyoye to Elizabeth Harding, 17.12.2002.

Letter by Mercy Amba Oduyoye to Margaret Umeagudosu and Rhodah Ada James, Geneva, 16.6.1993.

Letter by Mercy Amba Oduyoye to Rev Dr Dan Antwi, Principal, Trinity College, 12.8.1999.

Letter for Nyambura Njoroge, World Alliance of Reformed Churches, 19.11.1993.

Letter form Mercy Amba Oduyoye, WCC, 16.7. July 1993 to Monsieur le Pasteur Harry Henry.

Letter from Mercy Amba Oduyoye to Elizabeth Calvin, 17.9.2005.

Letter from Mercy Amba Oduyoye to Rachel Tetteh, Geneva, 3.6.1993.

Letter from Mercy Amba Oduyoye to Rev Janice Nessiboo, Women's Coordinator, PROCMURA, 14.7.1994.

Letter from Mercy Amba Oduyoye, the Director, Institute of Women in Religion and Culture, Trinity Theological College, addressed to all participants, 8.9.2003.

Letter from Musimbi Kanyoro to Friends, Circle, c/o World YWCA- 16, Ancienne Route Grand Saconnex, Geneva, Switzerland, 12.4.2001.

Letter from Musimbi Kanyoro to Mary Getui and Teresa Hinga, 21.9.1993.

Letter of Acknowledgement from Angela Dwamera Aboagye, Executive Director, The Ark Foundation, Ghana, 18.08.2003.

Letter of Invitation Mercy Amba Oduyoye, to all Participants, 8.9.2003.

Letter of Invitation to Elizabeth Calvin, 17.12.2002.

Letter of Invitation, Mrs Hannah Agyeman, National Women's Secretary, Apostolic Church, Ghana, 21.7.2003.

Letter to Prof Amoah from Mercy Amba Oduyoye, Correspondence File, accessed 15.9.2005.

Letter to Sisters by Mercy Amba Oduyoye, 24.3. 1993.

Letter, Institute of Women in Religion and Culture, Ghana to Teresa Hinga, 20.12. 2001.

Peggy Mulambya Kabonde, "Women and Health in Africa in the Face of HIV/Aids Based on Mt 8:14-17, Malaka-le Theologies 2005.

Phiri, Isabel Apawo, "1995: The Struggle of Women in the Church and the University of Malawi" Paper, no date, no publisher, accessed 2.3.2006.

Regional Circle Report 2005, Circle of Concerned African Women Theologians.

Report by Nyambura Njoroge 13.4.1998.

Report Circle Study Commissions, Institute of Women in Religion and Culture, Trinity Theological College, Legon, Ghana, 20-25.3.1998.

Report on the 1996 Institute of Women in Religion and Culture, no date, no author, accessed 14.9.2005.

Written Interview by Mercy Amba Oduyoye, Circle meeting, Kempton Park, Johannesburg 13.10.2003

A Brief Biography and Tribute to Dr Dorcas Akintunde

(Acting Head, Department of Religious Studies, University of Ibadan, Associate Professor in New Testament and Women Studies)

She was born on 22nd February 1961. She was fondly called a "child of the mission yard" because her father, the late Moses Ajibade Amusan, was a pastor with the Christ Apostolic Church.

After primary school education she obtained the Grade II Teacher's Certificate in Education. Afterwards, she had a Diploma in Religious Studies from the Department of Religious Studies, University of Ibadan, in 1984, followed by a Bachelor's Degree in 1988, a Master's Degree in 1991, and a PhD in 2001. She was an Associate Professor in New Testament and Women Studies and the Acting Head, Department of Religious Studies, University of Ibadan, Ibadan Nigeria at the time of her shocking demise at the age of 50. She was the first female head of the Department, even though in Acting Capacity.

She won many notable academic awards and fellowships including: Mrs Jokotola Sobanjo Memorial Prize for best female student in the Department of Religious Studies 1988; Bishop Kate award for best student in the Department of Religious Studies, University of Ibadan, 1988; Post-Doctoral Fellow Yale University, New Haven, USA, 2005-2006; and Post-Doctoral Fellow, Centre for African Studies, University of Edinburgh, Scotland 2008.

She belonged to, and played leadership roles in several learned bodies and organizations, both locally and internationally including: Society for Biblical Literature, West African Association of Theological Institutions; Ecumenical Association for Biblical Studies; Project for Christian-Muslim Relations in Africa, International Association for the Study of Religion.

She published over forty-five articles in learned journals, as well as several books and monographs. She was well travelled and contributed to international projects on HIV and AIDS in Africa, Europe and USA. She is fondly remembered for her courtesy, care and concern for other's welfare and efficiency at work. She is a great mentor and role model to many. Most students casually called her "Mummy Dorcas" while colleagues would occasionally refer to her as "Aunty Dorcas" because of her usual concern for people's welfare. She was a family woman, and indeed egalitarian. The love she shared with her family is extended to all. Up to the moment, we find it difficult to compose ourselves enough to comment meaningfully on her virtues because she is still so dear and near to us and our emotional sentiments for her are too deep. This was so glaring at her funeral.

Indeed, Africa has lost a gem of rare lustre."[333]

---

[333] www.sbl-site.org/assets/pdfs/AkintundeObit.pdf.

Index

Aaron 51
Abraham/Abram 52, 65, 66
Abusive 16, 53, 138-140, 143
Abusive marriages 53, 138f
Accommodation Approach 122
Accra 7, 36, 51f
Ackermann, Denise 46f, 57, 59
Adah 90
Adam 48, 58, 72, 76
Adama 72
Adekunbi, Helen Labedeodan 36, 53
Advocacy 34, 37f, 145
African American 45
African culture 7, 13-15, 27, 34f, 37, 55, 77, 118, 144,
African Feminist Hermeneutics 6-9, 27, 30-33, 41, 66, 152
African Feminist Theologies 7f, 10, 12, 21, 27, 117, 120, 144, 146f, 149-151
African Independent Churches 33
African Theology 7, 10, 13, 15f, 20, 29, 51, 62, 117, 141, 147, 150f
African Traditional Culture 36
African Traditional Religion 33
African Traditionalist 30
African Women's Theologies 21f
Akan 34, 37
Akintunde, Dorcas 3, 8, 43, 45-47, 59
Akintunde, Dorcas Olubanke 3, 43, 45-47
Alangizi 123, 125, 128, 136, 138, 141-145
Alternative interpretations 112
Amaro, elder 111
Amba Oduyoye, Mercy 34, 36, 51-53
American 14, 19-24, 28, 44f

Anderson, Cheryl Barbara 44-46
Androcentric 27, 43, 48-52, 117, 120, 132, 137
Androcentrism 127
Andronicus 107
Anglican 23, 124, 133, 135
Angola 35
Anna, prophet 94, 99, 110
Apartheid 14, 17, 22, 35, 42
Apodictic Law 66, 86f
Apollos 107
Apostles 100, 102, 108
Appropriation 45-47
Arranged marriages 32
Arthur, Dr John 38
Assemblies of God 41, 48
Athaliah 92
Authority 51, 58, 64, 92, 107, 114
Banja ndi kunjoya 140
Banja nkupirira 139f
Baptist Convention 30, 37, 41, 43, 123, 125f, 132, 137, 146, 149-151
Beads 141-143
Beauvoir, Simone de 11
Bedroom instructions 140-145
Bethany 25, 101
Bible interpreters 48f
Bible Schools 57
Biblical Feminist Hermeneutics 31
Biblical Hermeneutics 7, 27, 33, 40f, 43, 62, 146, 150
Biblical interpreters 48
Biblical reinterpretation 43, 45f, 49, 146f
Biblical Studies 23, 29, 42, 102

Birth 10, 14, 25, 35, 38, 65, 77, 82, 86, 148
Black American 20, 22
Black Theology 14, 22
Black women 7, 14, 21f
Blacks 14#
Blantyre Synod 59, 119
Blessed wedding 137, 141
Blessings 72, 76, 89
Blurred distinctions 22
Book of the Law 94
Booklet *chinamwali* 125f
Booth, Catherine 25
Boston 25, 27, 69
Botswana 46
Brethren 82, 102, 106, 109
Bridal Shower 117, 119, 135-140
Bruce, Patricia Frances 47
Buddhism 30
Burundi 35
Bwalo 119f, 125f, 151
Calvary Family Church 41
Canaanite 91
Canada 10, 12
Case law 66-68, 97
Catechetical School 56
CCAP 56, 59, 119, 148
Ceremonial law 67f
Chakanza, J.C. 78, 119f, 122, 137
Chameleon 64
Chancellor College 148
Charismatic 16, 33, 40, 55, 148, 150
Chewa 29, 64, 72, 74, 103, 106, 119-123, 125f, 128, 132, 137, 151
Chikuta 134
Chilangizo 125f
Chinamwali 119, 123, 125f

Chinkhoswe 119, 140f
Chinyela 142
Chitekwe 127
Christian marriages 118, 144f
Chrysostomos 22, 108
Church *chinamwali* 126
Church History 29
Church women groups 56, 59
Circle of Concerned African Women Theologians 6f, 10, 143
Circumcision 38f, 111, 138
Clergy 22f, 55
Colonization 35
Compassion 35
Conceptualization 47
Congo 35
Consequences of sin 76f, 89f
Contextual Bible Studies 40f, 46
Contextual Theologies 7, 10, 12, 15
Contextualization 13, 44f, 124, 128
Corinth 41, 103, 109, 112-114
Co-workers 105-107
Creation Stories 63-66, 68-73, 76, 85, 89, 103, 152
Cultural context 30, 35
Cultural Feminist Hermeneutics 31
Cultural heritage 30
Cultural Hermeneutics 8, 27, 31, 33f, 36f, 42, 118
Cultural identity 118, 126f
Dance 120, 123, 126, 142, 144
Daughters 18f, 21, 37, 39, 67, 80f, 83, 86, 96, 98-100, 108f
Daughters of Anowa 37
David, King 64, 87, 90, 92, 97
Deaconess 106, 109
Deacons 24, 56, 106f, 109

Death 38, 53, 56, 68, 79, 82, 83f, 101, 126, 129, 132f, 139, 146
Deborah 8, 51, 93f, 109
Delivery 38, 109, 134f
Department of Theology and Religious Studies 7, 119, 148
Descriptive 65f
Deuteronomy 66, 90f, 97
Diakonissen 106
Dickson, Kwesi 13
Dignity of women 14, 49, 52, 118, 140, 147
Dignity of women and men 32
Disciples 50, 52f, 97, 99-102, 114
Disclose 31
Discrimination 147
Distantiation 47
Distortion 76f
Divorce 11f, 38, 86f, 97, 127, 129, 132, 140, 146
Domestic violence 137
Dube, Musa 46f
Dutch Reformed Church Mission 123
Early marriages 39
EATWOT 20-22, 48, 50
Ecclesiastes 66, 84
Ecclesiology 6, 55-57, 104
Economic liberation 128
Economic security 138
Ecumenical Association of Third World Theologies 22
Ecumenical surroundings 10
Education 11, 47, 53, 64, 118, 137, 143, 151
Efik 25
Egypt 66, 74
Elberfeld Version of the Bible 106
Elkanah 88

Epistemology 31
Equal 11, 18f, 27, 33, 49f, 52, 55, 57, 59, 83f, 88, 109, 148f
Equal Leadership 57
Equality 7, 22, 24, 32f, 42, 49, 54f, 57, 71f, 75f, 84, 96, 99, 102, 104, 149, 152
Esther, Queen 51, 59, 87f
Ethical 38f
Eurocentric 10, 13, 61
Eurocentric Feminist Theologies 10
European 13, 16, 20, 37, 39, 61, 116
Evangelical Awakening 22, 25
Evangelical Church of Guinea Bissao 111
Evangelical Discoveries 22
Evangelical Feminist 7, 28, 40, 43, 50, 54, 60f, 63, 69, 79, 85, 87, 89, 96f, 117, 127, 146, 148, 152
Evangelical Feminist Theology 28, 88, 152
Evangelism 22f, 25f, 109, 111
Evil prophets 95
Exile 66, 68, 71, 95
Exousia 113f
Faith Missions 23, 25, 39
Family 8, 11f, 25, 37, 39-41, 55, 78, 81, 86, 96, 118, 137f, 142, 146
Fellow workers 105f
Female apostle 107
Female genital mutilation 38
Female subordination 69
Feminist Literary Research 37
Feminist Movement 7f, 10, 12, 22, 24, 27f, 50, 90, 145, 151f
Feminist theologians 6, 13, 15, 17f, 27, 31, 34, 36, 43, 49, 52, 54, 72, 83, 86-89, 91, 118, 122, 146, 147

Feminist theory 8, 19f, 28, 31-34, 41
Firestone, Shullamith 11
First creation story 64, 71-73
First Feminist Movement in North America 24
First World Feminist Theologies 13, 20
Fisi 120f, 133f
Folly 81-83, 98
Food taboos 97
Forced marriages 32
Forgiveness 92, 108, 114, 146
Franson, Frederick 23, 26, 110 112
Free Methodists 23
Galatians 3:28 28, 54, 112
Galatiya, Mary 125
Garden of Eden 73
Gender equality 7, 32f, 42, 49, 99, 102
Gendered analysis 32, 46
Genesis 3 58, 76f, 89, 96
Genesis 64f, 69-71, 75f, 84, 89f, 96, 103
Genre, literary 40, 62f, 69, 88, 152
Gentiles 68, 98, 101, 111
Getman, Eliza Jane 35
Getui, Mary 33, 42, 60
Ghana 7, 34, 37, 53, 60
Gift 54, 58, 85, 89, 99, 105, 111
Gikuyu 34, 38f
Gikuyu 64, 12
Girls' initiation 29, 37, 78, 120, 122, 142
God talk 32
God's image 8, 27f, 54, 72
Gospel 13f, 24-26, 51, 97, 100f, 104-106, 110, 114, 123f, 127f, 152,
Grasshopper tradition 117
Grassroots 17, 46, 60, 117f, 122-124, 128-130, 132, 138-140, 144, 146f, 149, 151

Grassroots theologies 147, 149
Great Awakening 24
Gutierrez, Gustavo 16-18
Hadassah/Esther, Queen 88
Haddad, Beverly 45, 59
Hannah 51, 87
Head 49, 53, 81, 91, 97, 109, 113f, 134, 138, 144
Headship 139
Healers 42, 54
Health 16, 21, 32, 36, 38, 48f, 53, 120, 124, 129, 131-133, 135, 143, 147
Hegemonic social relationships 118, 127, 135, 143
Help opposite-him 73
Hierarchical Feminism 50
Hierarchical structures 54, 55
High Priest 91
High risk cultural choices 36
Higher education 11, 137
Hinga, Teresa 55
Historical Texts 66, 70, 87, 88
Hitler, Adolf 110
HIV AIDS 42, 44-48, 56, 120, 122, 124, 129, 131f, 134, 139, 146f, 151, , 131, 132, 133, 135, 139
HIV/AIDS booklet 151
Holiness Feminist Movement 7, 10, 12
Holiness Movement 8, 10, 22f, 25, 110f
Holiness Revival 22, 23, 25
Holy Communion 41, 82
Holy Spirit 22, 68, 99, 102, 110, 112, 115, 152
Horned Chameleon 64
Huldah 8, 94, 109
Hultman, Rosa Salinas 28
Humankind 18, 28, 70f, 75, 98
Hyena 120, 122, 128, 133

Image of God 8, 27f, 54, 72
Immoral husband 121, 130
Immoral woman 79
Immorality 95, 98, 115, 122, 124, 128-132, 134
Inculturation 13, 24, 125
Indissolubility of marriage 55
Inheritance 55, 80, 86
Insiders 31
Interviews 29, 45, 57f, 60, 131, 140
Irruption within an irruption 7, 10
Isaiah 68, 98f
Ish 74
Isha 74
Israel 66, 68f, 71, 74, 87, 91-94, 98, 100, 109
Jairus 52
Jali 123, 132f
James, Rhoda Ada 51f, 140
Jealous 79, 85, 121
Jephthah 87, 88, 98
Jeremiah 92-95, 109
Jerusalem 88, 93f, 102, 109
Jesus and Women 97
Jewish 30, 51f, 87, 89, 98, 100, 110, 113f,
Jezebel 95, 115
Joanna 99, 100
Job 66
Joel 95, 98, 99, 102
Joseph 52, 134
Joseph, husband of Mary 52
Josiah 94
Judges 51, 87f, 93
Junias 104, 106-108
Junios 108
Justice 21, 35, 46f, 62

Kabonde, Peggy Mulambya 48
Kachiwala 127-131
Kalu, Ogbu O. 21, 33, 50
Kanyela 142
Kaphirintiwa Myth 64
Khundabwi 120, 122
Kikuyu 64, 123
Kinship 36f, 118
Kudika 134f
Kyriarchy 27, 128
Labia minora 144
Laissez faire approach 122
Lamech 86, 90
Landman, Christina 33
Lankfort, Sarah 23
Latin America 14, 20f, 124
Lazarus 51, 101
Leadership 8, 16, 31-33, 41, 43, 49-55, 91f, 94, 96, 105, 120, 137, 140, 149
Lecturers 58, 148
Legal Texts 62, 66, 85-87, 90f, 96
Leipzig Lutheran Mission 123
Lesbianism 11
Levirate marriage 42
Levitical laws 148
Leviticus 41, 53, 66, 68
Liberal 24, 40, 50, 60, 117f, 120, 141, 143-145
Liberal Feminism 50, 143
Liberate 8, 16-18, 20f, 25, 27, 34, 143
Liberation theologies 10, 15-17, 19, 117
Liberation Theology 7, 12, 15f, 18, 57
Liberation/Liberating 15f, 18-20, 36, 38, 42, 48, 58, 96, 126, 135
Lilongwe 41, 121, 123, 125, 140
Literary analysis 44, 46
Literary approach 40

Literary genre 40, 63
Livingstonia Synod 148
Liwombo 134
London's East End 25
Love 8, 14, 67, 85, 91, 95, 110, 138, 141f
Lovemaking 141-144
Low risk cultural choices 36
Lydia 8, 109
Lyon, Mary 25
Madoo Lengermann, Patricia 28
Magna Charta 28, 54
Male dominance 65, 92, 137
Male superiority 96
Mambo, Esther 59
Mangochi 41
Marriage counselling 117, 119
Marriage security 127, 144
Marriage send offs 119, 135-137, 139f, 145
Marriage stability 36
Marriage teaching 55
Martha 5, 100
Marxist 20
Mary Magdalene, 51, 99, 101
Mary, sister of Martha and Lazarus 51
Mary, the mother of Jesus 51, 102
Mary, the wife of Clopas 101
Masenya, Madipoane 17, 41, 45
Masks 18
Matriarchy 10f, 62
Matrilineal 36, 62, 118f, 125
Mbiti, John 13
Menstruation 29, 135, 142f, 148
Methodist Church of Ghana 53
Mexico 20

Ministry 23, 26, 48, 50f, 53-55, 59, 63, 68, 93, 99, 104, 148
Miriam 51, 93, 109
Misconceptions 36, 69
Mission History 28f, 48
Missionaries 13, 22-26, 33, 39, 53, 55f, 102, 105f, 109f, 123-126, 141
Mkhalapakati 56
Moe, Malla 25, 28
Moral law 67f
Mordecai 88
Morgenster Mission 25
Moses 42, 51, 86f, 89f, 92f, 97f, 109, 111
Mothers' Union 59
Mothers 11f, 21, 35, 47f, 51f, 66, 75, 77, 81, 85, 90, 101f, 104, 114, 118, 120, 131
Mount Holyoke College 25
Mouton, Elna 17, 42, 58f
Mozambique 35
Mujerista Theology 20
Munthu 70-76
Mwachukwu, Daisy 36
Mwambo 78, 117, 121, 136f, 145
Mwamuna 71, 75f, 78, 87, 122, 128, 137-139
Mwamuna ndi pamimba 137
Mwaura, Philomena Njeri 16, 33
Mzuzu University 7, 7, 86, 93, 119, 148
Nadar, Sarojini 21, 29, 46f, 87, 124, 129
Naomi 88
Nathan 92
National Initiative for Civic Education (NICE) 151
Nehemiah 66, 95
Neo-Pentecostal 16
New Covenant 95, 99

New Testament 7, 23f, 40, 43, 45f, 51, 60f, 68, 70, 82, 92, 94-97, 99f, 102f, 105f, 108-111, 113-115
NICE 151
Niebrugge-Brantley, Jill 28
Nigeria 33f, 36, 39, 43, 45, 53, 59
Nikolaites 115
Njolomole, Agnes 125
Njoroge, Nyambura 33f, 38f
Nkhoma Synod 53, 56, 125f
North America 16, 21f, 24
Obedience 120
Okeyere-Manu, Beatrice 49
Old Testament 7, 40, 42, 47, 51, 60-63, 66-68, 71f, 74, 85, 87-99, 108-111
Oppression 8, 14f, 17, 19-21, 27f, 33-36, 41-43, 61f, 65, 71, 76f, 79, 84f, 93, 97, 135f, 140f
Ordained 23, 32, 43, 49f, 55, 95, 100, 148
Ordination 8, 55, 59f, 92, 148
Origen 22f, 64, 71, 131
Orphan care 148
Ott, Martin 3, 55
Outsider 31, 39
PACWA 60
Pain in childbirth 77
Palmer, Phoebe 23, 25
Pastoral 17, 42, 112, 115, 149
Pastors 24, 41, 49, 54, 57, 92, 125f, 130, 133, 137, 140, 148f
Patriarchal society 62, 75, 84, 96, 108
Patriarchal structures 21, 129
Patriarchal theologies 15
Patriarchy 10f, 19, 27, 32, 38, 54, 62, 80, 85, 88, 117, 127, 129, 133, 144
Patrilineality 36, 118f
Paul's Magna Charta 28

Pauline letters 102, 104
Pentecost 95, 99, 102
Pentecostal 16, 33, 148, 150
Persian 88
Peter 48, 53, 68, 95, 99, 102, 108, 111
Philip 109
Phiri, Isabel Apawo 21f, 29, 33f, 37, 44f, 47, 53, 55f, 59, 119, 123-126, 129, 139
Phoebe 51, 53, 104, 106f
Poetry 68f, 152
Political Theology 14
Polygamy 42, 86, 87-91, 98
Polygamy, tolerated 86, 90
Poor 15, 18, 27, 49
Potamiaena 56
Power 7, 13, 16, 19, 27, 32-35, 42f, 51, 54f, 57, 59, 64f, 87, 102, 110, 114, 138, 144, 148, 152
Power balance 13, 16, 32, 148
Power relations 7, 27, 34, 152
Practical Theology 102f, 110
Praise poems 62, 69, 83, 152
Pregnancy 11, 25, 38f, 52, 62
Presbyterian 33, 37f, 55f, 59, 119, 140
Presbyterian Church of East Africa 38
Prescriptive 37, 65f, 70, 85, 103
Priest 71, 91f, 94, 96f, 99f
Priesthood of all believers 92
Primary sources 29, 45
Promiscuity 128-130, 140
Proper order of society 63
Prophesy 99, 101, 108f, 113, 132
Prophetesses 93, 95, 99, 115
Prophets 8, 54, 91-95, 99, 108f
Proverbs 68, 78-81, 83-85
Psalms 66, 68f

Puberty 38
Public spaces 11
Purity laws 67f
Queen of Sheba 88f
Rabbis 100
Radford Ruether, Rosemary 27, 33, 71
Rahab 51
Ramazanoglu, Caroline 19f
Rastafarianism 30
Reader Response Criticism 40
Rebecca 51
Redemption 27, 77, 94, 96, 99
Reinterpretation 13, 36, 39, 44, 46, 48, 53, 68, 87, 96, 136, 140, 143f, 146, 150
Rejectionist approach 122f
Rejectionist Feminism 50
Relational Feminist Hermeneutics 31, 33
Relational Hermeneutics 27, 33f, 148
Religions 7, 12, 14, 17, 19, 21f, 28, 30f, 33, 41, 60, 91, 119f, 130
Remarriage 38, 133
Rereading 45, 140, 146
Re-reading 77, 79
Revelation 14, 29f, 62, 70, 97, 115
Revival 22f, 25, 111
Roberts, Titus 23f
Romans 52, 104, 106f
Ruling elder 109
Ruth 57, 88, 90
Rwanda 35
Salvation Army 25
Salvation History 62f, 67, 97, 110
Samuel 51, 93
Sarah 51f
Sarai 66

Schirrmacher, Thomas 109, 114
Schüssler-Fiorenza, Elisabeth 27f, 33, 43, 57, 117f
Scriptural holiness 22
Second Evangelical Awakening 22
Security 36f, 39, 118, 127, 129, 131, 138, 144
Selective approach 15, 122, 124, 127
Servant 22, 67, 74, 78, 83, 96, 98-100, 107f, 115
Sexual immorality 95, 98, 115
Sexual overtures 115
Sexual relationships 117, 128, 133f, 142f, 145
Sexuality 32, 150f
Sign of authority 114
Silas 109
Silence 24, 55f, 94, 100, 103, 106f, 113
Sin 48f, 65, 70, 75-77, 79, 86, 89f, 96, 101
Single motherhood 12
Single women 12, 24f, 127, 129
Sisterhood 11, 19
Slave 28, 42, 54, 103f, 112
Slave trade 42
Slessor, Mary 25, 28
Smallbridge, Robert 12
Social justice 21
Social security 118, 127
Solomon 86-89
Song of Songs 66, 85
South African 14, 17, 19, 22, 25, 29, 35, 46, 59, 125
Southern Baptists 123
Spirit 18, 22, 53, 68, 96, 98f, 102, 108-110, 112, 115, 145, 151f
Spiritual warfare 124
Stegman, Mrs 123

Stigmatization 39f, 147
Subordination 16, 49, 56, 60, 64, 69, 77, 85, 113
Sunday School 150
Susanna 99f
Swahili 107, 114
Swaziland 25, 69
Swedish 23
Synagogue 113
Synod of Livingstonia 119, 148
Tamar 46, 87, 98
Tangents of oppression 27, 33-35, 41f, 62, 79
Teachers 54, 76, 81, 84, 95, 100, 107, 114f, 123
Ten Commandments 66, 87
Theological Colleges 57, 148
Theological training 35, 55, 57, 145, 148
Third Word Theologies 7
Third World 10, 14-16, 20-22, 48, 50
Third World Feminist Theologies 10, 20-22
Thogolo Hospital 38
Thyatira 95, 115
Traditional Religion 33, 128, 132
Transform 15, 18, 32, 39, 46, 52, 59, 117, 135, 141, 145, 151
Translation 8, 49, 61, 63, 71f, 74f, 93, 106-109, 113-115, 119, 138
Trible, Phyllis 49, 87
Tsempho 128
Twelve 50, 99f, 108
Ulangizi 117-119, 123, 126, 136
Umeagudosu, Margaret A. 34, 39f
Umodzi wa Amayi 150
University of Malawi 148
Until death do us part 53, 56, 146

Vagina 39, 121, 129f, 134
Vatican II 57
Vesico Vagina Fistula (VVF) 39
Virginity 47, 86
Vitamin K 129
Wamkulu ndani mbanja 78, 138f
Watson, Minnie 39
Wesley, John 23, 111
Wester, Blanche 123
Western Feminist Theology 27
White Queen of Calabar 25
White women 7, 21
Whole testimony of Scripture 62, 111
Widowhood Cleansing 128, 132
Widow<u>s</u> 67, 90, 127, 131, 133
Wife of Noble Character 69, 81
Wisdom 49, 52, 66, 68f, 78f, 81-85
Wisdom Literature 66, 68f, 79, 84f
Woman as a Blessing 80
Woman as a Nuisance 80
Woman church elders 109
Womanist Theologies 21
Women apostles 108
Women of colour 7, 14, 35, 59
Women of power 43, 51
Women prophets 108f
Women structures 150
Women's empowerment 7, 19, 34, 37, 40
Women's Guild 38, 136
Women's history 43
Women's liberation 8, 10-12, 14, 18-21, 26, 28, 34, 50, 65, 71, 79, 87, 122, 136, 140, 146, 149, 152
Women's Liberation Movement 19, 24, 26
Women's organizations 150

Women's Sunday 83
Word of God 18, 43, 62f, 71, 88, 100
Yao 41, 64
Yila, Othniel Mintang 50, 54
Zelophehad's daughters 86

Zillah 90
Zimbabwe 25, 102
Zomba 123, 125f, 131-133, 136, 140, 146

www.ingramcontent.com/pod-product-compliance
Lightning Source LLC
Chambersburg PA
CBHW051614230426
43668CB00013B/2104